Writing Arguments

Concise Edition

John D. Ramage

Arizona State University

John C. Bean

Seattle University

Allyn and Bacon

Boston ■ London ■ Toronto ■ Sydney ■ Tokyo ■ Singapore

Vice President: Eben W. Ludlow
Editorial Assistant: Linda M. D'Angelo
Marketing Manager: Lisa Kimball
Editorial Production Administrator: Susan Brown
Editorial-Production Service: Matrix Productions, Inc.
Text Designer: Denise Hoffman
Composition Buyer: Linda Cox
Manufacturing Buyer: Suzanne Lareau
Cover Administrator: Jennifer Hart

Copyright © 1999 by Allyn & Bacon
A Viacom Company
160 Gould St.
Needham Heights, Mass. 02194
Internet: www.abacon.com

Portions of this book first appeared in *Writing Arguments: A Rhetoric with Readings*, Fourth Edition, by John D. Ramage and John C. Bean. Copyright © 1998 by Allyn & Bacon.

Library of Congress Cataloging-in-Publication Data

Ramage, John D.
    Writing arguments : a rhetoric with readings / John D. Ramage,
John C. Bean. — Concise ed.
      p.   cm.
    Adapted from: Writing arguments. 4th ed., brief ed. 1997.
    Includes index.
    ISBN 0-205-26906-0
    1. English language—Rhetoric.   2. Persuasion (Rhetoric)
3. College readers. 4. Report writing.   I. Bean, John C.
II. Title.
PE1431.R33   1998b
808'.042—dc21   98-21160
                                                  CIP

Printed in the United States of America

10 9 8 7 6 5 4 3 2   RRDV   02 01 00 99

brief contents

contents

CHAPTER 3   Writing Arguments   40

❧ PART TWO
PRINCIPLES OF ARGUMENT   59

CHAPTER 4   The Core of an Argument:
A Claim with Reasons   61

CHAPTER 5   The Logical Structure of Arguments   73

CHAPTER 8 Accommodating Your Audience: Treating Differing Views 113

❧ PART THREE ARGUMENTS IN DEPTH: FIVE CATEGORIES OF CLAIMS 131

CHAPTER 9 Using the Categories of Claims to Generate Ideas 133

CHAPTER 15   Ethical Arguments   227

❧ APPENDICES   239

APPENDIX ONE   Informal Fallacies   239

❧ *p r e f a c e*

Overview

Through its four editions, *Writing Arguments* has emerged as the leading college textbook on the art of writing arguments. In this Concise Edition, adapted from the Fourth Edition of *Writing Arguments,* we have tried to create the most up-to-date, accessible, and affordable short rhetoric of argument on the market. Covering the essentials of argumentation without sacrificing clarity or flexibility, this Concise Edition can be used successfully either as a stand-alone rhetoric text or as a compact companion to an anthology of readings.

As in *Writing Arguments,* Fourth Edition, our aim is to integrate a comprehensive study of argument with a process approach to writing. The text treats arguments as a means of clarification and truth seeking, as well as a means of persuading audiences. In both its treatment of argumentation and its approach to teaching writing, the text is rooted in current research and theory.

Features of the Concise Edition

The Concise Edition is a careful redaction of *Writing Arguments,* Fourth Edition, aimed at retaining the conceptual strengths of the original. Among the key features of the Concise Edition are the following:

- Four different, complementary approaches to argument—the enthymeme (a claim with because clause); the Toulmin system; the classical appeals of *logos, ethos,* and *pathos;* and the stasis system (five categories of claims). These approaches allow flexibility for instructors and provide students with a range of argumentative strategies. Teachers can emphasize one, two, three, or all four of these complementary approaches.

- A comprehensive chapter on reading arguments (Chapter 2). Treating reading as a process, including reading as a "believer" and as a "doubter," this chapter helps students analyze and evaluate arguments and develop strategies for clarifying their own views when faced with complex disagreements among experts.

- A chapter on writing arguments (Chapter 3) treating composing as a process of learning and discovery. Presenting various heuristics for argument as well as strategies for structuring arguments, the chapter links writing to thinking and stresses both the truth seeking and the persuasive aims of argument.

- The treatment of argument as multi-sided conversation rather than as pro-con debate. Throughout we show how issues are embedded in a context of sub-issues, side issues, and larger issues that resist reduction to a simple pro-con focus. We have avoided such combative terms as "opponents" or "adversaries" in order to treat argument as a truth seeking inquiry among alternative views instead of a win-lose debate between two sides.

- Comprehensive treatment of audience showing how writers vary the content, tone, and structure of an argument to accommodate readers along a scale of resistance from sympathetic to hostile. We show how one-sided arguments are often best for friendly audiences; how classical arguments work best with neutral or undecided audiences; and how delayed thesis or Rogerian strategies work best with hostile audiences.

- Illustration of effective arguing through fourteen sample arguments. Seven of these are student arguments reflecting genuine student voices with which readers can identify.

- Class-tested exercises and assignments. Opportunities for students to practice what they have learned include numerous collaborative "For Class Discussion" exercises and a variety of sequenced writing assignments, including "microthemes."

- A "Concise Guide to Documentation" (Appendix 2), which provides brief, clear explanations and examples of how to cite sources illustrating both the MLA and APA styles. The text includes two student researched arguments, one in the MLA style and the other in APA.

Structure of the Text

The text has three main parts plus two appendixes. Part I gives an overview of argumentation. These first three chapters present our philosophy of argument, showing how argument helps writers clarify their own thinking. Throughout we link the process of arguing—articulating issue questions, formulating propositions, examining alternative points of view, and creating structures of supporting reasons and evidence—with the processes of reading and writing.

Part II examines the principles of argument. Chapters 4 through 6 show that the core of an argument is a claim with reasons. These reasons are often stated as enthymemes, the unstated premise of which must sometimes be brought to the surface and supported. Discussion of Toulmin logic shows students how to discover both the stated and unstated premises of their arguments and to provide structures of reasons and evidence to support them. Chapters 7 and 8 focus on the rhetorical context of arguments. These chapters discuss the writer's relationship with an audience, particularly with finding audience-based reasons, with using *pathos* and *ethos* effectively and responsibly, and with accommodating arguments to different kinds of audiences from sympathetic to neutral to hostile.

Part III discusses five different categories of argument: definitional arguments, causal arguments, resemblance arguments, evaluation arguments, and proposal arguments. These chapters introduce students to two recurring strategies of argument that cut across the different category types: criteria-match arguing in which the writer establishes criteria for making a judgment and argues whether a specific case does or does not meet those criteria, and causal arguing in which the writer shows that one event or phenomenon can be linked to others in a causal chain. The last chapter of Part III deals with the special complexities of moral arguments.

The text concludes with two appendices. Appendix 1 gives an overview of informal fallacies while Appendix 2 provides a concise overview of the MLA and APA systems for citing and documenting sources.

WRITING ASSIGNMENTS

The text provides a variety of sequenced writing assignments, including expressive tasks for discovering and exploring arguments, "microthemes" for practicing basic argumentative moves, and numerous other assignments calling for complete arguments. Thus, the text provides flexible assignment options on which to build a coherent course.

ACKNOWLEDGMENTS

We are happy for this opportunity to give public thanks to the scholars, teachers, and students who have influenced our approach to composition and argument. We would especially like to thank Darlene Panvini of Vanderbilt University for her advice on our treatment of the wetlands controversy in Chapter 10. We also thank the following reviewers who gave us helpful and cogent advice for producing the Concise Edition: Christopher Burnham, New Mexico State University; Tim McGee, The College of New Jersey; and Kathy Overhulse Smith, Indiana University, Bloomington.

We would also like to thank our editor Eben Ludlow, whose unflagging good humor and faith in our approach to both composition and argument have kept us writing and revising for the better part of fourteen years.

Finally, we would like to thank our families. John Bean: Thanks to Kit, Matthew, Andrew, Stephen, and Sarah for their love, support, good humor, rich conversation, and willingness to discuss argument in any context at any time. John Ramage: Thanks to my siblings for their extended support—brother Steve and sisters Carol Flinders, Wendy Hawkins, and Mary Beth Smith—and to my parents Gib and Jeanne Ramage for a lifelong dialectic. May the final synthesis never be achieved.

part one

Overview
of Argument

chapter 1

Argument
An Introduction

One ought to begin a book on argument by telling the reader straight out what argument is. But we can't. Philosophers and rhetoricians have disagreed for centuries about the meaning of the term and about the goals that arguers should set for themselves. So in place of a simple definition, we'll show you several different ways of thinking about argument as a way of helping you become a more powerful arguer yourself.

After explaining how arguments make claims and provide justifications for those claims, we will consider argument from two different perspectives—as product and process. We'll also explain how arguments combine two distinct and sometimes conflicting purposes—truth seeking and persuasion. Because of the importance of this last distinction, we'll explore extensively the debate over truth versus victory as the goal of argument.

WHAT DO WE MEAN BY ARGUMENT?

Let's begin by rejecting two popular synonyms for argument—fight and debate.

Argument Is Not a Fight or a Quarrel

The word *argument* often connotes anger, as when we say, "I just got in a huge argument with my roommate!" We may picture heated disagreements, rising pulse rates, and slamming doors. We may conjure up images of shouting talk show guests or fist-banging speakers.

But to our way of thinking, argument doesn't necessarily imply anger. In fact, arguing can be pleasurable. It can be a creative and productive activity that engages our minds and our hearts in conversations with people we respect about ideas that we cherish. For your primary image of argument, we invite you to think not of a fist-banging speaker but of a small group of reasonable persons seeking the best solution to a problem. We will return to this image throughout the chapter.

Argument Is Not Pro-Con Debate

Another popular conception of argument is debate—a presidential debate, perhaps, or a high school or college debate tournament, in which, according to one popular dictionary, "opposing speakers defend and attack a given proposition." While formal debates can develop our critical thinking powers, they stress winning and losing, often to the detriment of cooperative inquiry.

To illustrate the limitations of debate, consider one of our former students, a champion high school debater, who spent his senior year debating prison reform. Throughout the year he argued for and against such propositions as "The United States should build more prisons," and "We must find innovative alternatives to prison." One day we asked him, "What do you personally think is the best way to reform prisons?" "I don't know," he replied. "I've never thought about it that way."

Here was a bright, articulate student who had studied and debated prison reform for a year. But nothing in the atmosphere of pro-con debate propelled him to form his own view on the issue. As we emphasize throughout this text, argument *should* grow out of a desire for truth, not necessarily Truth with a capital *T* but truth in the sense of a better understanding of all sides of an issue and a desire to find the best solutions to complex problems. That doesn't mean that arguers don't passionately support their own points of view or expose weaknesses in other views. It just means that their passionate defenses and their relentless probing are in the service of truth.

Arguments Can Be Explicit or Implicit

Before we define argument further, we need to distinguish between two types of argument: explicit and implicit. An *explicit* argument directly states a claim and supports it with reasons and evidence. An *implicit* argument, in contrast, often doesn't look like an argument. It may be a poem or a short story, a photograph or cartoon, or an autobiographical narrative. But like an explicit argument, it persuades its audience of a certain point of view. Steinbeck's *Grapes of Wrath* is an implicit argument for the unionization of farm workers, just as the following poem is an implicit argument against the premise that it is sweet and fitting to die for one's country.

Dulce et Decorum Est

Bent double, like old beggars under sacks,
Knock-kneed, coughing like hags, we cursed through sludge
Till on the haunting flares we turned our backs,
And towards our distant rest began to trudge.
Men marched asleep. Many had lost their boots,
But limped on, blood-shod. All went lame, all blind;
Drunk with fatigue; deaf even to the hoots
Of gas-shells dropping softly behind.

Gas! Gas! Quick, boys—An ecstasy of fumbling,
Fitting the clumsy helmets just in time,
But someone still was yelling out and stumbling
And flound'ring like a man in fire or lime.
Dim through the misty panes and thick green light,
As under a green sea, I saw him drowning.

In all my dreams before my helpless sight
He plunges at me, guttering, choking, drowning.

If in some smothering dreams, you too could pace
Behind the wagon that we flung him in,
And watch the white eyes writhing in his face,
His hanging face, like a devil's sick of sin,
If you could hear, at every jolt, the blood
Come gargling from the froth-corrupted lungs
Bitter as the cud
Of vile, incurable sores on innocent tongues,—
My friend, you would not tell with such high zest
To children ardent for some desperate glory,
The old lie: *Dulce et decorum est
Pro patria mori.**

—Wilfred Owen

Here Wilfred Owen makes a powerful case against the "old lie"—that war is honorable, that dying for one's country is sweet and fitting. But the argument is implicit: It is carried in the horrible image of a soldier drowning in his own fluids from a mustard gas attack rather than through an ordered structure of thesis, reasons, and evidence.

---

*"How sweet and fitting it is to die for one's country." Wilfred Owen (1893–1918) was killed in World War I and wrote many of his poems while in the trenches.

❦ **FOR CLASS DISCUSSION** ▬▬▬▬▬▬▬▬▬▬▬▬▬▬▬▬▬▬▬▬▬▬▬▬▬▬▬

Working individually or in small groups, describe a photograph that would create an implicit argument persuading (1) teenagers to avoid smoking; (2) teenagers to avoid becoming sexually active; (3) the general public to ban handguns; or (4) the general public to save endangered species.

EXAMPLE: To create an implicit argument against legalizing hard drugs, you might photograph a blank-eyed, cadaverous teenager plunging a needle into her arm.

▬▬▬ ❦

We'll return to implicit arguments later, especially in Chapter 9 where we describe the persuasive power of stories and narratives. For now, however, and for most of this text, our predominant focus is on explicit argument.

ARGUMENT REQUIRES JUSTIFICATION OF ITS CLAIMS

To begin defining argument, let's turn to a humble but universal site of disagreement: the conflict between a parent and a teenager over rules. In what way and in what circumstances do these conflicts constitute arguments?

Consider the following dialogue:

YOUNG PERSON (*racing for the front door while putting coat on*):   Bye. See you later.

PARENT: Whoa! What time are you planning on coming home?

YOUNG PERSON (*coolly, hand still on doorknob*):   I'm sure we discussed this earlier. I'll be home around 2 A.M. (*The second sentence, spoken very rapidly, is barely audible.*)

PARENT (*mouth tightening*):   We did *not* discuss this earlier and you're *not* staying out till two in the morning. You'll be home at twelve.

At this point in the exchange, we have a quarrel, not an argument. Quarrelers exchange antagonistic assertions without any attempt to support them rationally. If the dialogue never gets past the "Yes-you-will/No-I-won't" stage, it either remains a quarrel or degenerates into a fight.

Let us say, however, that the dialogue takes the following turn:

YOUNG PERSON (*tragically*):   But I'm *sixteen years old*!

Now we're moving toward argument. Not, to be sure, a particularly well-developed or cogent one, but an argument all the same. It's now an argument because one of the quarrelers has offered a reason for her assertion. Her choice of curfew is satisfactory, she says, *because* she is sixteen years old.

The parent can now respond in one of several ways that will either advance the argument or turn it back into a quarrel. The parent can simply invoke parental authority ("I don't care—you're still coming home at twelve"), in which case argument ceases, or the parent can provide a reason for his or her view ("You will be home at twelve because your dad and I pay the bills around here!"), in which case the argument takes a new turn.

So far we've established two necessary conditions that must be met before we're willing to call something an argument: (1) a set of two or more conflicting assertions, and (2) the attempt to resolve the conflict through an appeal to reason.

But good argument demands more than meeting these two formal requirements. For the argument to be effective, an arguer must clarify and support the reasons presented. For example, "But I'm sixteen years old!" is not yet a clear support for the assertion "I should be allowed to set my own curfew." On the surface, Young Person's argument seems absurd. Her parent, of all people, knows precisely how old she is. What makes it an argument is that behind her claim lies an unstated assumption—all sixteen-year-olds are old enough to set their own curfews. What Young Person needs to do now is to support that assumption.* In doing so, she must anticipate the sorts of questions the assumption will raise in the minds of her parent: What is the legal status of sixteen-year-olds? How psychologically mature, as opposed to chronologically mature, is Young Person? What is the actual track record of Young Person in being responsible? and so forth. Each of these questions will force Young Person to reexamine and clarify her assumptions about the proper degree of autonomy for sixteen-year-olds. And her response to those questions should in turn force the parents to reexamine their assumptions about the dependence of sixteen-year-olds on parental guidance and wisdom. (Likewise, the parents will need to show why "paying the bills around here" automatically gives them the right to set Young Person's curfew.)

As the argument continues, Young Person and Parent may shift to a different line of reasoning. For example, Young Person might say: "I should be allowed to stay out until 2 A.M. because all my friends get to stay out that late." (Here the unstated assumption is that the rules in this family ought to be based on the rules in other families.) The parent might in turn respond, "But I certainly never stayed out that late when I was your age"—an argument assuming that the rules in this family should follow the rules of an earlier generation.

As Young Person and Parent listen to each other's points of view (trying to figure out why their initial arguments are unpersuasive), both parties find themselves in the uncomfortable position of having to examine their own beliefs and to

---

*In Chapter 5 we will call the assumption underlying a line of reasoning its *warrant*.

justify assumptions that they have taken for granted. Here we encounter one of the earliest senses of the term *to argue,* which is "to clarify." In response to her audience's failure to understand or assent to her view, the arguer must reshape her argument to help her audience "see" her position. In the process she may, perhaps for the first time, come to understand that position herself. Thus Young Person might recast her argument so that it relates more directly to her parent's values:

> I should be allowed to stay out until 2 A.M. on a trial basis because I need enough space to demonstrate my maturity and show you I won't get into trouble.

The assumption underlying this argument is that it is good to give teenagers freedom to demonstrate their maturity. Because this reason is apt to appeal to her parent's values (the parent wants the daughter to mature) and because it is tempered by the qualifier "on a trial basis" (which reduces some of the threat of Young Person's initial demands), it may prompt productive discussion.

Whether or not Young Person and Parent can work out a best solution, the preceding scenario illustrates how argument leads persons to clarify their reasons and provide justifications that can be examined rationally. The scenario also illustrates two specific aspects of argument that we will explore in detail in the next sections: (1) Argument is both a process and a product, and (2) arguments combine truth seeking and persuasion.

ARGUMENT IS BOTH A PROCESS AND A PRODUCT

In the preceding scenario, argument functioned as a *process* whereby two or more parties sought the best solution to a question or problem. But if we stopped the process at a given moment and looked at each person's contribution to the conversation, these contributions would be *products.* In an informal discussion, these products are usually brief, comprising a few sentences. In a more formal setting, such as an open-mike discussion of a campus issue or a presentation to a legislative subcommittee, the oral argument might be considerably longer.

Written versions of informal conversations occur online among members of chat groups or listservs. These e-mail messages are usually short and informal, albeit more carefully crafted than real-time oral rejoinders. And as these discussions (or *threads*) play out over several days, you may well see participants' ideas shift and evolve as they negotiate some sort of collectively agreeable view, or perhaps a simple truce.

Written versions of formal speeches, drafted over the course of days or weeks, may take the form of an academic argument for a college course; a grant proposal; a guest column for the op-ed (opinion-editorial) section of a newspaper; a legal brief; a letter to a congressperson; or an article for an organizational newsletter, popular magazine, or professional journal. In such instances, the written argument (a product) enters a conversation (a process)—in this case, a conversation of readers, many of whom will carry on the conversation by writing their own responses or by discussing the writer's views with others.

ARGUMENT COMBINES TRUTH SEEKING AND PERSUASION

In producing her argument, the writer will find herself continually moving back and forth between truth seeking and persuasion—that is, between questions about the subject matter (What is the best solution to this problem?) and about audience (What reasons and evidence best speak to my audience's values?). Back and forth she'll weave, alternately absorbed in the subject matter of her argument and in the persuasiveness of her argument to her audience.

Rarely is either focus ever completely ignored, but their relative importance shifts during different phases of the argument's development. We could thus place "concern for truthfulness" at one end of a continuum, "concern for persuasiveness" at the other, and fit any argument somewhere along that continuum. At the far truth-seeking end of the continuum might be an exploratory piece that lays out several alternative approaches to a problem and weighs the strengths and weaknesses of each. At the other end of the continuum would be outright propaganda, such as a political campaign advertisement that reduces a complex issue to sound bites. (At its most blatant, propaganda obliterates truth seeking; it will do anything, including distorting or inventing evidence, to win over an audience.) In the middle ranges of the continuum, writers shift their focuses back and forth between truth seeking and persuasion but with varying degrees of emphasis.

To illustrate the need for a shifting focus, consider the case of Kathleen, who, in her college argument course, addressed the definitional question "Should American Sign Language meet the university's foreign language requirement?" Kathleen had taken two years of ASL at a community college. When she transferred to a four-year college, her ASL proficiency was dismissed by the foreign language department chair. "ASL isn't a 'language,' " he said summarily. "It's not equivalent to learning French, German, or Japanese."

Kathleen disagreed and immersed herself in her argument. In her initial research she focused almost entirely on subject matter, searching for what linguists, brain neurologists, cognitive psychologists, and sociologists had said about ASL. She was only tacitly concerned with her audience, whom she mostly envisioned as her classmates and those sympathetic to her view. She wrote a well-documented paper, citing several scholarly articles, that made a good case to her classmates (and her professor) that ASL was indeed a distinct language.

Proud of the big red A the professor had placed on her paper and more secure in her position, Kathleen resubmitted her request (this time buttressed with a copy of her paper) to count ASL for her language requirement. The chair of the foreign language department read her paper, congratulated her on her good writing, but said her argument was not persuasive. He disagreed with the definition of language used in the paper and took issue with several of the linguists she cited. He again turned down her request.

Stung by what she considered a facile rejection of her argument, Kathleen embarked on a second ASL paper for her argument class—this time aimed directly at the foreign language chair. She researched the history of her college's foreign language requirement and discovered that after being dropped in the 1970s, the requirement was revived in the 1990s, partly (her math professor confided) to revive flagging enrollments in foreign languages. She also interviewed foreign language teachers to uncover their assumptions about ASL. She discovered that many of them thought ASL was "easy to learn" and that given the option, many students would take ASL to avoid the rigors of "real" language classes. Additionally, she learned that foreign language teachers valued immersing students in a foreign culture; in fact, the foreign language requirement was seen as a key component in the college's attempt to improve multicultural education.

With her newly acquired understanding of her target audience, Kathleen reconceptualized her argument. She emphasized how difficult ASL was to learn (to counter her audience's belief that learning ASL was easy), how the deaf community formed a distinct culture with its own customs and literature (to show how ASL met the goals of multiculturalism), and how few students would transfer in with ASL credits (to allay fears that accepting ASL would threaten language enrollments). She concluded by citing her college's mission statement, which called for eradicating social injustice and for reaching out to the oppressed. Surely, she argued, encouraging hearing people to learn ASL would help integrate the deaf community more fully into the larger campus community. In sum, all her revisions—the reasons selected, the evidence used, the arrangement and tone—were guided by her desire to persuade.

Our point, then, is that all along the continuum writers are concerned both to seek truth and to persuade, but not necessarily with equal balance. Kathleen could not have written her second paper, aimed specifically at persuading the chair of foreign languages, if she hadn't first immersed herself in truth-seeking research that convinced her that ASL was indeed a distinct language. Nor are we saying that her second argument was better than her first. Both fulfilled their purposes and met the needs of their intended audiences. Both involved truth seeking and persuasion, but the first focused primarily on subject matter whereas the second focused primarily on audience.

ARGUMENT AND THE PROBLEM OF TRUTH

The tension that we have just examined between truth seeking and persuasion raises one of the oldest issues in the field of argument: Is the arguer's first obligation to truth or to winning the argument? And just what is the nature of the truth to which arguers are supposed to be obligated? To this second question we now turn.

good question

When Does Argument Become Propaganda?
The Debate Between Socrates and Callicles

One of the first great debates on the issue of truth versus victory occurs in Plato's dialogue *The Gorgias,* in which the philosopher Socrates takes on the rhetorician Callicles.

By way of background to the dispute, Socrates was a great philosopher known to us today primarily through his student Plato, whose "dialogues" depict Socrates debating various friends and antagonists. Socrates' stated goal in these debates was to "rid the world of error." In dialogue after dialogue, Socrates vanquishes error by skillfully leading people through a series of questions that force them to recognize the inconsistency and implausibility of their beliefs. He was a sort of intellectual judo master who takes opponents' arguments the way they want to go until they suddenly collapse.

Callicles, on the other hand, is a shadowy figure in history. We know him only through his exchange with Socrates—hence only through Plato's eyes. But Callicles is easily recognizable to philosophers as a representative of the Sophists, a group of teachers who schooled ancient Greeks in the fine art of winning arguments. The Sophists were a favorite, if elusive, target of both Socrates and Plato. Indeed, opposition to the Sophists' approach to life lies at the core of Platonic philosophy. Having said all that, let's turn to the dialogue.

Early in the debate, Socrates is clearly in control. He easily—too easily, as it turns out—wins a couple of preliminary rounds against some less determined Sophists before confronting Callicles. But in the long and arduous debate that follows, it's not at all clear that Socrates wins. In fact, one of the points being made in *The Gorgias* seems to be that philosophers committed to "clarifying" and discovering truth may occasionally have to sacrifice winning the debate in the name of their higher ends. Although Plato makes an eloquent case for enlightenment as the goal of argument, he may well contribute to the demise of this noble principle if he should happen to lose. Unfortunately, it appears that Socrates can't win the argument without sinning against the very principle he's defending.

The effectiveness of Callicles as a debater lies in his refusal to allow Socrates *any* assumptions. In response to Socrates' concern for virtue and justice, Callicles responds dismissively that such concepts are mere conventions, invented by the weak to protect themselves from the strong. Indeed, the power to decide what's "true" belongs to the winner of the debate. For Callicles, a truth that never wins is no truth at all because it will soon disappear.

Based on what we've said up to this point about our belief in argument as truth seeking, you might guess that our sympathies are with Socrates. To a great extent they are. But Socrates lived in a much simpler world than we do, if by "simple" we mean a world where the True and the Good were, if not universally agreed-upon notions, at least ones around which a clear consensus formed. For Socrates, there was one True Answer to any important question. Truth resided in the ideal world of forms, and through philosophic rigor humans could transcend the changing, shadowlike world of everyday reality to perceive the world of universals where Truth, Beauty, and Goodness resided.

Callicles, on the other hand, rejects the notion that there is only one possible truth at which all arguments will necessarily arrive. For Callicles, there are different degrees of truth and different kinds of truths for different situations or cultures. In raising the whole nettlesome question—How "true" is a "truth" that you can't get anyone to agree to?—Callicles is probably closer to the modern world than is Plato. Let's expand on Callicles' view of truth by examining some contemporary illustrations.

What Is Truth? The Place of Argument in Contemporary Life

Although the debate between Socrates and Callicles appears to end inconclusively, many readers over the centuries conceded the victory to Socrates almost by default. Callicles was seen as cheating. The term *sophistry* came to be synonymous with trickery in argument. The Sophists' relativistic beliefs were so repugnant to most people that they refused to grant any merit to the Sophists' position. In our century, however, the Sophists have found a more sympathetic readership, one that takes some of the questions they raised quite seriously.

In the twentieth century, absolute, demonstrable truth is seen by many thinkers, from physicists to philosophers, as an illusion. Some would argue that truth is merely a product of human beings' talking and arguing with each other. These thinkers say that when considering questions of interpretation, meaning, or value one can never tell for certain whether an assertion is true—not by examining the physical universe more closely or by reasoning one's way toward some Platonic form or by receiving a mystical revelation. The closest one can come to truth is through the confirmation of one's views from others in a community of peers. "Truth" in any field of knowledge, say these thinkers, is simply an agreement of knowledgeable people in that field.

To illustrate the relevance of Callicles to contemporary society, suppose for the moment that we wanted to ask whether sexual fidelity is a virtue. A Socratic approach would assume a single, real Truth about the value of sexual fidelity, one that could be discovered through a gradual peeling away of wrong answers. Callicles, meanwhile, would assume that sexual morality is culturally relative; hence, he might point out all the societies in which monogamous fidelity for one or both sexes is not the norm. Clearly, our world is more like Callicles'. We are all exposed to multiple cultural perspectives directly and indirectly. Through television, newspapers, travel, and education we experience ways of thinking and valuing that are different from our own. It is difficult to ignore the fact that our personal values are not universally shared or even respected. Thus, we're all faced with the need to justify our views in such a diverse society.

It should be clear, then, that when we speak of the truth seeking aim of argument, we do not mean the discovery of an absolute "right answer," but the willingness to think through the complexity of an issue and to consider respectfully a wide range of views. The process of argument allows social groups, through the thoughtful exchange of ideas, to seek the best solution to a problem. The value of argument is its ability to help social groups make decisions in a rational and humane way without resorting to violence or to other assertions of raw power.

❦ FOR CLASS DISCUSSION

On any given day, newspapers provide evidence of the complexity of living in a pluralist culture. Issues that could be readily decided in a completely homogeneous culture raise many questions for us in a society that has few shared assumptions.

What follows are two brief news stories that appeared on recent Associated Press wires. Choose one of the stories and conduct a "simulation game" in which various class members role-play the points of view of the characters involved in the controversy. If you choose the first case, for example, one class member should role-play the attorney of the woman refusing the Caesarean section, another the "court-appointed representative of the woman's fetus," and another the doctor. If you wish, conduct a court hearing in which other members role-play a judge, cross-examining attorneys, and a jury. No matter which case you choose, your class's goal should be to represent each point of view as fully and sympathetically as possible to help you realize the complexity of the values in conflict.

Illinois Court Won't Hear Case of Mom Who Refuses Surgery

CHICAGO—A complex legal battle over a Chicago woman's refusal to undergo a Caesarean section, even though it could save the life of her unborn child, essentially was settled yesterday when the state's highest court refused to hear the case.   1

The court declined to review a lower court's ruling that the woman should not be forced to submit to surgery in a case that pitted the rights of the woman, referred to in court as "Mother Doe," against those of her fetus.   2

The 22-year-old Chicago woman, now in the 37th week of her pregnancy, refused her doctors' advice to have the surgery because she believes God intended her to deliver the child naturally.   3

4   The woman's attorneys argued that the operation would violate her constitutional rights to privacy and the free exercise of her religious beliefs.

5   Cook County Public Guardian Patrick Murphy, the court-appointed representative of the woman's fetus, said he would file a petition with the U.S. Supreme Court asking it to hear the case. He has 90 days to file the petition, but he acknowledged future action would probably come too late.

6   Doctors say the fetus is not receiving enough oxygen from the placenta and will either die or be retarded unless it is delivered by Caesarean section. Despite that diagnosis, the mother has stressed her faith in God's healing powers and refused doctors' advice to submit to the operation.

Homeless Hit the Streets
to Protest Proposed Ban

1   SEATTLE—The homeless stood up for themselves by sitting down in a peaceful but vocal protest yesterday in Seattle's University District.

2   About 50 people met at noon to criticize a proposed set of city ordinances that would ban panhandlers from sitting on sidewalks, put them in jail for repeatedly urinating in public, and crack down on "intimidating" street behavior.

3   "Sitting is not a crime," read poster boards that feature mug shots of Seattle City Attorney Mark Sidran, who is pushing for the new laws. . . . "This is city property; the police want to tell us we can't sit here," yelled one man named R. C. as he sat cross-legged outside a pizza establishment.

4   Marsha Shaiman stood outside the University Book Store holding a poster and waving it at passing cars. She is not homeless, but was one of many activists in the crowd. "I qualify as a privileged white yuppie," she said. "I'm offended that the privileged people in this country are pointing at the poor, and people of color, and say they're causing problems. They're being used as scapegoats."

5   Many local merchants support the ban saying that panhandlers hurt business by intimidating shoppers and fouling the area with the odor of urine, vomited wine, and sometimes even feces.

A SUCCESSFUL PROCESS OF ARGUMENTATION: THE WELL-FUNCTIONING COMMITTEE

We have said that neither the fist-banging speaker nor the college debate team represents our ideal image of argument. The best image for us, as we have implied, is a well-functioning small group seeking a solution to a problem. In professional life such small groups usually take the form of committees.

We must acknowledge that many people find committee deliberations hopelessly muddled and directionless—the very antithesis of good argumentation. Our collective suspicion of committees is manifest in the many jokes we make about them. (For example, do you know the definition of the word *committee*? It's a place where people keep minutes and waste hours. Or: What is a zebra? A horse designed by a committee.)

Our society relies on committees, however, for the same reason that Winston Churchill preferred democracy: However imperfect it may be, the alternatives are worse. A single individual making decisions may be quirky, idiosyncratic, and insensitive to the effects of a decision on different groups of people; worse yet, he or she may pursue self-interests to the detriment of an entire group. On the other hand, too large a group makes argumentative discussion impossible. Hence, people have generally found it useful to delegate many decision- and policy-making tasks to a smaller, representative group—a committee.

We use the word *committee* in its broadest sense to indicate all sorts of important work that grows out of group conversation and debate. The Declaration of Independence is essentially a committee document with Thomas Jefferson as the chair. Similarly, the U.S. Supreme Court is in effect a committee of nine judges who rely heavily, as numerous books and articles have demonstrated, on small group decision-making processes to reach their judgments and formulate their legal briefs.

To illustrate our committee model for argument, let's briefly consider the workings of a university committee on which coauthor John Ramage recently served, the University Standards Committee. The Arizona State University (ASU) Standards Committee plays a role in university life analogous to that of the Supreme Court in civic life. It's the final court of appeal for ASU students seeking exceptions to various rules that govern their academic lives (such as registering under a different catalog, waiving a required course, or being allowed to retake a course for a third time).

The Standards Committee is a large committee, comprising nearly two dozen members who represent the whole spectrum of departments and offices across campus. Every two weeks, the committee meets for two or more hours to consider between twenty and forty appeals. The issues that regularly come before the committee draw forth all the argumentative strategies discussed in detail throughout this text. For example, all of the argument types discussed in Part Three regularly surface during committee deliberations. The committee deals with definition issues ("Is math anxiety a 'learning disability' for purposes of exempting a student from a math requirement? If so, what criteria can we establish for math anxiety?"); cause/consequence issues ("What were the causes of this student's sudden poor performance during spring semester?" "What will be the consequences of approving or denying her appeal?"); resemblance issues ("How is this case similar to an earlier case that we considered?"); evaluation issues ("Which criteria should take precedence in assessing this sort of appeal?"); and proposal issues ("Should we make it a policy to allow course X to substitute for course Y in the General Studies requirements?").

On any given day, the committee's deliberations showed how dialogue can lead to clarification of thinking. On many occasions, committee members' initial views shifted as they listened to opposing arguments. In one case, for example, a student petitioned to change the catalog under which she was supposed to graduate because the difference in requirements would let her graduate a half year sooner. Initially, many committee members argued against the petition. They reminded the committee that in several earlier cases it had denied petitions to change catalogs if the petitioner's intent was to evade the more rigorous graduation requirements imposed by a new General Studies curriculum. Moreover, the committee was reminded that letting one student change catalogs was unfair to other students who had to meet the more rigorous graduation standards.

However, after emphatic negative arguments had been presented, a few committee members began to voice support for the student's case. While acknowledging the truth of what other committee members had said, they pointed out reasons to support the petition. The young woman in question had taken most of the required General Studies courses; it was mostly changes in the requirements for her major that delayed her graduation. Moreover, she had performed quite well in what everyone acknowledged to be a demanding course of study. Although the committee had indeed turned down previous petitions of this nature, in none of those cases had the consequences of denial been so dire for the student.

After extended negotiations between the two sides on this issue, the student was allowed to change catalogs. Although the committee was reluctant to set a bad precedent (those who resisted the petition foresaw a deluge of similar petitions from less worthy candidates), it recognized unique circumstances that legitimately made this petitioner's case different. Moreover, the rigor of the student's curriculum, the primary concern of those who opposed the change, was shown to be greater than the rigor of many who graduated under the newer catalog.

As the previous illustration suggests, what allowed the committee to function as well as it did was the fundamental civility of its members and their collective concern that their decisions be just. Unlike some committees, this committee made many decisions, the consequences of which were not trivial for the people involved. Because of the significance of these outcomes, committee members were more willing than they otherwise might have been to concede a point to another member in the name of reaching a better decision and to view their deliberations as an ongoing process of negotiation rather than a series of win-lose debates.

CONCLUSION

In this chapter we have explored some of the complexities of argument, showing you why we believe that argument is not a matter of fist banging or of win-lose debate but of finding, through a process of rational inquiry, the best solution to a problem or issue. What is our advice for you at the close of this introductory chapter? Briefly, to accept both responsibilities of argument: truth seeking and persuasion. To argue responsibly, you should seek out a wide range of views, especially ones different from your own, and treat those views as rationally defensible, paying special attention to the reasons and evidence on which they rest.

Our goal in this text is to help you learn skills of argument. If you choose, you can use these skills cynically to argue any side of any issue. And yet we hope you choose to use these skills in the service of your deepest beliefs—beliefs that you discover or clarify through open-minded inquiry. Thus we hope that on some occasions you will modify your position on an issue while writing a rough draft (a sure sign that the process of arguing has complicated your views). If our culture sets you adrift in pluralism, argument can help you take a stand, to say, "These things I believe." In this text we will not pretend to tell you what position to take on any given issue. But if this text helps you define and defend your beliefs—to say, "Here are the reasons that I consider Choice A better than Choice B, and why you ought to share my view"—then we'll consider it a success.

chapter 2

Reading Arguments

WHY READING ARGUMENTS IS IMPORTANT FOR WRITERS

In the previous chapter we explained how reading and writing arguments is a social phenomenon growing out of people's search for the best answers to important questions. In this chapter we'll focus on the first half of that social dynamic—the thoughtful reading that all good arguments require of us.

Much of the advice we offer about reading applies equally to listening. In fact, it is often helpful to think of reading as a conversation. We like to tell students that a college library is not so much a repository of information as a discussion frozen in time until you as reader bring it to life. Those books and articles, stacked neatly on library shelves, are arguing with each other, carrying on a great extended conversation. As you read, you bring those conversations to life. And when you write in response to your reading, you enter those conversations.

SUGGESTIONS FOR IMPROVING YOUR READING PROCESS

Before we offer specific strategies for reading argument, let's examine some general reading strategies applicable to any complex text.

1. Slow down: Ads for speedreading courses misleadingly suggest that the best readers are the fastest readers. They're not. Expert readers adjust their reading speed to the complexity of the text and often read complex texts several times. They hold confusing passages in suspension, hoping that their confusion will be dispelled later in the text. They interact with the text in the margins, often extensively and vigorously.

2. Get the dictionary habit: When you can't tell a word's meaning from context, look it up—but not necessarily right away. One strategy is to make tick marks next to troublesome words and look them up when you come to a resting place so as not to break your concentration.

3. Lose your highlighter/find your pen: Relying on those yellow highlighters makes you too passive. Next time you get the urge to highlight a passage, write in the margin *why* you think it's important. Use the margins to note new points or major evidence, to mark particularly strong or weak points, to jot down summaries of major points or connections to other texts, to ask questions—but don't just color the pages.

4. Reconstruct the rhetorical context: Train yourself to ask "Who is this author? To whom is he or she writing? Why? What's the occasion?" Writers are real people writing for a real purpose in a specific context. Knowing these specifics will help you make sense of the writing.

5. Explore your views on the text's subject before reading: Before reading the text, note the title, read the first few paragraphs carefully, and skim the opening sentences of paragraphs. Once you've determined the author's views, explore your own views on the topic. Thus prepared, you can read the text through more critically and more pleasurably.

6. Continue conversing with a text after reading: Soon after reading, complete the following statements in a journal: "The most significant question this essay raises is. . . ." "The most important thing I learned from this essay is. . . ." "I agree with the author about. . . ." "But I disagree about. . . ."

7. Try "translating" difficult passages: Translate difficult passages into your own words. Doing so may not yield up the author's intended meaning, but it will force you to focus on the precise meaning of the words and help you to discover the source of your confusion.

STRATEGIES FOR READING ARGUMENTS: AN OVERVIEW

The preceding strategies work for any sort of text. In what follows, we focus on reading strategies specific to arguments. All our strategies are grounded in the social nature of argument and the assumption that every argument is one voice in a larger conversation. We recommend, thus, the following sequence of strategies:

1. Read as a believer.
2. Read as a doubter.
3. Seek out alternative views and analyze sources of disagreement to clarify why participants in the conversation disagree with each other.
4. Evaluate the various positions.

STRATEGY 1: READING AS A BELIEVER

When you read as a believer, you practice what psychologist Carl Rogers calls *empathic listening*. Empathic listening requires you to see the world through the author's eyes, to adopt temporarily the author's beliefs and values, and to suspend your skepticism and biases long enough to hear what the author is saying.

To test your powers of empathic listening, we ask you to try them out on a controversial article first published in *The Wall Street Journal* by political writer Charles Murray. The article initiated a national debate about rising illegitimacy rates. According to syndicated columnist John Leo, Murray's article "may turn out to be the most potent op-ed article in about 10 years."*

Before reading the article, consider your own attitudes toward single parenthood. Is it a problem that 30 percent of American babies are now born to unmarried mothers? If so, why? Can a single parent raise a child as effectively as a married couple? Why have these illegitimacy rates risen so dramatically? How might this trend be reversed?

The Coming White Underclass

Charles Murray

1   Every once in a while the sky really is falling, and this seems to be the case with the latest national figures on illegitimacy. The unadorned statistic is that, in 1991, 1.2 million children were born to unmarried mothers, within a hair of 30 percent of all live births. How high is 30 percent? About four percentage points higher than the black illegitimacy rate in the early 1960s that motivated Daniel Patrick Moynihan to write his famous memorandum on the breakdown of the black family.[1]

2   The 1991 story for blacks is that illegitimacy has now reached 68 percent of births to black women. In inner cities, the figure is typically in excess of 80 percent. Many of us have heard these numbers so often that we are inured. It is time to think about them as if we were back in the mid-1960s with the young Moynihan and asked to predict what would happen if the black illegitimacy rate were 68 percent.

3   Impossible we would have said. But if the proportion of fatherless boys in a given community were to reach such levels, surely the culture must be *Lord of the Flies* writ large,[2]

---

*John Leo, "New Cultural Conscience Shifts the Welfare Debate," *Seattle Times* 14 Dec. 1993:B4

[1]A reference to a controversial Department of Labor study, *The Negro Family: The Case for National Action* (Office of Planning and Reasearch, March 1965).

[2]A reference to William Golding's novel *Lord of the Flies*, in which a group of adolescent males become stranded on an island and create their own society with no adult supervision. As soon as adult "norms" begin to fade, the boys' culture gradually descends into savagery and violence.

the values of unsocialized male adolescents made norms—physical violence, immediate gratification and predatory sex. That is the culture now taking over the black inner city.

But the black story, however dismaying, is old news. The new trend that threatens the U.S. is white illegitimacy. Matters have not yet quite gotten out of hand, but they are on the brink. If we want to act, now is the time.

In 1991, 707,502 babies were born to single white women, representing 22 percent of white births. The elite wisdom holds that this phenomenon cuts across social classes, as if the increase in Murphy Browns[3] were pushing the trendline. Thus, a few months ago, a Census Bureau study of fertility among all American women got headlines for a few days because it showed that births to single women with college degrees doubled in the last decade to 6 percent from 3 percent. This is an interesting trend, but of minor social importance. The real news of that study is that the proportion of single mothers with less than a high school education who gave birth jumped to 48 percent from 35 percent in a single decade.

These numbers are dominated by whites. Breaking down the numbers by race (using data not available in the published version), women with college degrees contribute only 4 percent of white illegitimate babies, while women with a high school education or less contribute 82 percent. Women with family incomes of $75,000 or more contribute 1 percent of white illegitimate babies, while women with family incomes under $20,000 contribute 69 percent.

The National Longitudinal Study of Youth, a Labor Department study that has tracked more than 10,000 youths since 1979, shows an even more dramatic picture. For white women below the poverty line in the year prior to giving birth, 44 percent of births have been illegitimate, compared with only six percent for women above the poverty line. White illegitimacy is overwhelmingly a lower-class phenomenon.

This brings us to the emergence of a white underclass. In raw numbers, European-American whites are the ethnic group with the most people in poverty, most illegitimate children, most women on welfare, most unemployed men, and most arrests for serious crimes. And yet whites have not had an "underclass" as such, because the whites who might qualify have been scattered among the working class. Instead, whites have had "white trash" concentrated in a few streets on the outskirts of town, sometimes a Skid Row of unattached white men in the large cities. But these scatterings have seldom been large enough to make up a neighborhood. An underclass needs a critical mass, and white America has not had one.

But now the overall white illegitimacy rate is 22 percent. The figure in low-income, working-class communities may be twice that. How much illegitimacy can a community tolerate? Nobody knows, but the historical fact is that the trendlines on black crime, dropout from the labor force, and illegitimacy all shifted sharply upward as the overall black illegitimacy rate passed 25 percent.

---

[3]Murphy Brown, the star of a TV sitcom by the same name, became a single mother on a TV episode made famous in 1992 by then Vice President Quayle, who used her as a symbol of the breakdown of the traditional family.

10   The causal connection is murky—I blame the revolution in social policy during that period, while others blame the sexual revolution, broad shifts in cultural norms, or structural changes in the economy. But the white illegitimacy rate is approaching that same problematic 25 percent region at a time when social policy is more comprehensively wrongheaded than it was in the mid-1960s, and the cultural and sexual norms are still more degraded.

11   The white underclass will begin to show its face in isolated ways. Look for certain schools in white neighborhoods to get a reputation as being unteachable, with large numbers of disruptive students and indifferent parents. Talk to the police; listen for stories about white neighborhoods where the incidence of domestic disputes and casual violence has been shooting up. Look for white neighborhoods with high concentrations of drug activity and large numbers of men who have dropped out of the labor force. Some readers will recall reading the occasional news story about such places already.

12   As the spatial concentration of illegitimacy reaches critical mass, we should expect the deterioration to be as fast among low-income whites in the 1990s as it was among low-income blacks in the 1960s. My proposition is that illegitimacy is the single most important social problem of our time—more important than crime, drugs, poverty, illiteracy, welfare or homelessness because it drives everything else. Doing something about it is not just one more item on the American policy agenda, but should be at the top. Here is what to do.

13   In the calculus of illegitimacy, the constants are that boys like to sleep with girls and that girls think babies are endearing. Human societies have historically channeled these elemental forces of human behavior via thick walls of rewards and penalties that constrained the overwhelming majority of births to take place within marriage. The past 30 years have seen those walls cave in. It is time to rebuild them.

14   The ethical underpinning for the policies I am about to describe is this: Bringing a child into the world is the most important thing that most human beings ever do. Bringing a child into the world when one is not emotionally or financially prepared to be a parent is wrong. The child deserves society's support. The parent does not.

15   The social justification is this: A society with broad legal freedoms depends crucially on strong nongovernmental institutions to temper and restrain behavior. Of these, marriage is paramount. Either we reverse the current trends in illegitimacy—especially white illegitimacy—or America must, willy-nilly, become an unrecognizably authoritarian, socially segregated, centralized state.

16   To restore the rewards and penalties of marriage does not require social engineering. Rather, it requires that the state stop interfering with the natural forces that have done the job quite effectively for millennia. Some of the changes I will describe can occur at the federal level; others would involve state laws. For now, the important thing is to agree on what should be done.

17   I begin with the penalties, of which the most obvious are economic. Throughout human history, a single woman with a small child has not been a viable economic unit. Not being a viable economic unit, neither have the single woman and child been a legitimate social unit. In small numbers they must be a net drain on the community's resources. In large numbers, they must destroy the community's capacity to sustain itself. *Mirabile dictu,*

communities everywhere have augmented the economic penalties of single parenthood with severe social stigma.

Restoring economic penalties translates into the first and central policy prescription: to 18 end all economic support for single mothers. The AFDC (Aid to Families with Dependent Children) payment goes to zero. Single mothers are not eligible for subsidized housing or for food stamps. An assortment of other subsidies and in-kind benefits disappear. Since universal medical coverage appears to be an idea whose time has come, I will stipulate that all children have medical coverage. But with that exception, the signal is loud and unmistakable. From society's perspective, to have a baby that you cannot care for yourself is profoundly irresponsible, and the government will no longer subsidize it.

How does a poor young mother survive without government support? The same way 19 she has since time immemorial. If she wants to keep a child, she must enlist support from her parents, boyfriend, siblings, neighbors, church or philanthropies. She must get support from somewhere, anywhere, other than the government. The objectives are threefold.

First, enlisting the support of others raises the probability that other mature adults are 20 going to be involved with the upbringing of the child, and this is a great good in itself.

Second, the need to find support forces a self-selection process. One of the most short- 21 sighted excuses made for current behavior is that an adolescent who is utterly unprepared to be a mother "needs someone to love." Childish yearning isn't a good enough selection device. We need to raise the probability that a young single woman who keeps her child is doing so volitionally and thoughtfully. Forcing her to find a way of supporting the child does this. It will lead many young women who shouldn't be mothers to place their babies for adoption. This is good. It will lead others, watching what happens to their sisters, to take steps not to get pregnant. This is also good. Many others will get abortions. Whether this is good depends on what one thinks of abortion.

Third, stigma will regenerate. The pressure on relatives and communities to pay for 22 the folly of their children will make an illegitimate birth the socially horrific act it used to be, and getting a girl pregnant something boys do at the risk of facing a shotgun. Stigma and shotgun marriages may or may not be good for those on the receiving end, but their deterrent effect on others is wonderful—and indispensable.

What about women who can find no support but keep the baby anyway? There are 23 laws already on the books about the right of the state to take a child from a neglectful parent. We have some 360,000 children in foster care because of them. Those laws would still apply. Society's main response, however, should be to make it as easy as possible for those mothers to place their children for adoption at infancy. To that end, state governments must strip adoption of the nonsense that has encumbered it in recent decades.

The first step is to make adoption easy for any married couple who can show reason- 24 able evidence of having the resources and stability to raise a child. Lift all restrictions on interracial adoption. Ease age limitations for adoptive parents.

The second step is to restore the traditional legal principle that placing a child for adop- 25 tion means irrevocably relinquishing all legal rights to the child. The adoptive parents are parents without qualification. Records are sealed until the child reaches adulthood, at which time they may be unsealed only with the consent of biological child and parent.

26   Given these straightforward changes—going back to the old way, which worked—there is reason to believe that some extremely large proportion of infants given up by their mothers will be adopted into good homes. This is true not just for flawless blue-eyed blond infants but for babies of all colors and conditions. The demand for infants to adopt is huge.

27   Some small proportion of infants and larger proportion of older children will not be adopted. For them, the government should spend lavishly on orphanages. I am not recommending Dickensian barracks. In 1993, we know a lot about how to provide a warm, nurturing environment for children, and getting rid of the welfare system frees up lots of money to do it. Those who find the "orphanages" objectionable may think of them as 24-hour-a-day preschools. Those who prattle about the importance of keeping children with their biological mothers may wish to spend some time in a patrol car or with a social worker seeing what the reality of life with welfare-dependent biological mothers can be like.

28   Finally, there is the matter of restoring the rewards of marriage. Here, I am pessimistic about how much government can do and optimistic about how little it needs to do. The rewards of raising children within marriage are real and deep. The main task is to shepherd children through adolescence so that they can reach adulthood—when they are likely to recognize the value of those rewards—free to take on marriage and family. The main purpose of the penalties for single parenthood is to make that task easier.

29   One of the few concrete things that the government can do to increase the rewards of marriage is make the tax code favor marriage and children. Those of us who are nervous about using the tax code for social purposes can advocate making the tax code at least neutral.

30   A more abstract but ultimately crucial step in raising the rewards of marriage is to make marriage once again the sole legal institution through which parental rights and responsibilities are defined and exercised.

31   Little boys should grow up knowing from their earliest memories that if they want to have any rights whatsoever regarding a child that they sire—more vividly, if they want to grow up to be a daddy—they must marry. Little girls should grow up knowing from their earliest memories that if they want to have any legal claims whatsoever on the father of their children, they must marry. A marriage certificate should establish that a man and a woman have entered into a unique legal relationship. The changes in recent years that have blurred the distinctiveness of marriage are subtly but importantly destructive.

32   Together, these measures add up to a set of signals, some with immediate and tangible consequences, others with long-term consequences, still others symbolic. They should be supplemented by others based on a re-examination of divorce law and its consequences.

33   That these policy changes seem drastic and unrealistic is a peculiarity of our age, not of the policies themselves. With embellishments, I have endorsed the policies that were the uncontroversial law of the land as recently as John Kennedy's presidency. Then, America's elites accepted as a matter of course that a free society such as America's can sustain itself only through virtue and temperance in the people, that virtue and temperance depend centrally on the socialization of each new generation, and that the socialization of each generation depends on the matrix of care and resources fostered by marriage.

34   Three decades after that consensus disappeared, we face an emerging crisis. The long, steep climb in black illegitimacy has been calamitous in black communities and painful for

the nation. The reforms I have described will work for blacks as for whites, and have been needed for years. But the brutal truth is that American society as a whole could survive when illegitimacy became epidemic within a comparably small ethnic minority. It cannot survive the same epidemic among whites.

So how well did you "listen" to Murray's article? Can you summarize his argument fairly and accurately in your own words? Can you identify experiences, values, and beliefs of your own that support his argument?

Summary Writing, Empathic Listening, and Reading to Believe

An excellent way of listening to an argument is to write a summary of it in your own words. A *summary* (also called an *abstract*, a *precis*, or a *synopsis*) presents only a text's major points and eliminates supporting data. While book summaries can be several pages long, article summaries typically range between 100 and 300 words.

Practicing the following steps will help you be a better summary writer.

1. Read the essay first for general meaning. Don't judge the argument; just follow the writer's meaning, trying to see the issue from the writer's perspective.

2. Read the argument slowly a second time, writing brief *says* and *does* statements for each paragraph. A *says* statement summarizes a paragraph's content. A *does* statement identifies a paragraph's function (e.g., "summarizes opposition," "provides supporting statistics," "offers illustrative anecdote"). What follows are *says* and *does* statements for the first eight paragraphs of Murray's article (boldface numbers refer to original paragraph numbers).

DOES/SAYS ANALYSIS OF MURRAY

Paragraphs 1–2: *Does:* Introduces and underscores significance of problem. *Says:* Illegitimate birthrates are soaring, far exceeding the 25 percent level that Daniel Moynihan once said would signal the breakdown of the black family.

Paragraph 3: *Does:* Lends presence to his claim by use of an analogy. *Says:* Like the marooned boys in *Lord of the Flies,* illegitimate children will create a savage society.

Paragraph 4: *Does:* Provides transition from discussion of black illegitimacy rates to white illegitimacy rates. *Says:* The white illegitimacy problem is growing but still controllable.

Paragraphs 5–7: *Does:* Supports and limits the claim that the white illegitimacy rate is growing. *Says:* While 22 percent of all white births are illegitimate, working class whites' rates are much higher.

Paragraph 8: *Does:* Defines illegitimacy problem as part of the larger problem of an "emergent white underclass." *Says:* The white underclass is now large enough to constitute a "critical mass."

❦ FOR CLASS DISCUSSION ━━━━━━━━━━━━━━━━━━━━━━━━━━━━━━━

Working individually or in groups, make *says* and *does* statements for the rest of Murray's article.

━━ ❦

3. Convert your *says* and *does* statements into a list of the major points and sub-points of the argument. If you are visually oriented, you may prefer to make a flow chart or diagram of the article. (See Figure 2.1 for our diagram of Murray's article.)

4. Turn your list, outline, flowchart, or diagram into a prose summary. Typically, writers do this in one of two ways. Some start with a lengthy paragraph-by-paragraph summary and then prune it in successive drafts. Others start with a one-sentence summary of the argument's thesis and major supporting reasons and then gradually flesh it out with more supporting ideas.

5. Continue writing drafts until your summary is the desired length and is sufficiently clear, complete, and concise that someone who hasn't read the original could read your summary and explain the original to a third party.

As illustrations, consider the following three summaries of Murray's article.

ONE-SENTENCE SUMMARY

To solve the problem of illegitimacy, which has long been at crisis levels for black culture and now is reaching crisis proportions among lower-class whites, the United States should end all economic support for single mothers, thereby reawakening social stigmas against single parenthood. (45 words)

100-WORD SUMMARY

The illegitimacy rate in America, now 30 percent of all live births, has increased most dramatically among lower-class whites, where we can now predict the same kind of social breakdown that characterized black inner-city culture when illegitimacy rates soared above 25 percent. The solution is to revitalize cultural constraints against illegitimacy by ending all economic support for single mothers. Three good results will follow: (1) More family and friends will be involved in raising the child; (2) more infants will be given for adoption; and (3) social stigmas against illegitimacy will be reawakened. This approach, although seemingly drastic, returns our nation to earlier policies. (101 words)

250-WORD SUMMARY

The illegitimacy rate in America has reached 30 percent of all live births, thus exceeding the 25 percent black illegitimacy rate in the 1960s that sparked Moynihan's prophetic warnings about the breakdown of the black family.

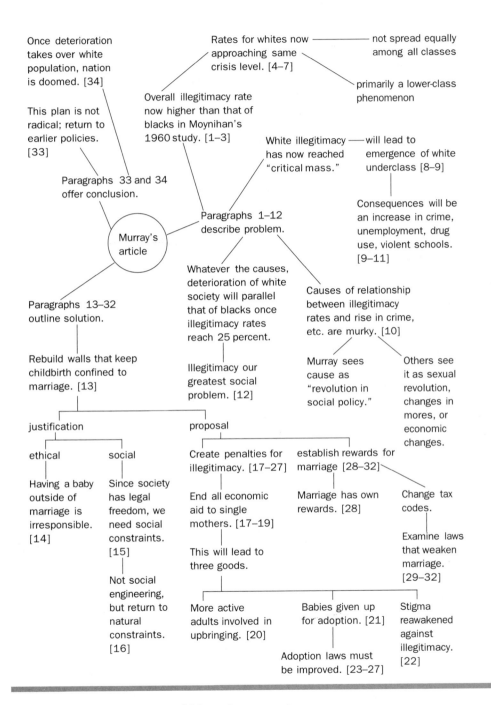

Once deterioration takes over white population, nation is doomed. [34]

This plan is not radical; return to earlier policies. [33]

Paragraphs 33 and 34 offer conclusion.

Murray's article

Rates for whites now —— not spread equally approaching same among all classes crisis level. [4–7]

primarily a lower-class phenomenon

Overall illegitimacy rate now higher than that of blacks in Moynihan's 1960 study. [1–3]

White illegitimacy ——will lead to has now reached emergence of white "critical mass." underclass [8–9]

Consequences will be an increase in crime, unemployment, drug use, violent schools. [9–11]

Paragraphs 1–12 describe problem.

Paragraphs 13–32 outline solution.

Rebuild walls that keep childbirth confined to marriage. [13]

Whatever the causes, deterioration of white society will parallel that of blacks once illegitimacy rates reach 25 percent.

Illegitimacy our greatest social problem. [12]

Causes of relationship between illegitimacy rates and rise in crime, etc. are murky. [10]

Murray sees cause as "revolution in social policy."

Others see it as sexual revolution, changes in mores, or economic changes.

justification

ethical

social

proposal

Having a baby outside of marriage is irresponsible. [14]

Since society has legal freedom, we need social constraints. [15]

Not social engineering, but return to natural constraints. [16]

Create penalties for illegitimacy. [17–27]

establish rewards for marriage [28–32]

End all economic aid to single mothers. [17–19]

Marriage has own rewards. [28]

Change tax codes.

Examine laws that weaken marriage. [29–32]

This will lead to three goods.

More active adults involved in upbringing. [20]

Babies given up for adoption. [21]

Stigma reawakened against illegitimacy. [22]

Adoption laws must be improved. [23–27]

FIGURE 2.1 Branch diagram of Murray's argument

Illegitimate births among lower-class whites have risen so dramatically that a new white underclass is beginning to emerge. We can thus predict the same kind of social breakdown among working-class whites (increase in crime, drug abuse, unemployment, unmanageable schools) that has characterized the black inner city. The solution, which can be justified on both ethical and social grounds, is to revitalize cultural constraints against illegitimacy. We should begin by ending all economic support for single mothers, forcing them to seek assistance from family, boyfriends, or charities. Three good results will follow: (1) more adults will be involved in raising the child; (2) many single mothers will decide against keeping infants and offer them for adoption; and (3) angry families will reawaken the social stigma against illegitimacy. To make the solution workable, we must ease adoption laws and be prepared to spend lavishly on orphanages. Finally, we must increase the rewards of marriage through restructured tax codes and reexamination of divorce laws and other regulations that undermine the social importance of marriage. Although this approach seems drastic, it merely returns our nation to the policies that prevailed up through John Kennedy's presidency. Unless we return to the values of virtue and temperance, the social catastrophe that has undermined black culture will sweep through white culture also, thus destroying our nation. (253 words)

We don't want to pretend that these summaries were easy to write. They weren't. Murray's argument is difficult to summarize because it is complex and occasionally lacks transitions and explicitly stated points. Consequently some readers may disagree with our selection of key points.

Incorporating Summaries into Your Writing

Suppose you wanted to incorporate a summary of Murray's argument into your own essay on welfare reform. You could do so by using *attributive tags* such as "Murray says" and "according to Murray." These tags announce that you are reporting someone else's views rather than your own. If you copy any of Murray's direct wording, you also need quotation marks around the borrowed language. The following example uses the documentation system of the Modern Language Association (MLA).*

SUMMARY OF MURRAY INCORPORATED INTO YOUR OWN ESSAY

Conservative social critic Charles Murray, writing in the *Wall Street Journal,* argues that America's skyrocketing illegitimacy rate is "the single most important social

---

*Most college handbooks explain the MLA documentation system (used primarily in the humanities) as well as the APA (American Psychological Association) system, used in the social sciences. In this example, numbers in parentheses indicate page numbers in this text where the quotations can be found. A listing of complete bibliographic information would be included on a separate page at the end of the essay under the heading "Works Cited."

problem of our time" (22). Citing extensive statistical evidence, Murray argues that the illegitimacy rate in America has reached 30 percent of all live births, thus exceeding the 25 percent black illegitimacy rate in the 1960s that sparked Daniel Patrick Moynihan's prophetic warnings about the breakdown of the black family. Murray's proposed solution is to revive cultural constraints against illegitimacy by ending all economic support for single mothers. Murray argues that three good results will follow: (1) More family and friends will be involved in raising the child, (2) more infants will be given for adoption, and (3) social stigmas against illegitimacy will be awakened. Murray believes that this approach, although drastic at first glance, returns our nation to earlier policies.

WORKS CITED

Murray, Charles. "The Coming White Underclass." *Wall Street Journal* 29 Oct. 1993: A13. Rpt. in *Writing Argument*, Concise Edition. John D. Ramage and John C. Bean. Needham, MA: Allyn and Bacon, 1998. 20–25.

Suspending Doubt: Willing Your Own Belief in the Writer's View

Summarizing an argument is only one aspect of trying to believe it. You must also suspend doubt and will yourself to adopt the writer's view, something easy to do when you already agree with the author. But if an author's views affront your own values, then "believing" can be a hard but valuable, exercise. By struggling to believe strange, dangerous, or unfamiliar views, we can grow as learners and thinkers.

To believe an author, search your mind for personal experiences, values, and beliefs that affirm his or her argument. Here is how one student, whose political values differ markedly from Murray's, tried to believe his argument in her journal.

JOURNAL ENTRY SHOWING STUDENT'S ATTEMPT TO BELIEVE MURRAY

Murray seems unconcerned about the fate of children (I can't stand the thought of putting babies in orphanages), but I admit that I can see the problem Murray is trying to address. I agree that a rising illegitimacy rate is a scary problem and that kids are better off with two parents who will love their children and not leave them to roam the streets. Anything that would put social pressure on families to keep their daughters from getting pregnant (and sons from seeking sex) might help. Although I don't think girls get pregnant for the welfare money, I can see how the absence of that money might lead adults to put more social pressure on teenagers to avoid sex or to have safe sex. I don't know what would happen to all the babies during the transition period, but I can see how we would be sending a strong message that you shouldn't have a baby unless you can support it. If there were only some way to punish the teenagers without abandoning the babies!

STRATEGY 2: READING AS A DOUBTER

But reading as a believer isn't enough. You must also read as a doubter by raising objections, asking questions, expressing skepticism, and withholding assent. In the margins you add a new layer of notations demanding more proof, doubting evidence, challenging the author's assumptions and values, and so forth.

❧ FOR CLASS DISCUSSION

Return now to Murray's article, reading it skeptically this time. Raise questions, offer objections, express doubts. Then, working as a class or in small groups, list all doubts you have about Murray's argument.

❧

Now that you've doubted Murray's article, compare your doubts to some of those raised by our students.

- Murray seems to have no compassion for those who would suffer from his proposal. He treats people like numbers.

- Murray initially calls the causes of the problem "murky" (paragraph 9) and says that the "revolution in social policy" is the primary culprit. But what if other changes—sexual revolution, shift in cultural norms, or changes in the economy—are more important?

- Will changing welfare rules really change behaviors of sexually active young adults? If poor women have babies to relieve the hopelessness of poverty, then Murray's proposal might increase illegitimacy by worsening poverty.

- If welfare payments suddenly stopped and single mothers were unable to get help from family and friends, how many babies might starve or be abandoned? Would these "lavish" orphanages really work?

- Our group felt the article was racist. Murray seems to have completely given up on Black America.

- Murray seems to view the past sentimentally. He assumes that all earlier cultures were modeled on 1950s two-parent nuclear families. He believes that what worked in the Fifties worked "for millennia." Were the Fifties really all that great?

- Murray is a sexist when it comes to sex. He assumes that only boys like sex while girls just want babies. He thus ignores improved sex education and family planning programs as part of his solution.

These are only some of the objections that might be raised against Murray's article. You and your classmates may have other important objections. Our point is that both doubting and believing are essential to a full reading. Whereas believing expands your view of the world and enlarges your sympathies, doubting protects you from being overpowered by others' arguments and teaches you to reflect thoughtfully on those arguments.

STRATEGY 3: SEEKING OUT ALTERNATIVE VIEWS AND ANALYZING SOURCES OF DISAGREEMENT

If you were an arbitrator, you wouldn't think of settling a dispute between A and B on the basis of A's testimony alone. You would also insist on hearing B's side of the story. By the same token, you can't fairly evaluate an argument detached from the controversy out of which it arose, or isolated from the alternative views to which it speaks. You must seek out those views.

In analyzing disagreements among various points of view, you'll find they typically fall into two categories: (1) disagreement about the facts or truth of the case, and (2) disagreements about underlying beliefs, values, or assumptions. Let's consider each in turn.

Disagreement about Facts or Truth

Theoretically, a fact is a piece of empirical data on which everyone agrees. Often, however, one person's "fact" is another person's "distortion." Thus, in the 1996 presidential elections Bob Dole claimed that Bill Clinton had pushed through "the largest tax increase in U.S. history." Clinton responded that a tax increase passed during the Bush administration (for which Dole had voted) was much higher in "adjusted dollars." Here Dole and Clinton disagree about "facts"—in this case, the proper way to represent numbers that can be expressed in a variety of ways. Disagreements can also arise over the way facts are interpreted. Thus, in arguing what to do about the problem of illegitimacy, disputants may agree that the illegitimacy rate is rising but disagree about causes and therefore about solutions.

Disagreement about Values, Beliefs, or Assumptions

A second source of disagreement concerns differences in values, beliefs, or assumptions. For example, Persons A and B may agree that a huge tax on gasoline would cut down on the consumption of petroleum. They may agree further that the world's supply of petroleum will eventually run out. Thus A and B agree at the level of facts. But they may disagree about whether the United States should enact a huge gas tax. Person A may support a tax increase to conserve oil, whereas person B may oppose it, perhaps because B believes that scientists will find alternative energy sources before the petroleum runs out or because B believes the short-term harm of such a tax outweighs distant benefits.

Sometimes disagreements about assumptions present themselves as disagreements about definitions or analogies. A and B may disagree whether *Playboy* is pornographic primarily because they define *pornography* differently. Similarly, people may disagree about the appropriateness of an analogy. Chief Justice William Rehnquist once argued that desecrating a flag is like desecrating the Washington Monument. By analogy, he concluded that we ought to forbid flag burning on the same grounds that we forbid desecrating national monuments. Opposing justices thought the analogy was inappropriate; they saw significant differences between burning a $30 mass-produced piece of symbolic cloth owned by the defendant and vandalizing a one-of-a-kind, multimillion dollar monument owned by the government.

❦ FOR CLASS DISCUSSION

As you might expect, the Murray piece provoked a great deal of controversy, particularly at the level of the values and assumptions it represented. What follows are two responses to Murray's piece. The first, a partial column by John Leo, is basically sympathetic to Murray's world view, while the second, by columnist Dorothy Gilliam, is decidedly less sympathetic.

1. What does each response reveal about the underlying beliefs, assumptions, and values of its author?

2. How do these two writers' underlying beliefs, assumptions, and values cause them to agree or disagree with Murray and with each other?

Response 1: Excerpt from "New Cultural Conscience Shifts Welfare Debate"

John Leo

1   . . . Reflecting the current state of the argument, President Clinton seems to say things like this, over and over: "Would we be a better-off society if babies were born to married couples? You bet we would." He told ministers in Memphis, Tenn., that if the Rev. Martin Luther King Jr. were to reappear today, he would say, among other things, "I did not live and die to see the American family destroyed." We are a long way here from last year's general babble about "family diversity" and "new family forms."

2   It says a lot about the current cultural moment that a Democratic president is starting to echo conservative scholar Charles Murray . . . Murray wants America to go cold-turkey on welfare—eliminating it completely. On Oct. 29, the *Wall Street Journal* published a piece by Murray that may turn out to be the most potent op-ed article in about 10 years. . . .

3   Murray's piece has had an explosive impact in policy discussions. He says it's like striking a spike into the earth and feeling "enormous pressure in the ground ready to explode."

He feels there's a chance now for "real radical reform." That's the new cultural moment. Like it or not, President Clinton seems to feel it, too. He said in an interview with Tom Brokaw that Murray's op-ed piece is "essentially right," though he questions the prescription of eliminating welfare entirely.

The debate on welfare will now take place on Murray's terms, not Clinton's, a rather   4
amazing phenomenon that nobody could have predicted a few weeks ago. Murray's analysis removes race from the welfare debate, since he sees whites and blacks going through the same process. And it calls into question all the sex programs and condom distribution schemes that sustain the highly sexualized youth culture driving the illegitimacy rate. Welcome to a new moment and a very different debate.

Response 2: Wrong Way to Reform Welfare
Dorothy Gilliam

With an eye toward reducing the rate of teenage pregnancy, the White House task force   1
on welfare reform wants to curtail additional benefits to unmarried mothers who have more children while on welfare.

Taking this drive to discourage out-of-wedlock births among young welfare recipients   2
a step further, Charles Murray, a fellow at the conservative American Enterprise Institute, wants to cut off all economic support to single mothers who have additional children while on welfare—no monetary assistance, no food stamps, no subsidized housing.

I agree with the underlying analysis that the problem of children born to poor, single   3
mothers is a crucial issue in welfare reform because it helps drive so many other social problems: crime, drugs, violence, poverty and illiteracy.

But the task force proposal and Murray's draconian "solutions" are not the answer.   4

Not only is there a lack of substantiated evidence linking welfare benefits to increases   5
in illegitimate births, but the task force's approach also is really a punitive, morally questionable attempt at social engineering on the backs of poor people.

President Clinton has not received the task force's final report on welfare reform,   6
which includes the aforementioned proposal and several others meant to discourage additional births among single, young mothers. But, thank God, he already has had the good sense to question whether that alternative would be "morally right."

Meanwhile, many children and family advocacy groups are working hard to turn the   7
tide against the idea.

"Frankly, I'm sick and tired of social engineering on the backs of poor women," said   8
David S. Liederman, executive director of the Child Welfare League of America.

Citing New Jersey's current experiment with "child exclusion" provisions for mothers   9
on public assistance, Liederman said trying to stop women from having additional children is "nonsense."

"There is no history that says these kinds of behavior-modification schemes have any   10
effect on whether or not women have children," Liederman said in an interview. "It

assumes women have children for money, and that is not true. The children suffer, and the baby who needs support doesn't get it."

11   Murray, writing recently in the *Wall Street Journal* that the United States is quickly developing a white underclass that is larger and potentially more devastating than the black underclass, goes on to propose a myriad of solutions to reduce the rising number of births among poor, single white women.

12   But the fallacy of Murray's argument is his belief that punitive action would change behavior. It's an argument that does not take into account why such behavior exists. Pamela J. Maraldo, president of Planned Parenthood Federation of America, believes too much attention is being paid to the issue of marital status, and too little to the more crucial issue of mutual commitment of parents to each other and their children.

13   "The issue is not whether a child is illegitimate, but whether that child is wanted or unwanted," Maraldo said.

14   Though a great deal of attention has been focused on the huge cost of welfare, Liederman notes that the budget for Aid to Families with Dependent Children equals 1 percent of the federal budget.

15   "To hear some folks rail about welfare, you'd think it's the terrible monster that is causing all of the evils," he said. "But to care for almost 10 million children with 1 percent of the budget is miraculous."

16   If Clinton is serious about "ending welfare as we know it," as he pledged in his campaign, his planners must take seriously what most advocates have long said: Most women do not want to be on welfare and would prefer jobs that position them to get off the rolls permanently.

17   Though welfare certainly includes a fringe of recipients who abuse the system, the focus should be on the majority of poor mothers and children who earnestly want better lives.

18   It's a quick-fix mentality that presumes that welfare can be reformed in isolation of all the root social problems that feed into it: poor housing, drug-related violence, joblessness, lack of opportunity. It's a cowardly mentality that targets the poor because they lack clout.

19   Why not, instead, exploit the current momentum for welfare reform by offering more continuing education and job-training opportunities for people who want meaningful work? That way reform would help them and their children, not punish them because they had the bad luck to be born disadvantaged and poor.

20   It would be a sad day if this country chooses the proposed alternative: to throw poor women and their children overboard.

STRATEGY 4: EVALUATING THE CONFLICTING POSITIONS

In asking you to evaluate an argument or a set of arguments, we don't mean for you simply to choose a winner. Rather, we ask you to make your own journey toward clarity. In the arguments you are examining, which lines of reasoning seem strong? Which seem weak? What facts are disputed? Where do people disagree about values? What additional research do you need to pursue? As we have seen in the dispute between Murray and Gilliam, writers don't always address neatly the questions you find most crucial. For example, neither Murray nor Gilliam satisfactorily analyzes the causes of rising illegitimacy rates. The one blames welfare benefits, the other blames hopelessness and poverty, but neither supports his or her claim with data.

To give you an extended example of how a person might evaluate conflicting positions in a controversy, we turn now to a new issue: the controversy over global warming. Early in your exploration of this issue, you come across the following newspaper editorial, which appeared in *USA Today:*

Imagine a world like this:

Omaha, Neb., sweats through the worst drought in its history. In July 2030, the mercury hits 100 on 20 days. Crops are wiped out; the Midwest is a dust bowl.

New Orleans is under water. The French Quarter has shut down; the Superdome holds a small lake. The governor says property damage will be in the billions.

Washington, D.C., suffers through its hottest summer—87 days above 90 degrees. Water is rationed; brownouts are routine because utilities can't meet demand for electricity. Federal employees, working half-days in unbearable heat, report an alarming rise in skin cancer across the USA.

Abroad, floods have inundated Bangladesh and Indonesia. The seas are four feet above 1986 levels. The United Nations reports millions will die in famines; shocking climate changes have ruined agriculture.

That sounds far-fetched, but if some scientists' worst fears come true, that could be what our children inherit.

Since the beginning of this century, man has been spewing pollutants into the atmosphere at an ever-increasing rate. Carbon dioxide and chlorofluorocarbons—CFC's—are fouling the air, our life support system. Everything that burns releases carbon dioxide. CFC's are used to make refrigerants, Styrofoam, computer chips, and other products.

In the past century, carbon dioxide in the atmosphere has risen 25 percent. The problem is that carbon dioxide holds in heat, just as the roof of a greenhouse does. That's why the Earth's warming is called the greenhouse effect.

CFC's retain heat, too, and break down the atmosphere's protective layer of ozone. If it is damaged, more of the sun's ultraviolet rays will reach Earth, causing skin cancer and damaging sea life.

Combined with the loss of forests that absorb carbon dioxide, the effects of this pollution could be disastrous. By 2030, Earth's temperature could rise 8 degrees, polar ice caps would melt, weather would change, crops would wilt.

There is growing evidence that these pollutants are reaching ominous levels. At the South Pole, the ozone layer has a "hole" in it—it's been depleted by 40 percent. NASA scientist Robert Watson says: "Global warming is inevitable—it's only a question of magnitude and time."

Some say don't panic, probably nothing will happen. The trouble with that is that we know these pollutants are building, and by the time we are sure of the worst effects, it may be too late. Action is needed, now. The USA must:

—Recognize that global warming may worsen and begin planning responses; more research is needed, too.

—Renew the search for safe, clean alternatives to fossil fuels, nuclear fission, and chlorofluorocarbons.

—Report on the extent of the problem to the world and press for international controls on air pollution.

The possible dimensions of this disaster are too big to just "wait and see." If a runaway train heads for a cliff and the engineer does nothing, the passengers are bound to get hurt. Let's check the brakes before it's too late.

When the students in one of our classes first read this editorial, they found it both persuasive and frightening. The opening scenario of potential disasters—New Orleans under water, unbearable heat, water rationing, floods, ruined agriculture, "alarming rise in skin cancer"—scared the dickens out of many readers. The powerful effect of the opening scenario was increased by the editorial's subsequent use of scientific data: carbon dioxide has increased 25 percent, the ozone layer has been depleted by 40 percent, a NASA scientist says that "[g]lobal warming is inevitable . . . " and so forth. Additionally, a plausible cause-and-effect chain explains the approaching disaster: the spewing of pollutants and the cutting down of forests lead to increased CO_2, which traps heat; use of CFC's breaks down the ozone layer, allowing more ultraviolet radiation to reach earth's surface, thereby causing cancer.

Inexperienced researchers might be tempted to quote this article. Unwittingly, they might even distort the article slightly by writing something like this:

According to *USA Today,* our civilization is on a train ride to disaster unless we put on the brakes. If global warming continues on its present course, by the year 2030, New Orleans will be under water, crops will be wiped out by droughts . . . [and so forth].

But a more careful reading of the *USA Today* piece suggests just how misguided this summary is. First of all, the article is couched in "coulds" and "mights." If we read carefully, we see that the opening scenario isn't represented as factual, inevitable, or even likely. Rather, it is represented as the "worst fears" of "some scientists." Near the end of the editorial we learn that "[s]ome say don't panic" but we aren't told whether these "some" are respectable scientists, carefree politicians, crackpots, or what. But the most puzzling aspect of this editorial is the gap between the alarming worst-case scenario at the beginning of the editorial and the tepid recommendations at the end. The final "call for action" calls for no real action at all. Recommendations 1 and 3 call for more research and for "international controls on air pollution"—nicely vague terms that create little reader discomfort. The second recommendation—renew the search for safe alternatives—reveals the writer's comfortable American optimism that scientists will find a way out of the dilemma without causing Americans any real distress. If the "possible dimensions of this disaster" are as great as the opening scenario leads us to believe, then perhaps wrenching changes in our economy are needed to cut down our dependence on fossil fuels.

But what is the actual truth here? How serious is the greenhouse effect and what should the United States do about it? A search for the truth involves us in the sequence of reading strategies suggested in this chapter: (1) reading as a believer, (2) reading as a doubter, (3) seeking out alternative views and asking why the various sides disagree with each other, and (4) evaluating the various positions. When our students applied this strategy to the greenhouse effect, they came to the unsettling realization that the experts disagree—about both the facts of the case and about underlying values.

So what do you do when the experts disagree? It is important to realize that experts can look at the same data, analyze the same arguments, listen to the same authorities, and still reach different conclusions. Seldom will one expert's argument triumph over another's. More often, one expert's argument will modify another's and in turn will be modified by yet another's. Your own expertise is not a function of your ability to choose the "right" argument, but of your ability to listen to alternative viewpoints, to understand why people disagree, and to synthesize your own argument from those disagreements.

Here is our brief analysis of some of the disagreements about the greenhouse effect.

Questions of Fact

At the heart of the controversy is the question "How serious is the greenhouse effect?" On the basis of our own research, we discovered that scientists agree on one fact: The amount of carbon dioxide in the earth's atmosphere has increased 7 percent since accurate measurements were first taken during the International Geophysical Year 1957/58. Additionally, scientists seem to agree that the percentage of carbon dioxide has increased steadily since the start of the Industrial Revolution in the 1860s. The statement in the *USA Today* editorial that carbon dioxide has increased by 25 percent is generally accepted by scientists as an accurate estimate of the total increase since 1860.

Where scientists disagree about the facts is on the projected effect of this increase. Predictions of global warming are derived from computer models, none of which seems able to encompass all the factors that contribute to global climate, particularly ocean currents and the movements of air masses above the oceans. Because of the enormous complexity of these factors, projections about the future differ considerably from scientist to scientist. *USA Today* took one of the worst-case projections.

Questions of Value

There is also widespread disagreement on what actions the United States or other countries should take in response to the potential warming of the earth. In general, these disputes stem from disagreements about value. In particular, participants in the conversation give different answers to the following questions:

1. In the face of uncertain threat, do we react as if the threat were definite or do we wait and see? If we wait and see, will we be inviting disaster?

2. How much faith can we place in science and technology? Some people, arguing that necessity is the mother of invention, assume that scientists will get us out of this mess. Others believe that technofixes are no longer possible.

3. How much change in our way of life can we tolerate? What, for example, would be the consequences to our economy if we waged an all-out war on global warming by drastically reducing our use of carbon fuels? To what extent are we willing to give up the benefits of industrialization?

4. How much economic disruption can we expect other nations to tolerate? What worldwide economic forces, for example, are making it profitable to cut down and burn tropical rain forests? What would happen to the economies of tropical countries if international controls suddenly prevented further destruction of rain forests? What changes in our own economy would have to take place?

Our whole point here is that the problem of global warming is interwoven into a gigantic web of other problems and issues. One of the benefits you gain from researching a complex technical and value-laden issue such as global warming is learning how to cope with ambiguity.

What advice can we give, therefore, when the experts disagree? Here is the strategy we tend to use. First, we try to identify the facts that all sides agree on. These facts give us a starting place on which to build an analysis. In the greenhouse controversy, the fact that all sides agree that the amount of CO_2 in the atmosphere has increased by 25 percent and that this amount increases the percentage of infrared radiation absorbed in the atmosphere suggests that there is scientific cause for concern.

Second, we try to determine if there is a majority position among experts. Sometimes dissenting voices stem from a small but prolific group of persons on the fringe. Our instincts are to trust the majority opinions of experts, even though we realize that revolutions in scientific thought almost always start with minority groups. In the case of the greenhouse effect, our own research suggests that the majority of scientists are cautiously concerned but not predicting doomsday. There seems to be a general consensus that increased greenhouse gases will contribute to global warming—but how much and how soon, they won't say.

Third, we try as much as possible to focus, not on the testimony of experts, but on the data the experts use in their testimony. In other words, we try to learn as much as possible about the scientific or technical problem and immerse ourselves in the raw data. Doing so in the case of the greenhouse effect helped us appreciate the problems of creating computer models of global climate and especially of gathering data about oceanic impact on climate.

Finally, we try to determine our own position on the values issues at stake because, inescapably, these values influence the position we ultimately take. For example, the authors of this text tend to be pessimistic about technofixes for most environmental problems. We doubt that scientists will solve the problem of greenhouse gases either through finding alternatives to petrocarbon fuels or by discovering ways to eliminate or counteract greenhouse gases. We also tend not to be risk takers on environmental matters. Thus, we prefer to take vigorous action now to slow the increase of greenhouse gases rather than take a wait-and-see attitude. The conclusion of our own research, then, is that the *USA Today* editorial is irresponsible in two ways: The opening scenario overstates the fears of most scientists, yet its conclusion understates the disruption of our present way of life necessary to a solution.

What we have attempted to do in this section is show you how we try to reach a responsible position in the face of uncertainty. We cannot claim that our position is the right one. We can only claim that it is a reasonable one and a responsible one—responsible to our own understanding of the facts and to our own declaration of values. Thus, when you evaluate opposing arguments, you don't simply pick the best one; you seek out the lines of the debate, the questions at issue, the unanswered questions. And you reexamine your own values to ensure that whatever position you ultimately take is consistent with your most important beliefs.

CONCLUSION

This chapter has offered four main strategies for enhancing your reading of argument: (1) Read as a believer, (2) read as a doubter, (3) seek out alternative views and analyze sources of disagreement, and (4) evaluate the various positions. In turn, we've shown you how to write summaries and how to incorporate summaries into your own writing.

In Chapter 3, we turn from reading arguments to writing arguments and suggest ways that you can improve your writing process.

c h a p t e r 3

Writing Arguments

As the opening chapters suggest, writing about an issue forces you to see it more complexly. By role-playing alternative views and by examining the logic of your own position, you may find your own views shifting, leading you to modify your position and seek stronger support. It follows, then, that writing is an act of discovering your argument, of developing and clarifying your thinking.

Insofar as writing is an act of discovery, it's also a process. Because a writer's ideas evolve through stages, a persuasive final product may be preceded by rambling, confusing drafts. Too often inexperienced writers cut the process short. They finish too soon, submitting arguments that are not yet "ready for strangers" but that are nonetheless promising drafts.

You should, thus, allow yourself plenty of time to write your argument—time for planning and talking, for drafting, and for extensive rethinking and revision. Be prepared to make major changes in your drafts; be willing even to throw them out and start over. As the following description of skilled writers' processes makes clear, a commitment to process means a commitment to take greater care with your writing.

A BRIEF DESCRIPTION OF WRITERS' PROCESSES

No two writers follow the same composing process. In fact, your own processes probably vary from essay to essay. There are, however, some similar stages that most writers go through. These stages may follow different sequences from writer to writer, and indeed most writers loop back to an earlier stage in the process whenever they encounter difficulties. Nevertheless, the stages can be described in a loose way as follows:

Stage 1—Starting point: Most writers begin with a sense of a problem or issue. Some writers are drawn to controversial conversation already in progress. Perhaps they don't hear their point of view precisely articulated, or they believe the prevailing voices are missing the point. Writers sometimes begin with their positions already decided, sometimes not.

Stage 2—Exploration and rehearsal: Writers explore the issue by reading, interviewing, and recalling personal experiences. They identify disagreements about the facts of the case as well as conflicts about values, assumptions, and beliefs. At this stage, many writers begin exploring and rehearsing their own arguments in journals or notes.

Stage 3—Writing a discovery draft: The writer's attention now shifts from gathering data and exploring issues to composing a draft. At this stage, writers often ignore potential audiences and concentrate on clarifying ideas for themselves. Consequently, discovery drafts are often messy, jumbled, and incoherent to others.

Stage 4—Re-vision or "seeing again": After completing a discovery draft, many writers feel the need to rethink the problem, frequently discussing their ideas with others. Often they dismantle much of their first draft and start again. They may also need to reshape their writing for readers, worrying now about such audience-based concerns as unity, coherence, and emphasis. Often several drafts are needed at the revision stage.

Stage 5—Editing: Writers now polish their drafts, finding just the precise word, clarifying each sentence and the links between sentences. They also turn finally to surface features such as spelling, punctuation, and grammar as well as the appearance and form of the final manuscript.

STRATEGIES FOR IMPROVING YOUR WRITING PROCESSES

The writing process just described is based on observations of skilled writers. Unskilled writers, however, generally go through a quite different process, one that takes less time and is less rigorous in its demand for clarity. For example, too few novice writers use drafts for exploration and rehearsal. Fewer still revise with the needs of readers in mind. Most college writers could greatly accelerate their writing growth by enriching their composing processes. To that end, here are some strategies you might try.

Talking about ideas in small groups: This is especially helpful early on, when you may have an issue in mind but no particular claim to make, let alone a sense of how to develop that claim. The greatest power of groups is their ability to generate ideas and multiple perspectives. In particular, listen to your classmates' doubts and objections to determine where your reasons and evidence are weak.

Using exploratory writing: Exploratory writing is like talking to yourself on paper. Its purpose is to help you discover ideas without worrying about someone reading over your shoulder. At the end of this chapter we provide some exploratory writing tasks that will help you discover ideas for arguments and deepen your thinking.

Talking your draft: Talking through a draft with another person is a good way to begin role-playing your audience. Without looking at your draft, present your argument orally to your listener. When your listener looks confused or skeptical, explain your point in new language. Look for ways to make the argument clearer to your listener and yourself.

Doing research: Among the most powerful ways to generate ideas is to read about your issue in the library or on the Internet or World Wide Web, where you can examine various points of view, explore evidence and counterevidence, and analyze the argumentative strategies used by others. Inventive researchers perform a kind of reverse engineering on the arguments they read, taking them apart to see how they work and to gain insights on how to construct their own.

Using heuristic strategies: Another way to generate ideas is to use one or more structured processes called *heuristics* (derived from the Greek word *heuresis*, meaning "to discover"). In the next section we discuss several heuristic strategies in detail.

Using visual techniques for brainstorming and shaping: Cognitive psychologists recommend supplementing verbal modes of thinking with visual modes to enhance our understanding. In our own teaching, we have found that visual techniques such as idea maps and tree diagrams can help writers imagine the content and shape of their emerging arguments. Later in this chapter we will explain these strategies.

Seeking out alternative views: Once you're reasonably confident in your argument, your best audience may be someone who's downright opposed to your views. Unlike friendly audiences, who will usually assure you that your argument is excellent, skeptical audiences will challenge your thinking. Skeptics may find holes in your reasoning, argue from different values, surprise you by conceding points you thought had to be developed at length, and dismay you by demanding development of points you thought could be conceded. In short, opponents will urge you to "re-see" your draft.

Extensive revising: Don't manicure your drafts, rebuild them. If you draft by hand, leave lots of white space between lines and in the margins for rewriting. If you draft by computer, we recommend revising off double-spaced hard copy (so that you can easily get a global view of the whole as you add, delete, crossout, and rewrite); then type your changes into your draft, giving the new draft a different file name. And be sure to apply some of the systematic strategies for testing your argument's logic and evidence described later in this text.

Exchanging drafts: Get other people's reactions to your work in exchange for your reactions to theirs. Exchanging drafts is different from conversing orally with a skeptic. Conversation with a skeptic usually leads to changes in content. An exchange of drafts, however, leads to changes in organization, development, and style as well as content.

Saving "correctness" for last: Save your concern for sentence correctness, spelling, and punctuation for last. Focusing on it at the early stages of writing can dampen your creative spirit.

USING EXPLORATORY WRITING TO DISCOVER IDEAS AND DEEPEN THINKING

What follows is a compendium of strategies to help you discover and explore ideas. None of these strategies works for every writer. But all of them are worth trying. Each requires practice, so don't give up on the strategy if it doesn't work at first. We recommend that you keep your exploratory writing in a journal or in easily identified files in your word processor so you can review it later and test the "staying power" of ideas produced by the different strategies.

Freewriting or Blind Writing

Freewriting is useful at any stage of the writing process. When you freewrite, you put pen to paper and write rapidly *nonstop,* usually ten to fifteen minutes at a stretch. The object is to think of as many ideas as possible without stopping to edit your work. On a computer, freewriters often turn off the monitor so that they can't see the text being produced. Such "blind writing" frees the writer from the urge to edit or correct the text and simply to let ideas roll forth. Some freewriters or blind writers achieve a stream-of-consciousness style, recording their ideas at the very moment they bubble into consciousness, stutters and stammers and all. Others produce more focused chunks, though without clear connections among them. You will probably find your initial reservoir of ideas running out in three to five minutes. If so, force yourself to keep writing or typing. If you can't think of anything to say, write "relax" or "I'm stuck" over and over until new ideas emerge.

Here is an example of a freewrite from a student named Steve, exploring his thoughts on the question "What can be done about the homeless?" (Steve eventually wrote the proposal argument found on pages 216–225.)

Lets take a minute and talk about the homeless. Homeless homeless. Today on my way to work I passed a homeless guy who smiled at me and I smiled back though he smelled bad. What are the reasons he was out on the street? Perhaps an extraordinary string of bad luck. Perhaps he was pushed out onto the street. Not a background of work ethic, no place to go, no way to get someplace to live that could be afforded, alcoholism. To what extent do government assistance, social spending, etc, keep people off the street? What benefits could a person get that stops "the cycle"? How does welfare affect homelessness, drug abuse programs, family planning? To what extent does the individual have control over homelessness? This question of course goes to the depth of the question of how community affects the individual. Relax, relax. What about the signs that I see on the way to work posted on the windows of businesses that read, "please don't give to panhandlers it only promotes drug abuse etc" a cheap way of getting homeless out of the way of business? Are homeless the natural end of unrestricted capitalism? What about the homeless people who are mentally ill? How can you maintain a living when haunted by paranoia? How do you decide if someone is mentally ill or just laughs at society? If one can't function obviously. How many mentally ill are out on the street? If you are mentally ill and have lost the connections to others who might take care of you I can see how you might end up on the street. What would it take to get treatment? To what extent can mentally ill be treated? When I see a homeless person I want to ask, How do you feel about the rest of society? When you see "us" walk by how do you think of us? Do you possibly care how we avoid you.

FOR CLASS DISCUSSION

Individual task: Choose one of the following controversial claims (or another chosen by your instructor) and freewrite your response to it for ten to fifteen minutes. **Group task:** Working in pairs, in small groups, or as a whole class, share your freewrite with classmates. Don't feel embarrassed if your freewrite is fragmentary or disjointed. Freewrites are not supposed to be finished products; their sole purpose is to generate a flow of thought. The more you practice the technique, the better you will become.

1. A student should report a fellow student who is cheating on an exam or plagiarizing an essay.
2. States should legalize marriages between homosexuals.
3. Recycling cans, bottles, plastics, and paper does little to help the environment.
4. Spanking children should be considered child abuse.
5. State and federal governments should legalize hard drugs.
6. For grades 1–12, the school year should be extended to eleven months.
7. Taxpayer money should not be used to fund professional sports stadiums.

8. Violent video games such as Mortal Kombat should be made illegal.

9. Rich people are morally obligated to give part of their wealth to the poor.

10. Women should be assigned to combat duty equally with men.

Idea Mapping

Another good technique for exploring ideas is *idea mapping*. When you make an idea map, draw a circle in the center of the page and write some trigger idea (a broad topic, a question, or working thesis statement) in the center of the circle. Then record your ideas on branches and subbranches extending from the center circle. As long as you pursue one train of thought, keep recording your ideas on the branch. But when that line of thinking gives out, start a new branch. Often your thoughts jump back and forth between branches. That's a major advantage of "picturing" your thoughts; you can see them as part of an emerging design rather than as strings of unrelated ideas.

Idea maps usually generate more ideas, though less well-developed ones, than freewrites. Writers who practice both techniques report that each strategy causes them to think about their ideas very differently. When Steve, the freewriter on homelessness, created an idea map (Figure 3.1), he was well into an argument disagreeing with a proposal by columnist Charles Krauthammer advocating the confinement of the homeless mentally ill in state mental hospitals. Steve's idea map helped him find some order in his evolving thoughts on homelessness and his reasons for disagreeing with Krauthammer.

 FOR CLASS DISCUSSION

Choose a controversial issue—national, local, or campus—that's interesting to the class. The instructor will lead a class discussion on the issue, recording ideas on an idea map as they emerge. Your goal is to appreciate the fluidity of idea maps as a visual form of idea generation halfway between an outline and a list.

Playing the Believing and Doubting Game

The believing/doubting game* is an excellent way to imagine views different from your own and to anticipate responses to those views.

As a believer, your role is to be wholly sympathetic to an idea, to listen carefully to it, and to suspend all disbelief. You must identify all the ways in which the

---

*A term coined by Peter Elbow, *Writing Without Teachers* (New York: Oxford UP,1973), 147–90.

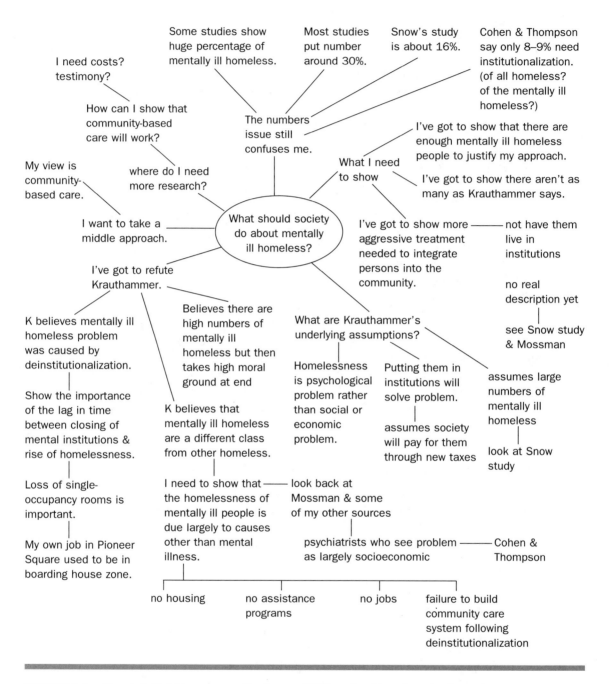

FIGURE 3.1 Steve's initial idea map on the issue of "What should society do about the mentally ill homeless?"

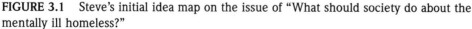

idea might appeal to different audiences and all the reasons for believing the idea. The believing game is easy so long as you already accept an idea. But in dealing with ideas that strike you as shaky, false, or dangerous, you will find that the believing game can be difficult, even frightening.

The doubting game is the opposite of the believing game. As a doubter, your role is to be judgmental and critical, to find faults with an idea. You do your best to find counterexamples and inconsistencies that undermine it. Again, it is easy to play the doubting game with ideas you reject, but doubting those you're invested in can be threatening.

Here is how one student played the believing and doubting game with the assertion "Pornography serves a useful function in society."

DOUBT

Pornography is smutty, indecent, outlandish usage of the human body. People who look at that have to be indecent nonmoralistic sexists with nothing better to do. Pornography uses the human body to gain pleasure when the human body is supposed to be like a temple that you take care of. I feel very strongly against pornography especially when they use it with young children and pets, etc. I just don't understand how people can get such a big kick out of it. It really surprised me how Dr. Jones [a guest speaker in this student's psychology course] admitted that he had bought pornographic materials, etc. I would think that it would be something that someone wouldn't readily admit to. It seems socially unacceptable to me.

BELIEVE

Pornography is something that people look at when they are feeling sexually frustrated or lonely. It is a form of escape that everyone needs at one time or another. There is always a time where one is unhappy with their sexual relationships and looking at pornography helps. Pornography is an art form. The human body is a beautiful thing and these pictures are for everyone to see the beauty of it all. People should not be afraid to be open about sex and their bodies. Everyone feels the same things. Why not share the experience with others? There is nothing dirty or smutty about being open. It is so individualistic, another way of getting out of the rut of conformity. Sex is beautiful and pornography helps share it with others that aren't quite so lucky to share these moments. (I feel this doubting game with this topic for me opens no new ideas because my mind is so set against pornography but I guess it is good to open up the new avenues of thinking.)

It is easy to see from this entry how the believing game threatens this student's moral views. Yet she does a good job of starting to get inside the head of someone who believes that pornography serves a useful purpose. Although she denies at the end of her entry that playing this game opened up new ideas, the game certainly helped her to see what the issue is and to appreciate that not all people share her values.

When you play the believing and doubting game with an assertion, simply write two different chunks, one chunk arguing for the assertion (the believing game) and one chunk opposing it (the doubting game). Freewrite both chunks, letting your ideas flow without censoring. Or, alternatively, make an idea map with believing and doubting branches.

❦ FOR CLASS DISCUSSION

Return to the ten controversial claims in the For Class Discussion exercise following the section on freewriting (pp. 44–45). **Individual task:** Choose one of the claims and play the believing and doubting game with it by freewriting for five minutes trying to believe the claim and then for five minutes trying to doubt the claim. Or, if you prefer, make an idea map by creating a believing spoke and a doubting spoke off the main hub. Instead of freewriting, enter ideas onto your idea map, moving back and forth between believing and doubting. **Group task:** Share what you produced with members of your group or with the class as a whole.

Repeat the exercise with another claim.

❦

Brainstorming for Pro and Con *Because* Clauses

This activity is similar to the believing and doubting game in that it asks you to brainstorm ideas for and against a controversial assertion. In the believing and doubting game, however, you simply freewrite or make an idea map on both sides of the issue. In this activity, you try to state your reasons for and against the proposition as *because* clauses. The value of doing so is discussed in depth in Chapter 4, which shows how a claim with *because* clauses can form the core of an argument.

Here is an example of how you might create *because* clauses for and against the claim, "Pornography serves a useful function in society."

PRO

Pornography serves a useful function in society

- because it provides a sexual outlet for lonely men.
- because what some people call pornography might really be an art form.
- because it helps society overcome Victorian repression.

- because many people obviously enjoy it.
- because it may relieve the sexual frustration of a person who would otherwise turn to rape or child molestation.

CON

Pornography is harmful to society

- because it is degrading and oppressive to women.
- because it depersonalizes and dehumanizes sexuality.
- because it gives teenagers many wrong concepts about loving sexuality.
- because it is linked with racketeering and crime and destroys neighborhoods.
- because it often exploits children.
- because it might incite some people to commit rape and violence (serial murderer Ted Bundy's claim).

FOR CLASS DISCUSSION

Generating *because* clauses like these is an especially productive discussion activity for groups. Once again return to the ten controversial claims in the For Class Discussion exercise in the freewriting section (pp. 44–45). Select one or more of these claims (or others provided by your instructor) and, working in small groups, generate pro and con *because* clauses supporting and attacking the claim. Share your group's *because* clauses with those of other groups.

Later on we'll introduce several other strategies for exploring and developing arguments, including the Toulmin Schema, the principles/consequences/analogies strategy, and the stock issues strategy.

Brainstorming a Network of Related Issues

The previous exercise helps you see how certain issues can provoke strong pro-con stances. Occasionally in civic life, an issue is presented to the public in just such a pro-con form, as when voters are asked to approve or disapprove a referendum or when a jury must decide the guilt or innocence of a defendant.

But in most contexts, the argumentative situation is more open ended and fluid. You can easily oversimplify an issue by reducing it to two opposing sides. Because most issues are embedded in a network of subissues, side issues, and larger issues, seeing an issue in pro-con terms can often blind you to other ways to join a conversation. For example, an arguer might propose a middle ground between adversarial positions, examine a subissue in more depth, connect an issue to a related side issue, or redefine an issue to place it in a new context.

Consider, for example, the previous assertion, "Pornography serves a useful function in society." Rather than arguing for or against this assertion, a writer might focus on pornography in a variety of other ways:

- How can pornography be defined?
- Should pornography be censored?
- Can violence be considered pornographic?
- Should pornography be allowed on the World Wide Web? If so, how could children be denied access to it?
- Does pornography exploit or degrade women?
- What effect does pornography have on sexual offenders?
- Is Demi Moore's character as a stripper and single mom in the movie *Striptease* a role model for feminism or an embarrassment?

 FOR CLASS DISCUSSION

Working as a whole class or in small groups, choose one or more of the controversial assertions on pages 44–45. Instead of arguing for or against them, brainstorm a number of related issues (subissues, side issues, or larger issues) on the same general subject. For example, brainstorm a number of issues related to the general topics of cheating, gay marriage, recycling, and so forth.

SHAPING YOUR ARGUMENT

We turn now from discovery strategies to organizing strategies. As you begin drafting, you need some sort of plan. How elaborate that plan is varies considerably from writer to writer. Some writers plan extensively before writing; others write extensively before planning. But somewhere along the way, all writers must decide on a structure. This section offers two basic organizing strategies: (1) using the conventional structure of "classical argument" as an initial guide, and (2) using a tree diagram instead of a traditional outline.

Classical Argument as an Initial Guide

In drafting, writers of argument often rely on knowledge of typical argument structures to guide their thinking. One of the oldest models is the *classical argument*—so called because it follows a pattern recommended by ancient rhetoricians. In traditional Latin terminology, classical argument has the following parts: the *exordium* (which gets the audience's attention); the *narratio* (which provides needed background); the *propositio* (which introduces the speaker's proposition or thesis);

the *partitio* (which forecasts the main parts of the speech); the *confirmatio* (which presents arguments supporting the proposition); the *confutatio* (which refutes opposing views); and the *peroratio* (which sums up the argument, calls for action, and leaves a strong last impression).

In slightly homelier terms (see Figure 3.2), writers of classical argument typically begin with a dramatic story or a startling statistic that commands our attention. Then they focus the issue, often by stating it directly as a question and perhaps by briefly summarizing opposing views. Next, they contextualize the issue by providing needed background, explaining the immediate context, or defining key terms. They conclude the introduction by presenting the thesis and forecasting the argument's structure.

Next, in usually the longest part of the classical argument, writers present the major reasons and evidence supporting their thesis. Typically, each reason is developed in its own section. Each section opens with a statement of the reason, which is then supported with evidence or chains of other reasons. Along the way, writers guide their readers with appropriate transitions.

Subsequently, alternative views are summarized and critiqued. (Some writers put this section *before* the presentation of their own argument.) If opposing arguments consist of several parts, writers may either (1) summarize all opposing arguments before responding, or (2) summarize and respond one part at a time. Writers may respond to opposing views either by refuting them or by conceding their strengths but shifting to a different field of values where these strengths are less decisive.

Finally, in their conclusion, writers will sum up their argument, often calling for some kind of action, thereby creating a sense of closure and leaving a strong final impression.

For all its strengths, the classical argument may not always be your best model. In some cases, for example, delaying your thesis or ignoring alternative views may be justified (see Chapter 8). Even in these cases, however, the classical argument is a useful planning tool. Its call for a thesis statement and a forecasting statement in the introduction helps you see the whole of your argument in miniature. And by requiring you to summarize and consider opposing views, classical argument alerts you to the limits of your position and to the need for further reasons and evidence. Moreover, the classical argument is a particularly persuasive mode of argument when you address a neutral or undecided audience.

The Power of Tree Diagrams

The classical argument offers a general guide for shaping arguments, but it doesn't help you wrestle with particular ideas. It is one thing to know that you need one or more reasons to support your thesis, but quite another to figure out what those reasons are, to articulate them clearly, and to decide what evidence supports them. Traditionally, writers have used outlines to help them flesh out a structure. We prefer to use tree diagrams.

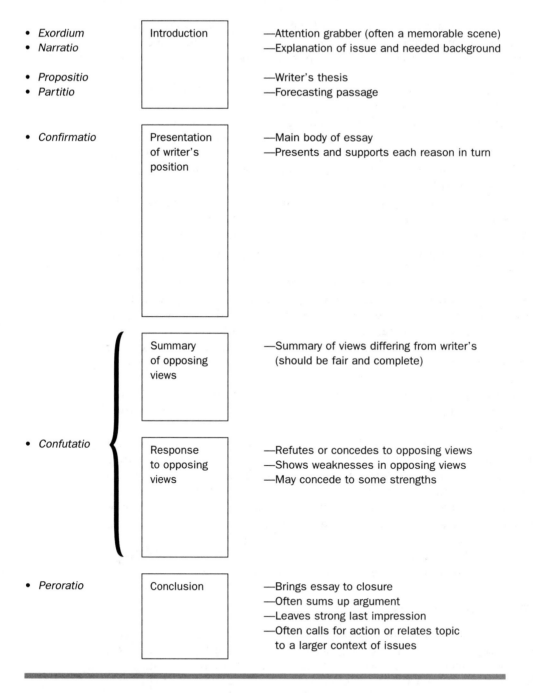

• *Exordium* • *Narratio*	Introduction	—Attention grabber (often a memorable scene) —Explanation of issue and needed background
• *Propositio* • *Partitio*		—Writer's thesis —Forecasting passage
• *Confirmatio*	Presentation of writer's position	—Main body of essay —Presents and supports each reason in turn
• *Confutatio*	Summary of opposing views	—Summary of views differing from writer's (should be fair and complete)
	Response to opposing views	—Refutes or concedes to opposing views —Shows weaknesses in opposing views —May concede to some strengths
• *Peroratio*	Conclusion	—Brings essay to closure —Often sums up argument —Leaves strong last impression —Often calls for action or relates topic to a larger context of issues

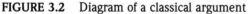

FIGURE 3.2   Diagram of a classical argument

A *tree diagram* differs from an outline in that headings and subheadings are indicated by spatial relationships rather than by a system of letters and numerals. Figure 3.3 reveals the plan for a classical argument opposing a campus ban on hate speech. The inverted triangle at the top of the tree represents the writer's introduction. The main reasons appear on branches beneath the claim, and the supporting evidence and arguments for each reason are displayed beneath each reason.

The same argument displayed in outline form would look like this:

THESIS: Colleges should not try to ban hate speech.

I.   A ban on hate speech violates the First Amendment.

II. A ban on hate speech doesn't solve the problem of hate.
     A. It doesn't allow people to understand and hear each other's anger.
     B. It disguises hatred instead of bringing it out in the open where it can be dealt with.
     C. The ability to see both sides of an issue would be compromised.

III. Of course, there are good arguments in support of a ban on hate speech.
     A. Banning hate speech creates a safer environment for minorities.
     B. It helps eliminate occasions for violence.
     C. It teaches good manners and people skills.
     D. It shows that ignorant hate speech is not the same as intelligent discussion.

IV. Although these arguments have strengths, they conceal a major flaw.
     A. I concede that a hate speech ban might make a safer, less violent campus and might help teach good manners.
     B. But in the long run, it doesn't change people's prejudices; it just drives them underground.

V.   CONCLUSION: There are better ways to deal with prejudice and hatred.
     A. Instead of repressing hate, let ugly incidents happen.
     B. Create discussions around the ugly incidents.

In our experience, tree diagrams lead to fuller, more detailed, and more logical arguments than do traditional outlines. Their strength results from their several advantages. First, they are visual. The main points are laid out horizontally and support is displayed vertically. Writers can literally "see" where they need more support and can move freely between dimensions as they construct their argument.

Second, they are flexible. While traditional outlines require a division of each whole into two or more parts (every A must have a B—based on the principle that no whole can logically have just one part), tree diagrams can represent additional relationships. For example, a tree diagram can logically show a single line descending vertically from a higher-level point to represent, say, a generalization illustrated by a single example. Additionally, the descending lines on a tree diagram

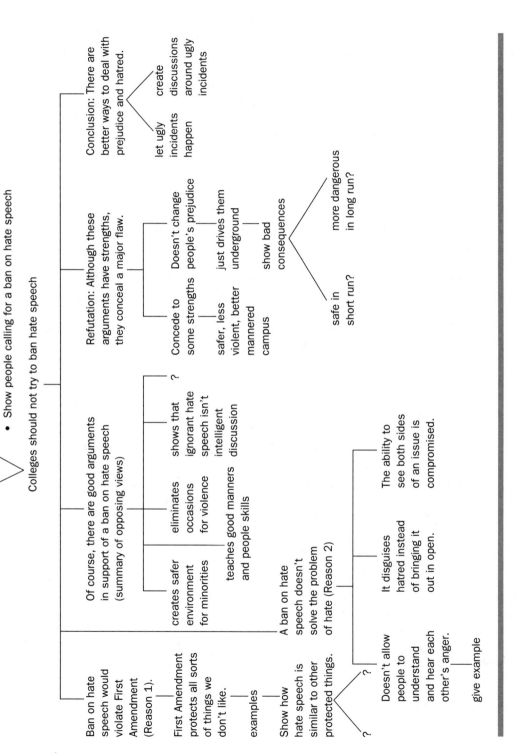

FIGURE 3.3   Tree diagram of an argument opposing a ban on hate speech

function as an informal flowchart, letting you plan out a chain of reasons. (This flexibility explains why the tree diagram in Figure 3.3 contains so much more information than the outline for the same argument.)

Finally, tree diagrams are powerful aids to invention because they invite you to insert question marks as placeholders for information you know you need but haven't yet found. For instance, if you know you need more data to support a point, you can write out your point on the tree diagram and place one or more question marks on descending lines below the point. (See the writer's use of question marks in Figure 3.3.)

USING EXPLORATORY WRITING TO DISCOVER IDEAS AND DEEPEN THINKING: TWO SETS OF EXPLORATORY TASKS

The following tasks use exploratory writing to help you generate ideas. The first set of tasks helps you gather ideas early in a writing project either by helping you think of issues to write about or by deepening and complicating your response to readings. The second set of tasks helps you think about your ideas systematically before you compose a first draft.

Set 1: Starting Points

Task 1: Make an Inventory of Issues that Interest You

Using one or more of the following "trigger questions," make a list of ten to fifteen possible issues or topic areas that you might like to write about. Share your list with classmates, adding their ideas to yours.

My friends and I disagree about . . .

I think it is wrong when . . .

Our campus (this city, my hometown, our state, the country) would be better if . . .

Person X believes . . . ; however, I believe . . .

When people discuss X, what do they disagree about?

Task 2: Choose Several Areas of Controversy for Exploration

For this task, choose two or three possible controversies from the above list and explore them through freewriting or idea mapping. Try responding to the following questions: (a) What is my position on this issue and why? (b) What are opposing or alternative positions on this issue? (c) Why do people disagree about this issue? (Do they disagree about the facts of the case? About underlying values, assumptions, and beliefs?) (d) To argue a position on this issue, what evidence do I need to find and what further research will be required?

Task 3: Identify and Explore Issues that Are Problematic for You

A major assignment often given in argument courses is to write a research-based argument on an issue or problem initially puzzling to you. Perhaps you don't know enough about the issue (for example, establishing international controls on pesticides) or perhaps the issue draws you into an uncomfortable conflict of values (for example, assisted suicide, legalization of drugs, noncriminal incarceration of sexual predators). Your goal for this task is to identify several issues about which you are undecided, to choose one, and to explore your current uncertainty. Why can't you make up your mind on this issue?

Task 4: Deepen Your Response to Readings

This task requires you to read a collection of arguments on an issue and to explore them thoughtfully. As you read the arguments assigned by your instructor, annotate the margins with believing and doubting notes as explained in Chapter 2. Then respond to one or more of the following prompts, using freewriting or idea mapping.

- Why do the writers disagree? Are there disagreements about facts? About underlying values, beliefs, and assumptions?
- Identify "hot spots" in the readings—passages that evoke strong agreement or disagreement, anger, confusion, or any other memorable response—and explore your reaction to these passages.
- Explore the evolution of your thinking as you read and later review the essays. What new questions have they raised? How did your thinking change? Where do you stand now and why?
- If you were to meet one of the authors on a plane or at a ball game, what would you say to him or her?

Set 2: Exploration and Rehearsal

The following tasks are designed to help you once you have chosen a topic and begun to clarify your thesis. While these tasks may take two or more hours to complete, the effort pays off by helping you produce a full set of ideas for your rough draft. We recommend using these tasks each time you write a paper for this course.

Task 1

What issue do you plan to address in this essay? Try wording the issue as a one-sentence question. Reword your question in several different ways because each version will frame the issue somewhat differently. Then put a box around your best version of the question.

Task 2

Explain why people disagree on this issue. Is there insufficient evidence to resolve the issue? Is the evidence controversial? Do the disputants hold different values, assumptions, or beliefs? Do they disagree about key definitions? What do people fear in others' positions?

Task 3

What personal connections do you have with the issue? What direct experience do you have with it? What have you read, seen, or heard about it? How does it affect your life?

Task 4

What is your current position on this issue? Write your major claim as a one-sentence response to the issue question you posed in Task 1.

Task 5

In this task, you will rehearse the main body of your paper. Using freewriting or idea mapping, think of all possible reasons and evidence supporting your position. Be expansive, brainstorming every possible point you can think of. As you generate reasons and evidence, you are likely to discover gaps in your knowledge. Where could your argument be bolstered by additional data such as statistics, examples, expert testimony? How do you plan on filling those gaps? Interviews? Library research? Internet or World Wide Web?

Task 6

Reread your response to Task 5. Reconsider your argument from the perspective of neutral or hostile audiences. What values, beliefs, or assumptions must they hold in order to accept your argument? Which of these values, beliefs, or assumptions do you think they hold, and which don't they hold?

Task 7

Assume the role of someone who opposes your position. Writing from that person's perspective, brainstorm the arguments he or she would make to refute your argument and make a counterargument. In other words, make the best case you can against your position.

Task 8

Why is this an important issue? What are its broader implications and consequences? What other issues does it relate to? (Your responses to these questions will help you write your introduction and conclusion.)

WRITING ASSIGNMENTS FOR CHAPTERS 1–3

OPTION 1: *An argument summary.*   Write a 250-word summary of an argument selected by your instructor. Then write a one-sentence summary of the same argument. Use as models the summaries of Charles Murray's essay in Chapter 2 (pp. 26–28).

OPTION 2: *An analysis of the sources of disagreement in opposing arguments.* Write an analysis of any two arguments that take differing views on the same issue. Where do the writers disagree about questions of fact or truth? Where do they disagree about beliefs, assumptions, and values, including disagreements about definitions or appropriate analogies?

OPTION 3: *A debate essay.*   Write a debate essay on an issue of your own choosing. Write your essay as a miniplay in which two or more characters argue about an issue. Create any kind of fictional setting for your debate. Have the characters disagree with each other, but make your characters reasonable people who are tying to argue logically and intelligently. The debate format frees you from a strict structure, allowing you to explore your issue from many perspectives without having to take sides.

part two

 Principles of
Argument

The Core of an Argument
A Claim with Reasons

THE RHETORICAL TRIANGLE

Before we examine the structure of arguments, we should explain briefly their social context, which can be visualized as a triangle with interrelated points labeled *message, writer/speaker,* and *audience.* Effective arguments consider all three points on this *rhetorical triangle.* As we will see in later chapters, when you alter one point of the triangle (for example, when you change the audience for whom you are writing), you often need to alter the other points (by restructuring the message itself and perhaps by changing the tone or image you project as writer/speaker). We have created a series of questions based on the "rhetorical triangle" to help you plan, draft, and revise your argument (see Figure 4.1).

Each point on the triangle in turn corresponds to one of the three kinds of persuasive appeals that ancient rhetoricians named *logos, ethos,* and *pathos.*

Logos (Greek for "word") refers primarily to the internal consistency and clarity of the message and to the logic of its reasons and support. The impact of *logos* on an audience is referred to as its *logical appeal.*

Ethos (Greek for "character") refers to the credibility of the writer/speaker. *Ethos* is mostly a function of the tone and style of the message and the care with which alternative views are considered. In some cases, it's also a function of the writer's reputation for honesty and expertise independent of the message. The impact of *ethos* on an audience is referred to as its *ethical appeal* or *appeal from credibility.*

Our third term, *pathos* (Greek for "suffering" or "experience") is often associated with emotional appeal. But *pathos* appeals more specifically to our

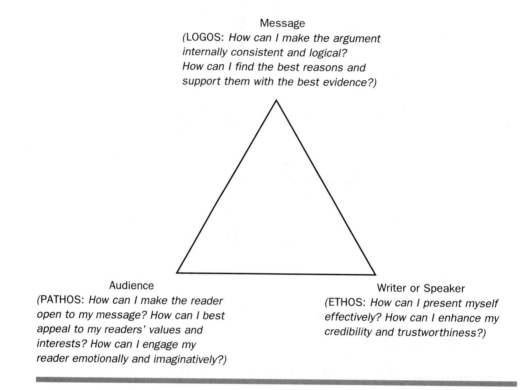

Message
(LOGOS: *How can I make the argument internally consistent and logical? How can I find the best reasons and support them with the best evidence?*)

Audience
(PATHOS: *How can I make the reader open to my message? How can I best appeal to my readers' values and interests? How can I engage my reader emotionally and imaginatively?*)

Writer or Speaker
(ETHOS: *How can I present myself effectively? How can I enhance my credibility and trustworthiness?*)

FIGURE 4.1   The rhetorical triangle

audience's imaginative sympathies—their capacity to feel and see what the writer feels and sees. Thus, when we turn the abstractions of logical discourse into a palpable and immediate story we are making a pathetic appeal. While *logos* and *ethos* may incline an audience to agree with our beliefs, *pathos* moves the audience to decision or action.

In Part Two, we treat all three elements of the rhetorical triangle in detail. Although all three terms overlap, Chapters 4–6 focus primarily on *logos*, and Chapters 7 and 8 focus primarily on *ethos* and *pathos*.

Given this background on the rhetorical triangle, let's turn now to *logos*—the logic and structure of arguments.

ISSUE QUESTIONS AS THE ORIGINS OF ARGUMENT

At the heart of any argument is a controversial question, or issue question, that gives rise to alternative answers. Any topic area, such as "criminal rights" or "health care," has embedded within it a number of issue questions. Thus the topic area "abortion" gives rise to issue questions such as "Should abortions be legal?" "Should the federal government underwrite the cost of abortion?" and "When does a fetus become a human being?" Each of these issue questions opens up one strand of the complex debate on abortion.

The Difference Between an Issue Question and an Information Question

Of course, not all questions are issue questions. Some may simply call for more information, not argument. Keeping this distinction in mind, consider the following two questions:

> How does the abortion rate in the United States compare with the rate in Sweden?
>
> If the rates are different, why?

On the surface, both seem like noncontroversial information questions. But the latter could be an issue question if reasonable people disagreed on the answer. Thus, one person might attribute Sweden's higher abortion rate to the absence of a large Catholic or conservative Protestant population. But a second might attribute the higher rate to Sweden's generous national health coverage or to differences in sex education in the schools. In this case, the *why* question provokes alternative points of view rather than a simple informational answer.

To determine if a given question is an issue question or an information question, examine the role it calls you to play in relation to your audience. If the question asks you to be a teacher providing new information or knowledge, then it is probably an information question. But if the question asks you to be an advocate, persuading your audience toward your point of view in a controversy, then it is probably an issue question. Sometimes context will determine if a given question is an issue question or an information question. Consider the following examples:

- How does a diesel engine work? (Almost surely an information question, posed by an audience of learners who regard you as a teacher.)
- What is the most cost-effective way to produce diesel fuel from crude oil? (This would be an information question if experts agreed on the answer and you were teaching this knowledge to new learners. But if experts disagreed—imagine a roomful of petroleum engineers seeking ways to reduce the production costs of diesel fuel—it would be an issue question.)
- Should the tax on diesel fuel be reduced? (A slam-dunk issue question sure to provoke controversy in almost any context.)

❦ FOR CLASS DISCUSSION ═══════════════════

Working as a class or in small groups, decide whether the following questions are information questions or issue questions. Some questions could be either, depending on the context. For such questions, create a hypothetical context that justifies your choice.

1. What percentage of single-parent families receive welfare support?

2. What caused the recent leap in America's out-of-wedlock birthrate?

3. Should the United States eliminate welfare support for unwed mothers?

4. Are chiropractors legitimate health professionals?

5. How does chiropractic treatment of illness differ from a medical doctor's treatment?

❦

DIFFERENCE BETWEEN A GENUINE ARGUMENT AND A PSEUDO-ARGUMENT

While every argument features an issue question with alternative answers, not every dispute over answers is a rational argument. Rational arguments require two additional factors: (1) reasonable participants who operate within the conventions of reasonable behavior, and (2) potentially sharable assumptions that can serve as a starting place or foundation for the argument. Lacking one or both of these conditions, disagreements remain stalled at the level of pseudo-arguments.

Pseudo-Arguments: Fanatical Believers and Fanatical Skeptics

A reasonable argument assumes the possibility of growth and change; disputants may modify their views as they acknowledge strengths in an alternative view or weaknesses in their own. Such growth becomes impossible—and argument degenerates to pseudo-argument—when disputants are fanatically committed to their positions. Consider the case of the fanatical believer or the fanatical skeptic.

Fanatical believers believe their claims are true because they say so, period. They may cite some authoritative text—the *Bible*, the *Communist Manifesto*, or *The Road Less Traveled*—but in the end it's their narrow and quirky reading of the text or their faith in the author (which others might not share) that underlies their argument. Disagreeing with a fanatical believer is like ordering the surf to quiet down. The only response is another crashing wave.

The fanatical skeptic, on the other hand, dismisses the possibility of proving anything. So what if the sun has risen every day of recorded history? That's no proof that it will rise tomorrow. Short of absolute proof, which never exists, fanatical skeptics accept nothing. In a world where the most we can hope for is increased audience adherence to our ideas, the fanatical skeptic demands an ironclad logical demonstration of our claim's rightness. In the presence of fanatical believers or skeptics, then, genuine argument is impossible.

Another Source of Pseudo-Arguments: Lack of Shared Assumptions

A reasonable argument is difficult to conduct unless the participants share common assumptions on which the argument can be grounded. Like axioms in geometry, these shared assumptions serve as the starting point for the argument. Consider the following conversation, in which Randall refuses to accept Rhonda's assumptions.

RHONDA: Smoking should be banned because it causes cancer.

RANDALL: So it causes cancer. What's so bad about that?

RHONDA: Don't be perverse, Randy. Cancer causes suffering and death.

RANDALL: Rhonda, my dear girl, don't be such a twinkie. Suffering and death are just part of the human condition.

RHONDA: But that doesn't make them desirable, especially when they can be avoided.

RANDALL: Perhaps in particular cases they're avoidable for a while, but in the long run, we all suffer and we all die, so who cares if smoking causes what's inevitable anyway?

This, we would suggest, is a doomed argument. Without any shared assumptions (for example, that cancer is bad, that suffering should be minimized and death delayed), there's no "bottom" to this argument, just an endless regress of reasons based on more reasons. While calling assumptions into question is a legitimate way to deepen and complicate our understanding of an issue, the unwillingness to accept any assumption makes argument impossible.

While our smoking example may be a bit heavyhanded, less obvious variants of this debate happen all the time. Whenever we argue about purely personal opinions—opera is boring, soccer is better than baseball, pizza is tastier than nachos—we're condemned to a bottomless dispute. Because there are no common criteria for "boring" or "better" or "tastier," we can't put our claims to any common test. We can only reassert them.

Of course, reasonable arguments about these disputes become possible once common assumptions are established. For example, a nutritionist could argue that pizza is better than nachos because it provides more balanced nutrients per calorie. Such an argument can succeed if the disputants accept the nutritionist's assumption that "more balanced nutrients per calorie" is a criterion for "better." But if one of the disputants responds, "Nah, nachos are better than pizza because nachos taste better," then he makes a different assumption—"My sense of taste is better than your sense of taste." This is a wholly personal standard, an assumption that others are unable to share.

❧ FOR CLASS DISCUSSION

The following questions can all be answered in alternative ways. However, not all of them will lead to reasonable arguments. Try to decide which questions will lead to reasonable arguments and which will lead only to pseudo-arguments:

1. Is Spike Lee a good film director?
2. Is postmodern architecture beautiful?
3. Should cities subsidize professional sports venues?
4. Is this abstract oil painting by a monkey smearing paint on a canvas a true work of art?
5. Is Mel Gibson better looking than Mel Brooks?

FRAME OF AN ARGUMENT: A CLAIM SUPPORTED BY REASONS

In writing an argument, you take a position on an issue and support it with reasons and evidence. You state your position in the form of a claim, which functions as the thesis statement of your argument. A claim should provide a one-sentence answer to the issue question. Your task, then, is to make a claim and support it with reasons and evidence, which together comprise your argument's framework.

What Is a Reason?

A reason is a claim used to support another claim. Reasons are usually linked to their claims with words like *because, thus, since, consequently,* and *therefore* to underscore their logical connection.

Let's take an example. In one of our recent classes, a female naval ROTC student ignited a heated discussion by suggesting that women not be allowed to serve on submarines. The ensuing discussion expanded into a more general debate about women's fitness to serve in combat units. Here are frameworks the class developed for two alternative positions on this issue.

One View

CLAIM: Women should be barred from military combat units.

REASON 1: Most women lack the strength and endurance needed for combat.

REASON 2: Serving in combat isn't necessary for female soldiers' career advancement.

REASON 3: Female soldiers would hurt morale by introducing sexual jealousy into combat units.

REASON 4: Pregnancy or need to care for infants would render women unreliable soldiers.

REASON 5: Women haven't been socialized into warrior roles and thus would be more reluctant than males to kill the enemy.

Alternative View

CLAIM: Women should be allowed to serve as combat soldiers.

REASON 1: Millions of women do have the strength and endurance to serve in combat roles.

REASON 2: Female combat soldiers would offer a positive role model to young women and help society overcome harmful gender stereotyping.

REASON 3: Serving in combat would open up new career advancement opportunities for female soldiers.

REASON 4: Simple justice demands that women be allowed to serve in combat units.

Formulating a list of reasons in this way breaks your persuasive task into a series of more manageable subtasks. Thus, in the first view given, five possible lines of support are laid out. A writer might use all five or select only two or three, depending on which would most persuade the intended audience. Each line of reasoning would comprise a distinct section of the argument.

For example, one section of an argument opposing women in combat might open with the following sentence: "Women should be excluded from combat units because they lack strength or endurance necessary for combat roles." The writer thereby assumes the burden of showing that women can't meet the prescribed physical requirements for combat duty. Further, the writer may also need to support the unstated assumption underlying this reason—namely, that meeting these physical requirements is a necessary condition for combat effectiveness.

The writer could develop each section of the argument in the same way. After a clear statement of the reason to be developed, the writer would offer evidence or chains of reasons in support. Depending on the intended audience, the writer might also articulate and support assumptions underlying the reason.

To summarize the gist of this section, the frame of an argument consists of a claim (the thesis statement of the essay), which is supported by one or more reasons, which are in turn supported by evidence or chains of further reasons.

Advantages of Expressing Reasons in *Because* Statements

Chances are that when you were a child the word *because* contained magical explanatory powers:

DOROTHY: I want to go home now.

TOMMY: Why?

DOROTHY: Because.

TOMMY: Because why?

DOROTHY: Just because.

Somehow *because* seemed decisive. It persuaded people to accept your view of the world; it changed people's minds. Later, you discovered that *because* only introduced your arguments and that it was the reasons following *because* that made the difference. But for most of us the word retains some residual magic and is persuasive in and of itself.

Of course, there are many other ways to express the logical connection between a reason and a claim. Our language is rich in ways of stating *because* relationships:

- Women shouldn't be allowed to join combat units because they don't have the strength or endurance for combat roles.
- Women don't have the strength or endurance for combat roles. Therefore women should not be allowed to join combat units.
- Women don't have the strength or endurance for combat roles, so they should not be allowed to join combat units.
- One reason that women should not be allowed to join combat units is that they don't have the strength or endurance for combat roles.

Even though logical relationships can be stated in various ways, writing out one or more *because* clauses remains the most succinct way to clarify an argument for oneself. We therefore suggest that sometime in the writing process you create a *working thesis statement* that summarizes your main reasons as because clauses attached to your claim.* Some writers compose their working thesis statements before they write their rough drafts. Others discover their thesis as they write. Still others compose their working thesis statement mid-draft in order to rein in an argument headed off in too many directions. Some wait until the very end, using their thesis statement to check the unity of the final product.

No matter when you write your working thesis statement, you will find doing so simultaneously thought provoking and frustrating. On the plus side, composing *because* clauses can be a powerful discovery tool, causing you to think of many different kinds of arguments to support your claim. But it is often difficult to wrestle your ideas into the *because* clause shape, which sometimes seems to be overly tidy for the complex network of ideas you are trying to work with. In the end, though, constructing a scale-model version of your argument in your working thesis statement is immensely helpful and worth the effort.

❦ FOR CLASS DISCUSSION

Try the following group exercise to help you see how writing *because* clauses can be a discovery procedure.

Divide into small groups. Each group member should contribute an issue that he or she might like to explore. Discussing one person's issue at a time, help each member develop a claim supported by several reasons. Express each reason as a *because* clause. Then write out the working thesis statement for each person's argument by attaching the *because* clauses to the claim. Finally, try to create *because* clauses in support of an alternative claim for each issue. Recorders should select two or three working thesis statements from the group to present to the class as a whole.

❦

APPLICATION OF THIS CHAPTER'S PRINCIPLES TO YOUR OWN WRITING

In Chapter 2, we discussed the difficulties of summarizing various types of arguments. Generally, an argument is easiest to summarize when the writer places her thesis in the introduction and uses explicit transitions to highlight the

---

*A working thesis statement for an argument opposing women in combat units might look like this: *Women should not be allowed to join combat units because they lack the strength, endurance, and "fighting spirit" needed in combat; because being pregnant or having small children would make them unreliable for combat at a moment's notice; and because women's presence would hurt morale of tight-knit combat units.* (A working thesis statment for an argument supporting women in combat is found on p. 70.)

You might not put a bulky thesis statement like this into your essay itself; rather, a working thesis statment is a behind-the-scenes way of summarizing your argument for yourself so that you can see it whole and clear.

argument's reasons and structural frame. Such arguments are said to have a *self-announcing structure* because they announce their thesis (and sometimes supporting reasons) and forecast their shape at the outset. Such self-announcing arguments typically follow the conventional format of classical argument discussed in Chapter 3. The invention strategies set forth in this chapter—generating parallel *because* clauses and nutshelling them in a working thesis statement—lead naturally to a classical argument with a self-announcing structure. Each *because* clause, together with its supporting evidence, becomes a separate section of the argument.

An argument with an *unfolding structure,* on the other hand, is considerably harder to summarize. In an unfolding structure, the thesis is delayed until the end or is unstated and left to be inferred by the reader from a narrative that may be both complex and subtle. As we explain in Chapter 8, unfolding structures can be especially effective when dealing with hostile audiences or with troubling or tangled issues. In contrast, classical arguments are often best for neutral or undecided audiences weighing alternative views on a clearcut issue.

In our own classes, we ask students initially to write arguments with self-announcing structures, thereby forcing them to articulate their arguments clearly to themselves and helping them to master the art of organizing complex ideas. Later on in the course, we invite them to experiment with structures that unfold their meanings in subtler, more flexible ways.

In writing classical arguments, students often ask how much of the argument to summarize in the introduction. Consider the following options. You might announce only your claim:

Women should be allowed to join combat units.

Or you could also predict a series of parallel reasons:

Women should be allowed to join combat units for several reasons.

Or you could forecast the actual number of reasons:

Women should be allowed to join combat units for four reasons.

Or you could forecast the whole argument:

Women should be allowed to join combat units because they are physically capable of doing the job; because the presence of women in combat units would weaken gender stereotypes; because opening combat units to women would expand their military career opportunities; and because it would advance the cause of civil rights.

These, of course, are not your only options. If you choose to delay your thesis until the end (a typical kind of unfolding argument), you might place the issue question in the introduction without giving away your own position.

Is the nation well served by allowing women to join combat units?

No formula can tell you how much of your argument to forecast in the introduction. In Chapters 7 and 8 we discuss how forecasting or withholding your thesis affects your *ethos*. We also show how a delayed thesis argument may be a better option for hostile audiences. It is clear at this point, though, that the more you forecast, the clearer your argument is to your reader, whereas the less you forecast, the more surprising your argument will be. The only general rule is this: Readers sometimes feel insulted by too much forecasting. In writing a self-announcing argument, forecast only what is needed for clarity. In short arguments readers often need only your claim. In longer arguments, however, or in especially complex ones, readers appreciate your forecasting the complete structure of the argument (claim with reasons).

APPLICATION OF THIS CHAPTER'S PRINCIPLES TO THE READING OF ARGUMENTS

When you read a complex argument that lacks explicit forecasting, it is often hard to discern its structural core, to identify its claim, and to sort out its reasons and evidence. The more "unfolding" its structure, the harder it is to see exactly how the writer makes his or her case. Moreover, extended arguments often contain digressions and subarguments. Thus there may be dozens of small interlinked arguments going on inside a slowly unfolding main argument.

When you feel yourself getting lost in an unfolding structure, try converting it to a self-announcing structure. (It might help to imagine that the argument's author must state the argument as a claim with *because* clauses. What working thesis statement might the writer construct?) Begin by identifying the writer's claim. Then ask yourself: What are the one, two, three, or four main arguments this writer puts forward to support that claim? State those arguments as *because* clauses attached to the claim. Then compare your *because* clauses with your classmates'. You can expect disagreement—indeed, that disagreement can enrich your understanding of a text—because the writer has left it to you to infer her intent. You should, however, find considerable overlap in your responses.

Once you have converted the support for the claim to *because* clauses and reached consensus on them, you will find it much easier to analyze the writer's reasoning, underlying assumptions, and use of evidence.

CONCLUSION

This chapter has introduced you to the rhetorical triangle with its key concepts of *logos, ethos,* and *pathos.* It has also shown how arguments originate in issue questions, how issue questions differ from information questions, and how arguments differ from pseudo-arguments. At the heart of this chapter we explained that the frame of an argument is a claim supported by reasons. As you generate reasons to support your own arguments, it is often helpful to articulate them as because clauses attached to the claim. Finally, we explained how you can apply the principles of this chapter to your own writing and reading of arguments.

In the next chapter we will see how to support a reason by examining its logical structure, uncovering its unstated assumptions, and planning a strategy of development.

c h a p t e r 5

❖ ▍ The Logical Structure of Arguments

In Chapter 4 you learned that the core of an argument is a claim supported by reasons and that these reasons can often be stated as *because* clauses attached to a claim. In the present chapter we examine the logical structure of arguments in more depth.

OVERVIEW TO *LOGOS:* WHAT DO WE MEAN BY THE "LOGICAL STRUCTURE" OF AN ARGUMENT?

As you will recall from our discussion of the rhetorical triangle, *logos* refers to the strength of an argument's support and its internal consistency. *Logos* is the argument's logical structure. But what do we mean by "logical structure"?

First of all, what we *don't* mean by logical structure is the kind of precise certainty you get in a philosophy class in formal logic. Logic classes deal with symbolic assertions that are universal and unchanging, such as "If all *p*s are *q*s and if *r* is a *p*, then *r* is a *q*." This statement is logically certain so long as *p*, *q*, and *r* are pure abstractions. But in the real world, *p*, *q*, and *r* turn into actual things, and the relationships among them suddenly become fuzzy. For example, *p* might be a class of actions called "Sexual Harassment," while *q* could be the class of "Actions that Justify Dismissal from a Job." If *r* is the class "Telling Off-Color Stories," then the logic of our *p*–*q*–*r* statement suggests that telling off-color stories (*r*) is an instance of sexual harassment (*p*), which in turn is an action justifying dismissal from one's job (*q*).

Now, most of us would agree that sexual harassment is a serious offense that might well justify dismissal from a job. In turn, we might agree that telling off-color stories, if the jokes are sufficiently raunchy and are inflicted on an unwilling

73

audience, constitutes sexual harassment. But few of us would want to say categorically that all people who tell off-color stories are harassing their listeners and ought to be fired. Most of us would want to know the particulars of the case before making a final judgment.

A key difference, then, between formal logic and real-world argument is that real-world arguments are not grounded in abstract, universal statements. Rather, as we shall see, they must be grounded in beliefs, assumptions, or values granted by the audience. A second important difference is that in real-world arguments these beliefs, assumptions, or values are often unstated. So long as writer and audience share the same assumptions, then it's fine to leave them unstated. But if these underlying assumptions aren't shared, the writer has a problem. To illustrate the nature of this problem, consider one of the arguments we introduced in the last chapter.

> Women should be allowed to join combat units because the image of women in combat would help eliminate gender stereotypes.

On the face of it, this is a plausible argument. But the argument is persuasive only if the audience agrees with the writer's assumption that it is a good thing to eliminate gender stereotyping. The writer assumes that gender stereotyping (for example, seeing men as the fighters who are protecting the women and children back home) is harmful and that society would be better off without such fixed gender roles. But what if you believed that some gender roles are biologically based, divinely intended, or otherwise culturally essential and that society should strive to maintain these gender roles rather than dismiss them as "stereotypes"? If such were the case, you might believe as a consequence that our culture should socialize women to be nurturers, not fighters, and that some essential trait of "womanhood" would be at risk if women served in combat. If these were your beliefs, the argument wouldn't work for you because you would reject its underlying assumption. To persuade you with this line of reasoning, the writer would have to show not only how women in combat would help eliminate gender stereotypes but also why these stereotypes are harmful and why society would be better off without them.

The previous core argument ("Women should be allowed to join combat units because the image of women in combat would help eliminate gender stereotypes") is what the Greek philosopher Aristotle would call an enthymeme. An *enthymeme* is an incomplete logical structure that depends, for its completeness, on one or more unstated assumptions (values, beliefs, principles) that serve as the starting point of the argument. The successful arguer, said Aristotle, is the person who knows how to formulate and develop enthymemes so that the argument is rooted in the audience's values and beliefs.

To clarify the concept of "enthymeme," let's go over this same territory again more slowly, examining what we mean by "incomplete logical structure." The original claim with *because* clause is an enthymeme. It combines a claim (women should be allowed to join combat units) with a reason expressed as a *because* clause (because the image of women in combat would help eliminate gender stereotypes). To render this enthymeme logically complete, you must supply an unstated assumption—that gender stereotypes are harmful and should be eliminated. If your audience accepts this assumption, then you have a starting place on which to build an effective argument. If your audience doesn't accept this assumption, then you must supply another argument to support it, and so on until you find common ground with your audience. To sum up:

1. Claims are supported with reasons. You can usually state a reason as a *because* clause attached to a claim (see Chapter 4).

2. A *because* clause attached to a claim is an incomplete logical structure called an enthymeme. To create a complete logical structure from an enthymeme, the unstated assumption (or assumptions) must be articulated.

3. To serve as an effective starting point for the argument, this unstated assumption should be a belief, value, or principle that the audience grants.

Let's illustrate this structure by putting the previous example—plus a new one—into schematic form.

INITIAL ENTHYMEME:	Women should be allowed to join combat units because the image of women in combat would help eliminate gender stereotypes.*
CLAIM:	Women should be allowed to join combat units.
STATED REASON:	because the image of women in combat would help eliminate gender stereotypes
UNSTATED ASSUMPTION:	Gender stereotypes are harmful and should be eliminated.
INITIAL ENTHYMEME:	Cocaine and heroin should be legalized because legalization would eliminate the black market in drugs.
CLAIM:	Cocaine and heroin should be legalized.
STATED REASON:	because legalization would eliminate the black market in drugs
UNSTATED ASSUMPTION:	An action that eliminates the black market in drugs is good.

*Most arguments have more than one *because* clause or reason in support of the claim. Each enthymeme thus develops only one line of reasoning, one piece of your whole argument.

❧ FOR CLASS DISCUSSION ▬▬▬▬▬▬▬▬▬▬▬▬▬▬

Working individually or in small groups, identify the claim, stated reason, and unstated assumption that completes each of the following enthymemic arguments.

EXAMPLE:
Rabbits make good pets because they are gentle.

CLAIM:	Rabbits make good pets.
STATED REASON:	because they are gentle
UNSTATED ASSUMPTION:	Gentle animals make good pets.

1. We shouldn't elect Joe as committee chair because he is too bossy.
2. Buy this stereo system because it has a powerful amplifier.
3. Drugs should not be legalized because legalization would greatly increase the number of drug addicts.
4. Practicing the piano is good for kids because it teaches discipline.
5. Welfare benefits for unwed mothers should be eliminated because doing so will greatly reduce the nation's illegitimacy rate.
6. Welfare benefits for unwed mothers should not be eliminated because these benefits are needed to prevent unbearable poverty among our nation's most helpless citizens.
7. We should strengthen the Endangered Species Act because doing so will preserve genetic diversity on the planet.
8. The Endangered Species Act is too stringent because it severely damages the economy.
9. The doctor should not perform an abortion in this case because the mother's life is not in danger.
10. Abortion should be legal because a woman has the right to control her own body. (This enthymeme has several unstated assumptions behind it; see if you can recreate all the missing premises.)

❧

ADOPTING A LANGUAGE FOR DESCRIBING ARGUMENTS: THE TOULMIN SYSTEM

Understanding a new field usually requires us to learn a new vocabulary. For example, if you were taking biology for the first time, you'd spend days memorizing dozens of new terms. Luckily, the field of argument requires us to learn a mere handful of new terms. A particularly useful set of argument terms, one we'll be using throughout the rest of this text, comes from philosopher Stephen Toulmin. In the 1950s, Toulmin rejected the prevailing models of argument based on formal logic in favor of a very audience-based courtroom model.

Toulmin's courtroom model differs from formal logic in that it assumes (1) that all assertions and assumptions are contestable by "opposing counsel," and (2) that all final "verdicts" about the persuasiveness of alternative arguments will be rendered by a neutral third party, a judge or jury. Keeping in mind the "opposing counsel" forces us to anticipate counterarguments and to question our assumptions; keeping in mind the judge and jury reminds us to answer opposing arguments fully, without rancor, and to present positive reasons for supporting our case as well as negative reasons for disbelieving the alternative views. Above all else, Toulmin's model reminds us not to construct an argument that appeals only to those who already agree with us.

The system we use for analyzing arguments combines Toulmin's system with Aristotle's concept of the enthymeme. The purpose of this system is to provide writers with an economical language for articulating the structure of argument and, in the process, to help them anticipate their audience's needs. More particularly, it helps writers see enthymemes—in the form of a claim with because clauses—as the core of their argument, and the other structural elements from Toulmin as strategies for elaborating and supporting that core.

This system builds on the one you have already been practicing. We simply need to add a few more key terms from Toulmin. The first key term is Toulmin's *warrant,* the name we will now use for the unstated assumption that turns an enthymeme into a complete logical structure. For example:

INITIAL ENTHYMEME:	Women should be allowed to join combat units because the image of women in combat would help eliminate gender stereotypes.
CLAIM:	Women should be allowed to join combat units.
STATED REASON:	because the image of women in combat would help eliminate gender stereotypes
WARRANT:	Gender stereotypes are harmful and should be eliminated.
INITIAL ENTHYMEME:	Cocaine and heroin should be legalized because legalization would eliminate the black market in drugs.
CLAIM:	Cocaine and heroin should be legalized.
STATED REASON:	because legalization would eliminate the black market in drugs
WARRANT:	An action that eliminates the black market in drugs is good.

Toulmin derives his term warrant from the concept of "warranty" or "guarantee." The warrant is the value, belief, or principle that the audience has to hold if the soundness of the argument is to be guaranteed or warranted. We sometimes make similar use of this word in ordinary language when we say "That is an unwarranted conclusion."

But arguments need more than claims, reasons, and warrants. These are simply one-sentence statements—the frame of an argument, not a developed argument. To flesh out our arguments and make them convincing, we need what Toulmin calls *grounds* and *backing*. Grounds are the evidence you use to support your *because* clause (your stated reason). Toulmin suggests that grounds are "what you have to go on" in an argument—the facts, data, statistics, testimony, or examples you use to support your reason. It sometimes helps to think of grounds as the answer to a "How do you know that . . . ?" question prefixed to your stated reason. (How do you know that letting women into combat units would help eliminate gender stereotypes? How do you know that legalizing drugs will end the black market?) Here is how grounds fit into our emerging argument schema.

CLAIM:	Women should be allowed to join combat units.
STATED REASON:	because the image of women in combat would help eliminate gender stereotypes
GROUNDS:	data and evidence showing that a chief stereotype of women is that they are soft and nurturing whereas men are stereotyped as tough and aggressive. The image of women in combat gear packing a rifle, driving a tank, firing a machine gun from a foxhole, or radioing for artillery support would shock people into seeing women not as "soft and nurturing" but as equal to men.
CLAIM:	Cocaine and heroin should be legalized.
STATED REASON:	because legalization would eliminate the black market in drugs
GROUNDS:	data and evidence showing how legalizing cocaine and heroin would eliminate the black market (statistics, data, and examples showing the size of the current black market and explaining why legalization would eliminate it).

In many cases, successful arguments require just these three components: a claim, a reason, and grounds. If the audience already accepts the unstated assumption behind the reason (the warrant), then the warrant can safely remain in the background unstated and unexamined. But if there is a chance that the audience will question or doubt the warrant, then the writer needs to back it up by providing an argument in its support. *Backing* is the argument that supports the warrant. Backing answers the question, "How do you know that . . . ?" or "Why do you believe that . . . ?" prefixed to the warrant. (Why do you believe that gender stereotyping is harmful? Why do you believe that ending the black market is good?) Here is how *backing* is added to our schema.

WARRANT:	Gender stereotypes are harmful and should be eliminated.
BACKING:	arguments showing how the existing stereotype of soft and nurturing women and tough and aggressive men is harmful to

both men and women (examples of how the stereotype keeps men from developing their nurturing sides and women from developing autonomy and power; examples of other benefits that come from eliminating gender stereotypes include more egalitarian society, no limits on what persons can pursue; deeper respect for both sexes)

WARRANT: An action that eliminates the black market in drugs is good.

BACKING: an argument supporting the warrant by showing why the benefits of eliminating the black market outweigh the social cost of legalizing drugs (statistics and examples about the ill effects of the black market, data on crime and profiteering, evidence that huge profits make drug dealing more attractive than ordinary jobs, the high cost of crime created by the black market, the cost to taxpayers of waging the war against drugs, the high cost of prisons to house incarcerated drug dealers, etc.)

Finally, Toulmin's system asks us to imagine how a shrewd adversary would try to refute our argument. Specifically, the adversary might attack our reason and grounds or our warrant and backing or both. In the case of the argument supporting women in combat, an adversary might offer one or more of the following rebuttals:

CONDITIONS OF REBUTTAL

Rebutting the reasons and grounds: evidence that letting women join combat units wouldn't overcome gender stereotyping (very few women would want to join combat units; those who did would be considered freaks; most girls would still identify with Barbie doll models, not with female infantry)

Rebutting the warrant and backing: arguments showing it is important to maintain gender role differences because they are biologically based, divinely inspired, or otherwise important culturally; women should be nurturers and mothers, not fighters; essential nature of "womanhood" sullied by putting women in combat

Likewise, a skeptical audience might rebut the legalization of drugs argument in one or more of the following ways:

CONDITIONS OF REBUTTAL

Rebutting the reasons and grounds: evidence that legalizing drugs might not end the black market (perhaps taxes would keep prices high or constraints on buyers would send them to the streets rather than to federal drug stores; or perhaps new designer drugs would be developed and sold on the black market)

Rebutting the warrant and backing: arguments showing that the costs of eliminating the black market by legalizing drugs outweigh the benefits (an unacceptably high number of new drug users and addicts; a catastrophic increase in health care costs because of increased drug use; harm to the social structure from increased acceptance of drugs; high social costs to families and communities associated with addiction or erratic behavior during drug-induced "highs")

Toulmin's final term, used to limit the force of a claim and indicate the degree of its probable truth, is *qualifier*. The qualifier reminds us that real-world arguments almost never prove a claim. We may add words like *very likely, probably,* or *maybe* to indicate the strength of the claim we are willing to draw from our grounds and warrant. Thus if your grounds or warrant can be rebutted, you will have to qualify your claim. For example, you might say, "Except in rare cases, women should not be allowed in combat units," or "With full awareness of the potential dangers, I suggest that legalizing drugs may be the best way to eliminate the social costs of the black market."

 FOR CLASS DISCUSSION

Working individually or in small groups, imagine that you have to write arguments developing the ten enthymemes listed in the For Class Discussion exercise on page 76. Use the Toulmin schema to help you determine what you need to consider when developing each enthymeme. As an example, we have applied the Toulmin schema to the first enthymeme.

ORIGINAL ENTHYMEME: We should not choose Joe as committee chair because he is too bossy.

CLAIM: We should not choose Joe as committee chair.

STATED REASON: because he is too bossy

GROUNDS: various examples of Joe's bossiness; testimony about his bossiness from people who have worked with him

WARRANT: Bossy people make bad committee chairs.

BACKING: arguments showing that other things being equal, bossy people tend to bring out the worst rather than the best in those around them; bossy people tend not to ask advice, make bad decisions; etc.

CONDITIONS OF REBUTTAL: *Rebuttal of reason and grounds:* perhaps Joe isn't really bossy (counterevidence of Joe's cooperativeness and kindness; testimony that Joe is easy to work with; etc.)

Rebuttal of the warrant and backing: perhaps bossy people sometimes make good chairpersons (arguments showing that at times a group needs a bossy person who can make decisions and get things done); perhaps Joe has other traits of good leadership that outweigh his bossiness (evidence that, despite his bossiness, Joe has many other good leadership traits such as high energy, intelligence, charisma, etc.)

QUALIFIER: In most circumstances, bossy people make bad committee chairs.

USING TOULMIN'S SCHEMA TO DETERMINE A STRATEGY OF SUPPORT

Having introduced you to Toulmin's terminology for describing the logical structure of arguments, we can turn directly to a discussion of how to use these concepts for developing your own arguments. As we have seen, the claim, supporting reasons, and warrant form the frame for a line of reasoning. The majority of words in an argument, however, are devoted to grounds and backing—the supporting sections that develop the argument frame. Generally these supporting sections take one of two forms: either (1) *evidence* such as facts, examples, case studies, statistics, testimony from experts, and so forth; or (2) a *sequence of reasons*—that is, further conceptual argument. The Toulmin schema can help you determine what kind of support your argument needs. Let's look at each kind of support separately.

Evidence as Support

It's often easier for writers to use evidence rather than chains of reasons for support because using evidence entails moving from generalizations to specific details—a basic organizational strategy that most writers practice regularly. Consider the following hypothetical case. A student, Ramona, wants to write a complaint letter to the head of the Philosophy Department about a philosophy professor, Dr. Choplogic, whom Ramona considers incompetent. Ramona plans to develop two different lines of reasoning: first, that Choplogic's courses are disorganized and, second, that Choplogic is unconcerned about students. Let's look briefly at how she can develop her first main line of reasoning, which is based on the following enthymeme:

Dr. Choplogic is an ineffective teacher because his courses are disorganized.

The grounds for this argument will be evidence that Choplogic's courses are disorganized. Using the Toulmin schema, Ramona lists under "grounds" all the evidence she can muster that Choplogic's courses are disorganized. Here is how this argument might look when placed into written form:

Claim and reason	One reason that Dr. Choplogic is ineffective is that his courses are poorly organized. I have had him for two courses—Introduction to Philosophy and Ethics—and both were disorganized. He never gave
Grounds (evidence in support of reason)	us a syllabus or explained his grading system. At the beginning of the course he wouldn't tell us how many papers he would require, and he never seemed to know how much of the textbook material he planned to cover. For Intro he told us to read the whole text, but he covered only half of it in class. A week before the final I asked him how much of the text would be on the exam and he said he hadn't decided. The Ethics class was even more disorganized. Dr. Choplogic told us to read the text, which provided one set of terms for ethical arguments, and then he told us he didn't like the text and presented us in lecture with a wholly different set of terms. The result was a whole class of confused, angry students.

As you can see, Ramona has plenty of evidence to support her contention that Choplogic is disorganized. But how effective is this argument as it stands? Is this all she needs? The Toulmin schema also encourages Ramona to examine the warrant, backing, and conditions of rebuttal for this argument. She believes that no one can challenge her reason and grounds—Choplogic is indeed a disorganized teacher. But she recognizes that some people might challenge her warrant ("Disorganized teachers are ineffective"). A supporter of Dr. Choplogic might say that some teachers, even though they are hopelessly disorganized, might nevertheless do an excellent job of stimulating thought and discussion. Moreover, such teachers might possess other valuable traits that outweigh their disorganization. Ramona therefore decides to address these concerns by adding another section to this portion of her argument.

Backing for warrant (shows why disorganization is bad)	Dr. Choplogic's lack of organization makes it difficult for students to take notes, to know what to study, or to relate one part of the course to another. Moreover, students lose confidence in the teacher because he doesn't seem to care enough to prepare for class.
Response to conditions of rebuttal	In Dr. Choplogic's defense, it might be thought that his primary concern is involving students in class discussions or other activities to teach us thinking skills or get us involved in philosophical discussions. But this isn't the case. Students rarely get a chance to speak in class. We just sit there listening to rambling, disorganized lectures.

This section of her argument backs the warrant that disorganized teachers are ineffective and anticipates some of the conditions for rebuttal that an audience might raise to defend Dr. Choplogic. Throughout her draft, Ramona has supported her argument with evidence. Although Ramona takes her evidence from personal experience, in other cases evidence might come primarily from reading and research. Chapter 6 is devoted to a more detailed discussion of evidence in arguments.

Sequence of Reasons As Support

So far we have been discussing how reasons can be supported with evidence. Often, however, reasons cannot be supported this way; rather, they must be supported with a sequence of other reasons. Consider, for example, a writer proposing a mandatory death penalty for convicted serial killers. Let's assume that this writer, living in a state where the death penalty is legal but seldom used, is angry that a recently convicted serial killer was sentenced to life imprisonment. His claim, along with his main supporting reason, is as follows:

The law should mandate capital punishment for serial killers because this crime is exceptionally heinous.

This argument cannot be supported simply with evidence that serial killing is heinous. Rather, the writer must show that serial killing is *exceptionally* heinous, an argument requiring a sequence of further reasons. So why should the law single out serial killers for a mandatory death sentence but not other murderers? Since all murders are heinous, what is unique about serial killers that justifies their execution while other murderers' crimes might not warrant the death penalty? In distinguishing serial murderers from other murderers, the writer develops the following list of potential reasons:

- By definition, serial killers have murdered more than one person.
- Serial killers are not capable of rehabilitation.
- The cost of capturing serial killers is extraordinarily high because they kill more or less at random and force police to deploy a large detective staff to one case.
- Serial murders are calculated crimes, often requiring extensive planning that goes far beyond the mere "intent" required in first-degree murder cases.
- Serial murders typically involve torture of at least some of the victims in order to satisfy the serial killer's deep need not just to kill but to dominate his (there are few documented cases of female serial killers) victims.
- They inflict widespread emotional distress on a community and incite 'copycat' killers because of the highly publicized nature of their crimes.
- The chances of mistakenly executing a defendant, which are minuscule to begin with, are virtually nonexistent with serial killers.

Having developed a list of reasons for singling out serial killers, the writer is ready to draft the argument in essay form. Here is a portion of that argument, picking up after the writer has used evidence (in the form of gruesome narratives) to demonstrate the heinous nature of serial murders.

These stories show the heinous nature of serial murders. "But aren't all murders heinous?" some might ask. What makes serial murders *exceptionally* heinous? Why single them out for a mandatory death sentence while leaving the fate of other murderers to the discretion of judges and juries?

First, serial murderers by definition have killed more than one person. Moreover, these killings are ruthless and brutal. Typically they involve torture of at least some of the victims to satisfy the serial killer's deep need not just to kill but to humiliate and dominate his victims. Whereas most killers kill for a particular purpose (greed, jealousy), the serial killer kills for pleasure. Moreover, because the drive to kill is potentially inexhaustible, serial murderers are psychologically incapable of remorse and rehabilitation. Yet they are not insane in any legal sense; what makes them so frightening is their rational intelligence as they plot the next victim. Their crimes are *calculated,* often requiring extensive planning that goes beyond the mere "intent" required for other first degree murder convictions.

Serial murders are exceptionally heinous in another way as well because of the economic and psychological harm they bring the nation. Serial killers inflict panic on a community, and widespread publicity often incites "copycat" killers. Moreover, serial killers are exceedingly expensive to catch because vast teams of detectives must be assembled to investigate multiple slayings and work feverishly to prevent future ones.

Ironically, though, when a serial killer is finally caught, he has left behind so many signature marks that it is virtually impossible to execute the wrong person. This frequent objection to capital punishment—that an innocent person may be executed—isn't an issue with serial killers.

As you can tell, this section is considerably more complex than one that simply cites data as evidence in support of a reason. Here the writer must use a sequence of other reasons to make his point, showing all the ways that serial killers differ from other first degree murderers and thus should be punished differently. Certainly it's not a definitive argument, but it is considerably more compelling than simply asserting your claim without elaboration. Although sequences of further reasons are harder to construct than bodies of evidence, many arguments will require them.

CONCLUSION

Chapters 4 and 5 have provided an anatomy of argument. They have shown that the core of an argument is a claim with reasons that usually can be summarized in one or more because clauses attached to the claim. Often, it is as important to support the unstated premises in your argument as it is to support the stated ones. In order to plan out an argument strategy, arguers can use the Toulmin schema, which helps writers discover grounds, warrants, and backings for their arguments and to test them through conditions for rebuttal. Finally, we saw how stated reasons and warrants are supported through the use of evidence or chains of other reasons. In the next chapter we will look more closely at the uses of evidence in argumentation.

 FOR CLASS DISCUSSION

1. Working individually or in small groups, consider ways you could use evidence from personal experience to support the stated reason in each of the following partial arguments:
   a. Another reason to oppose a state sales tax is that it is so annoying.
   b. Professor X should be rated down on his (her) teaching because he (she) doesn't design homework effectively to promote real learning.

   c. Professor X is an outstanding teacher because he (she) generously spends so much time outside of class counseling students with personal problems.

2. Now try to create a sequence-of-reasons argument to support the warrants in each of the above partial arguments. The warrants for each of the arguments are stated below.
   a. Support this warrant: We should oppose taxes that are annoying.
   b. Support this warrant: The effective design of homework to promote real learning is an important criterion for rating teachers.
   c. Support this warrant: Time spent counseling students with personal problems is an important criterion for rating teachers.

3. Using Toulmin's conditions of rebuttal, work out a strategy for refuting either the stated reasons or the warrants or both in each of the above arguments.

c h a p t e r 6

Evidence in Argument

In the previous chapter, we examined two basic ways to support arguments: through reasons supported by evidence and through reasons supported by sequences of other reasons. In this chapter we return to a discussion of evidence—how to find, use, and evaluate it. We focus on four categories of evidence: (1) data from personal experience—either from memory or from observation; (2) data from interviews, surveys, and questionnaires; (3) data from reading, especially library research, and (4) numerical or statistical data. Finally, we discuss how to evaluate evidence in order to use it fairly, responsibly, and persuasively.

USING EVIDENCE FROM PERSONAL EXPERIENCE

Your own life can be the source of supporting evidence in many arguments. Personal narratives can illustrate important points or underscore the human significance of your issue. Such stories build bridges to readers, who often find personal experience more engaging and immediate than dry lists of facts or statistics. Moreover, when readers sense a writer's personal connection to an issue, they are more likely to find the writer's position credible.

Using Personal Experience Data Collected from Memory

Many arguments can be supported extensively, even exclusively, by data recalled from memory. Here, for example, is how a student from a small Montana town used her memories to support the claim "Small rural schools provide a quality education for children."

Another advantage of small rural schools is the way they create in students a sense of identity with their communities and a sense of community pride. When children see the active support of the community toward the school, they want to return this support with their best efforts. I remember our Fergus Grade School Christmas programs. Sure, every grade school in Montana has a Christmas program, but ours seemed to be small productions. We started work on our play and songs immediately after Thanksgiving. The Fergus Community Women's Club decorated the hall a few days before the program. When the big night arrived, the whole community turned out, even Mr. and Mrs. Schoenberger, an elderly couple. I and the eleven other students were properly nervous as we performed our play, "A Charlie Brown Christmas." As a finale, the whole community sang carols and exchanged gifts. One of the fathers even dressed up as Santa Claus. Everyone involved had a warm feeling down inside when they went home.

The community bonding described in this paragraph—the father playing Santa Claus, the attendance of the elderly couple, the communal singing of Christmas carols—supports the writer's stated reason that small rural schools help students feel an identity with their communities.

Using Personal Experience Data Collected from Observations

For other arguments you can gather evidence through personal observations, as in the following example:

The intersection at 5th and Montgomery is particularly dangerous. Traffic volume on Montgomery is so heavy that pedestrians almost never find a comfortable break in the flow of cars. On April 29, I watched fifty-seven pedestrians cross this intersection. Not once did cars stop in both directions before the pedestrian stepped off the sidewalk onto the street. Typically, the pedestrian had to move into the street, start tentatively to cross, and wait until a car finally stopped. On fifteen occasions, pedestrians had to stop halfway across the street, with cars speeding by in both directions, waiting for cars in the far lanes to stop before they could complete their crossing.

USING EVIDENCE FROM INTERVIEWS, SURVEYS, AND QUESTIONNAIRES

In addition to direct observations, you can gather evidence by conducting interviews, taking surveys, or passing out questionnaires.

Conducting Interviews

Interviewing people is a useful way not only to gather expert testimony and important data, but also to learn about alternative views. To conduct an effective interview, you must have a clear sense of purpose, prepare in advance, be punctual, and respect your interviewee's time.

When you use interview data in your own writing, put quotation marks around any direct quotations. Except when unusual circumstances might require anonymity, identify your source by name and indicate his or her title or credentials—whatever will convince the reader that this person's remarks are to be taken seriously. Here is how one student used interview data to support an argument against carpeting dorm rooms.

> Finally, university-provided carpets will be too expensive. According to Robert Bothell, Assistant Director of Housing Services, the cost will be $300 per room for the carpet and installation. The university would also have to purchase more vacuum cleaners for the students to use. Altogether, Bothell estimated the cost of carpets to be close to $100,000 for the whole campus.

Using Surveys or Questionnaires

Still another form of field research data can come from surveys or questionnaires. Sometimes an informal poll of your classmates can supply evidence persuasive to a reader. One of our students, in an argument supporting public transportation, asked every rider on her bus one morning the following two questions:

Do you enjoy riding the bus more than commuting by car? If so, why?

She was able to use her data in the following paragraph:

> Last week I polled forty-eight people riding the bus between Bellevue and Seattle. Eighty percent said they enjoyed riding the bus more than commuting by car, while 20 percent preferred the car. Those who enjoyed the bus cited the following reasons in this order of preference: It saved them the hassle of driving in traffic; it gave them time to relax and unwind; it was cheaper than paying for gas and parking; it saved them time.

More formal research can be done through developing and distributing questionnaires. Plan your questionnaire carefully, write nonambiguous questions, and keep it short. Type it neatly so that it looks clean, uncluttered, and easy to complete. At the head of the questionnaire you should explain its purpose. Your tone should be courteous and, if possible, you should offer the reader some motivation to complete the questionnaire.

USING EVIDENCE FROM READING

Although you can base some arguments on evidence from personal experience or from questionnaires and interviews, most arguments require research evidence gleaned from reading: books, magazines, journals, newspapers, government documents, Internet sources, chat groups, specialized encyclopedias and almanacs, corporate bulletins, and so forth. When you use research data from reading, it often takes one or more of the following forms: facts and examples, summaries of research studies, and testimony.

Facts and Examples

A common way to incorporate evidence from reading is to cite facts and examples. Here is how one student writer argues that plastic food packaging and styrofoam cups aren't necessarily damaging to the environment.

> It's politically correct today to scorn plastic food wrapping and styrofoam cups. But in the long run these containers may actually help the environment. According to Tierney, a typical household in countries that don't use plastic food wrapping produces one-third more garbage from food spoilage than do U.S. households. Those plastic wrappers on foods allow us to buy foods in small quantities and keep them sterile until use. Tierney also claims that plastic packaging requires far less energy to produce than does paper or cardboard and is lighter to transport (27). Similarly, he claims that the energy costs of producing a ceramic coffee mug and of washing it after each use make it less environmentally friendly than throwaway styrofoam cups (44).

Knowing that experts can disagree about what is a "fact," this writer attributes her evidence to Tierney ("Tierney claims . . . ") rather than stating Tierney's claims baldly as facts and simply citing him in parentheses. (This writer is using the Modern Language Association documentation style: The numbers in parentheses are page numbers in the Tierney article where the cited information can be found. At the end of her paper, she will provide complete bibliographic information about the Tierney source in her "Works Cited" page. See Appendix 2, "A Concise Guide to Documentation.")

Summaries of Research

An argument can often be supported by summarizing research studies. Here is how a student writer used a summary statement to support his opposition to mandatory helmet laws for motorcycle riders:

> However, a helmet won't protect against head injury when one is traveling at normal traffic speeds. According to a U.S. Department of Transportation study, "There is no evidence that any helmet thus far, regardless of cost or design, is capable of rejecting impact stress above 13 mph" ("Head Injuries" 8).

Testimony

Research data can also take the form of *testimony*, an expert's opinion that you cite to help bolster your case. Testimony, which we might call secondhand evidence, is often blended with other kinds of data. Using testimony is particularly common wherever laypersons cannot be expected to be experts; thus, you might cite an authority on the technical feasibility of cold fusion, the effects of alcohol on fetal tissue development, or the causes of a recent airplane crash. Here is how a student writer used testimony to bolster an argument on global warming.

> We can't afford to wait any longer before taking action against global warming. At a recent Senate hearing of the Subcommittee on Environmental Pollution, Senator Chafee warned: "There is a very real possibility that man—through ignorance or indifference or both—is irreversibly altering the ability of our atmosphere to [support] life" (qtd. in Begley 64). At this same hearing, Robert Watson of the National Aeronautics and Space Administration (which monitors the upper atmosphere) claimed: "Global warming is inevitable—it's only a question of magnitude and time" (qtd. in Begley 66).

Here the writer uses no factual or statistical data that global warming is occurring; rather, she cites the testimony of experts.

USING NUMERICAL DATA AND STATISTICS

Among the most pervasive kinds of evidence in modern arguments are numerical data and statistics. Many of us, however, are understandably mistrustful of numerical data. "There are three kinds of lies," we have all heard: "lies, damned lies, and statistics."

Those who gather, use, and analyze numerical data have their own language for degrees of data manipulation. *Teasing* and *tweaking* data are usually legitimate attempts to portray data in a better light; *massaging* data may involve a bit of subterfuge but is still within acceptable limits. When the line is crossed and manipulation turns into outright, conscious misrepresentation, however, we say the data have been *cooked*—an unsavory fate for data and people alike. If we are to use data responsibly and protect ourselves from others' abuses of them, it's important for us to understand how to analyze them.

In this section we examine ways to use numerical data both responsibly and persuasively.

Using Graphics for Effect

Any time a writer presents numerical data pictorially, the potential for enhancing the rhetorical presence of the argument, or of manipulating the audience outright, increases markedly. By *presence,* we mean the immediacy and impact of the material. For example, raw numbers and statistics, in large doses, are apt to dull people's minds and perplex them. But numbers turned into pictures are very immediate. Graphs, charts, and tables help an audience see at a glance what long strings of statistics can only hint at.

We can have markedly different effects on our audience according to how we design and construct a graphic. For example, by coloring one variable prominently and enlarging it slightly, a graphic artist can greatly distort the importance of that variable. Although such depictions may carry warnings that they are "not to scale," the visual impact is often more memorable than the warning.

One of the subtlest ways of controlling an audience's perception of a numerical relationship is the way you construct the grids on the X/Y axes (the X axis being horizontal, the Y axis vertical) of a line graph. Consider, for example, the graph in Figure 6.1 depicting the monthly net profits of an ice cream sandwich retailer. If you look at this graph, you'd think that the net profits of "Bite O' Heaven" were themselves shooting heavenward. But if you were considering investing in an ice cream sandwich franchise yourself, you would want to consider how the graph was constructed. Note the quantity assigned to each square on the grid. Although the graph does represent the correct quantities, the designer's choice of increments leads to a wildly inflated depiction of success. If the "Bite O' Heaven" folks had chosen a larger increment for each square on the vertical axis—say, $5,000 instead of $1,000—the company's rise in profitability would look like the graph in Figure 6.2. One can easily distort or overstate a rate of change on a graph

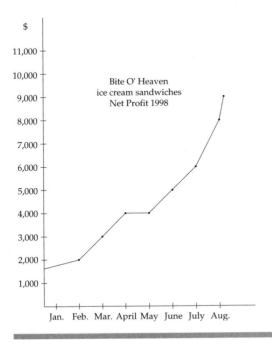

FIGURE 6.1   A line graph that distorts the data

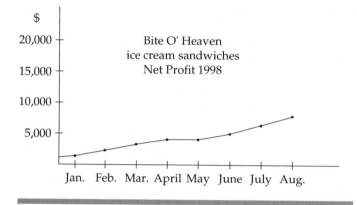

FIGURE 6.2   A line graph that more accurately depicts data

by consciously selecting the quantities assigned to each scale unit on the horizontal or vertical axis.

Another way to create a rhetorical effect with a line graph is to vary the scope of time it covers. Note that the two graphs just presented cover net sales from January through August. What do you think the sales figures for this company might typically be from September through December?

❦ FOR CLASS DISCUSSION

In small groups, create a line graph for the net profits of the Bite O' Heaven company for a whole year based on your best estimates of when people are most apt to buy ice cream sandwiches. Then draw graphs of net profits, quarter by quarter, over a three-year period to represent the following conditions:

1. The Bite O' Heaven company maintains a stable market share with no increase or decrease in the rate of profits over the three years.

2. The Bite O' Heaven company increases its market share, with each year more profitable than the preceding one.

3. The Bite O' Heaven company loses market share with each year leaner than the previous one.

❦

Using Numbers Strategically

As we have suggested, your choice and design of a graphic can markedly affect your audience's perception of your subject. But you can also influence your audience through the kinds of numbers you use: raw numbers versus percentages;

or raw numbers versus "adjusted" numbers (for example, wages "adjusted for inflation"); or a statistical presentation versus a narrative one. The choice always depends on the audience you're addressing and the purpose you want to achieve.

One of the most common choices writers have to make is between citing raw numbers or citing percentages or rates. In some cases, for example, a raw number will be more persuasive than a percentage. If you were to say that the cost of attending a state college will increase at a rate 15 percent greater than the Consumer Price Index over the next decade, most audiences would be lost—few would know how to translate that number into terms they could understand. But if you were to say that in the year 2007, the cost of attending a state college for one year will be about $21,000, you would surely grab your audience's attention. So, if you were a financial planner trying to talk a young couple into saving money for their children's college education, you would be more prone to use the raw number rather than the percent increase. But if you were a college administrator trying to play down the increasing costs of college to a hostile legislator, you might well use the percentage increase rather than the raw number.

In turn, how you state raw numbers can markedly increase or decrease their impact on an audience. For example, to say that newspapers consume huge amounts of wood pulp is mildly interesting. To say that publication of the *New York Times* requires 248 million tons of pulp each year is even more impressive. To say that publication of just one Sunday edition of the *New York Times* requires the cutting of 75,000 trees is mind boggling. Again, translate the number into what is most meaningful to your audience and the impact you wish to have on that audience.

WRITING YOUR OWN ARGUMENT: USING EVIDENCE PERSUASIVELY

Once you have arrived at a position on an issue, often after having written a draft that enables you to explore and clarify your own views, you need to select the best evidence possible and to use it persuasively. Whether your evidence comes from research or from personal experience, the following guidelines may be helpful.

When Possible, Select Your Data from Sources Your Reader Trusts

Other things being equal, choose data from sources you think your reader will trust. After immersing yourself in an issue, you will get a sense of who the participants in a conversation are and what their reputations tend to be. One needs to know the political biases of sources and the extent to which a source has a financial or personal investment in the outcome of a controversy. When the greenhouse controversy first struck the national consciousness, two prolific writers on the subject were Carl Sagan and Dixie Lee Ray, both of whom are now deceased. Both writers held Ph.D. degrees in science and both had national reputations for speaking out in the popular press on technical and scientific issues. Carl Sagan, however, was an environmentalist while Dixie Lee Ray tended to support business and industry. To some audiences, neither of these writers was as persuasive as more cautious and less visible scientists who publish primarily in scientific journals. Similarly, citing a conservative magazine such as *Reader's Digest* is apt to be ineffective to liberal audiences, just as citing a Sierra Club publication would be ineffective to conservatives.

Increase Persuasiveness of Factual Data by Ensuring Recency, Representativeness, and Sufficiency

Other things being equal, choose data that are recent, representative, and sufficient. The more your data meet these criteria, the more persuasive they are.

Recency: Although some timeless issues don't depend on recent evidence, most issues, especially those related to science and technology or to current political and economic issues, depend on up-to-date information. Make sure your supporting evidence is the most recent you can find.

Representativeness: Supporting examples are more persuasive when the audience believes they are typical examples instead of extreme cases or rare occurrences. Assuring representativeness is an especially important concern of statisticians, who seek random samples to avoid bias toward one point of view. Seeking representative examples helps you guard against selective use of data—starting with a claim and then choosing only those data that support it, instead of letting the claim grow out of a careful consideration of all the data.

Sufficiency: One of the most common reasoning fallacies, called *hasty generalization* (see p. 243), occurs when a person leaps to a sweeping generalization based on only one or two instances. The criterion of sufficiency (which means having enough examples to justify your point) helps you guard against hasty generalization. In our experience, lack of sufficiency occurs frequently in personal experience arguments. The student praised earlier for her personal experience data in an argument about rural schools suffers from this problem in the following paragraph:

My primary reason for supporting the small, rural grade schools over the larger urban schools is the amount of learning that occurs. I am my own proof. I was the only member of my grade from the third to the eighth grade at Fergus Grade School. I relished the privilege of being able to work on two chapters of math, instead of one, especially if I enjoyed the subject. Upon graduation from the eighth grade, I attended a large high school and discovered that I had a better background than students from larger grade schools. I got straight A's.

The problem here is that the writer's one example—herself—isn't sufficient for supporting the claim that rural schools provide quality learning. To support that claim, she would need either more examples or statistical data about the later achievements of students who attended rural grade schools.

In Citing Evidence, Distinguish Fact from Inference or Opinion

In citing research data, you should be careful to distinguish facts from inferences or opinions. A *fact* is a noncontroversial piece of data that is verifiable through observation or through appeal to communally accepted authorities. Although the distinction between a fact and an inference is a fuzzy one philosophically, at a pragmatic level all of the following can loosely be classified as facts.

The Declaration of Independence was signed in 1776.

An earthquake took place in San Francisco on the opening day of the World Series in 1989.

The amount of carbon dioxide in the atmosphere has increased by 7 percent since 1955.

An *inference*, on the other hand, is an interpretation or explanation of the facts that may be reasonably doubted. This distinction is important because, when reading as a doubter, you often call into question a writer's inferences. If you treat these inferences as facts, you are apt to cite them as facts in your own arguments, thereby opening yourself up to easy rebuttal. For the most part, inferences should be handled as testimony rather than as fact.

WEAK:	Flohn informs us that the warming of the atmosphere will lead to damaging droughts by the year 2035. [treats Flohn's inference as a fact about global warming]
BETTER:	Flohn interprets the data pessimistically. He believes that the warming of the atmosphere will lead to damaging droughts by the year 2035. [makes it clear that Flohn's view is an inference, not a fact]

CONCLUSION

Good arguers use evidence effectively. As we have seen, evidence includes facts, examples, statistics, testimony, and other forms of data, and it can come from personal experience as well as from reading and research. It is important to select data from sources that your reader will trust, to ensure the recency, representativeness, and sufficiency of your evidence, and to distinguish between facts and inference.

❦ WRITING ASSIGNMENTS FOR CHAPTERS 4–6

OPTION 1: *A microtheme that supports a reason with personal experience data*
Write a one- or two-paragraph argument in which you support one of the following enthymemes, using evidence from personal experience. Most of your microtheme should support the stated reason with personal experience data. However, also include a brief passage supporting the implied warrant. The opening sentence of your microtheme should be the enthymeme itself, which serves as the thesis statement for your argument.

1. Reading fashion magazines can be detrimental to teenage girls because such magazines can lower a girl's self-esteem.
2. Learning to surf the Web might harm your studying because it causes you to waste time.
3. Getting a part-time job in college might improve your grades because the job will teach you time management.
4. X (a teacher/professor of your choosing) is an outstanding teacher because she (he) generously spends time counseling students with personal problems.
5. Any enthymeme (a claim with because clause) of your choice that can be supported through personal experience. Clear your enthymeme with your instructor.

OPTION 2: *A microtheme that uses evidence from research*   The purpose of this microtheme is to help you learn how to support reasons with evidence gathered from research. The following presentation of data attempts to simulate the kinds of research evidence one might typically gather during a research project.
   The situation: By means of startling "before and after" photographs of formerly obese people, the commercial diet industry heavily advertises rapid weight loss diets that use liquids and powders or special low-calorie frozen dinners. **Your task:**   Drawing on the following data, write a short argument warning people of the hazards of these diets.

Source: Representative Ron Wyden (D–Oregon), chairman of a congressional subcommittee investigating the diet industry:

- Wyden fears that diet programs now include many shoddy companies that use misleading advertisements and provide inadequate medical supervision of their clients.
- "This industry has been built almost overnight on a very shaky foundation."
- "All the evidence says that losing large amounts of weight very fast does more harm than good."
- Wyden believes that the diet industry may need to be federally regulated.

Source: Theodore B. VanItallie, M.D., a founder of the Obesity Research Center at St. Luke's Roosevelt Hospital Center in New York:

- Rapid weight loss systems (such as liquid diets) were originally designed for morbidly obese individuals.
- For people who are only slightly overweight, rapid weight loss can be hazardous.
- When weight loss is too rapid, the body begins using lean muscle mass for fuel instead of excess fat. The result is a serious protein deficiency that can bring on heart irregularities.
- "If more than 25 percent of lost weight is lean body mass, the stage is set not only for early regain of lost weight but for a higher incidence of fatigue, hair loss, skill changes, depression and other undesirable side effects."

Source: Bonnie Blodgett, freelance writer on medical/health issues:

- Rapid weight loss may accelerate formation of gallstones. Currently 179 people are suing a major diet company because of gallstone complications while pursuing the company's diet. The company denies responsibility.
- For every five people who start a commercial weight-loss program, only one stays with it long enough to lose a significant amount of weight.
- Up to 90 percent of dieters who lose more than 25 pounds gain it all back within two years.
- Only one in fifty maintains the weight loss for seven years.
- The best way to lose weight is through increased exercise, moderate reduction of calories, and a lifelong change in eating habits.
- Unless one is grossly obese and dieting under a physician's supervision, one should strive to lose no more than 1 or 2 pounds per week.

Source: Philip Kern, M.D., in a study appearing in *The New England Journal of Medicine:*

- Rapid weight loss programs result in the "yo-yo" syndrome—a pattern of compulsive fasting followed by compulsive bingeing.

- This pattern may upset the body's metabolism by producing an enzyme called lipoprotein lipase.
- This protein helps restore fat cells shrunken by dieting.
- It apparently causes formerly fat people to crave fatty foods, thereby promoting regain of lost weight.*

OPTION 5:   *A formal argument using at least two reasons in support of your claim*
Write a multiparagraph essay in which you develop two or more reasons in support of your thesis or claim. Each of your reasons should be summarizable in a because clause attached to your claim. If you have more than two reasons, develop your most important reason last. Give your essay a self-announcing structure in which you highlight your claim at the end of your introduction and begin your body paragraphs with clearly stated reasons. Open your essay with an attention-grabbing lead that attracts your readers' interest; your introduction should also explain the issue being addressed as well as provide whatever background is needed.

Note that this assignment does not ask you to refute opposing views. Nevertheless, it is a good idea to summarize an opposing view briefly to help the reader see the issue more clearly. Because you will not be refuting this view, the best place to summarize it is in your introduction prior to presenting your own claim. (If you place an opposing view in the body of your essay, its prominence obligates you to refute it or concede to it—issues addressed in Chapter 8 of this text. If you briefly summarize an opposing view in the introduction, however, you use it merely to clarify the issue and hence do not need to treat it at length.)

The following essay illustrates this assignment. It was written by a freshman student whose first language is Vietnamese rather than English.

Choose Life!

Dao Do (student)

1   Should euthanasia be legalized? My classmate Paula and her family think it should be. Paula's grandmother was blind from diabetes. For three years she was constantly in and out of the hospital, but then her kidneys shut down and she became a victim of life supports. After three months of suffering, she finally gave up. Paula believes the three-month period was unnecessary, for her grandmother didn't have to go through all of that suffering. If euthanasia were legalized, her family would have put her to sleep the minute her condition worsened. Then, she wouldn't have had to feel pain, and she would have died in peace and with dignity. Despite Paula's strong argument for legalizing euthanasia, I find it is wrong.

2   First, euthanasia is wrong because no one has the right to take the life of another person. Just as our society discourages suicide, it should discourage euthanasia because in both

---

*Source of these data is Bonnie Blodgett, "The Diet Biz," *Glamour* Jan. 1991: 136ff.

the person is running away from life and its responsibilities. Some people say that euthanasia or suicide will end suffering and pain. But what proofs do they have for such a claim? Death is still mysterious to us; therefore, we do not know whether death will end suffering and pain or not. What seems to be the real claim is that death to those with illnesses will end *our* pain. Such pain involves worrying over them, paying their medical bills, and giving up so much of our time. Their deaths end our pain rather than theirs. And for that reason, euthanasia is a selfish act, for the outcome of euthanasia benefits us, the non-sufferers, more. Once the sufferers pass away, we can go back to our normal lives.

My second opposition to euthanasia is its unfavorable consequences. Today, euthanasia is performed on those who we think are suffering from incurable diseases or brain death. But what about tomorrow? People might use euthanasia to send old parents to death just to get rid of them faster, so they can get to the money, the possessions, and the real estate. Just think of all the murder cases on TV where children killed their parents so they can get to the fortune. Legalizing euthanasia will increase the number of these murder cases. The right of euthanasia not only encourages corruption, it encourages discrimination. People who suffer pain would be put into categories according to which should live longer and which shouldn't. Perhaps poor people or people of color will be more apt to be euthanized than rich people, or perhaps people with AIDS will be euthanized sooner so that society won't have to spend money on this very expensive disease. 3

My third objection to euthanasia is that it fails to see the value in suffering. Suffering is a part of life. We only see the value of suffering if we look deeply within our suffering. For example, I never thought my crippled uncle from Vietnam was a blessing to my grandmother until I talked to her. My mother's little brother was born prematurely. As a result of oxygen and nutrition deficiency, he was born crippled. His tiny arms and legs were twisted around his body, preventing him from any normal movements such as walking, picking up things, and lying down. He could only sit. Therefore, his world was very limited, for it consisted of his own room and the garden viewed through his window. Because of his disabilities, my grandmother had to wash him, feed him, and watch him constantly. It was hard but she managed to care for him for forty-three years. He passed away after the death of my grandfather in 1982. Bringing this situation out of Vietnam and into Western society shows the difference between Vietnamese and West's views. In West, my uncle might have been euthanized as a baby. Supporters of euthanasia would have said he wouldn't have any quality of life and that he would have been a great burden. But he was not a burden on my grandmother. She enjoyed taking care of him, and he was always her company after her other children got married and moved away. Neither one of them saw his defect as a form of suffering because it brought them closer together. My uncle was there for us to be thankful to God for not letting us be born with such disabilities. We should appreciate our lives, for they are not so limited. 4

In conclusion, let us be reminded that we do not have the right to take life, but we do have the right to live. We are free to live life to its fullest. Why anticipate death when it ends everything? Why choose a path we know nothing of? There's always room for hope. In hoping, we'll see that forced death is never a solution. Until we can understand the world after, we should choose to live and not to die. 5

chapter 7

Moving Your Audience

Audience-Based Reasons, *Ethos*, and *Pathos*

In Chapters 5 and 6 we discussed *logos*—the logical structure of reasons and evidence in an argument. In this chapter and the next, we show you how to make your arguments as persuasive as possible. Particularly, we show you how to connect your argument to your audience's values and beliefs (audience-based reasons), how to appear credible and trustworthy (*ethos*), and how to engage your audience's sympathies (*pathos*). In Chapter 8 we show you how to vary the tone, content, and structure of your argument depending on whether your audience is initially sympathetic, neutral, or hostile to your views.

While all these persuasive strategies can be used cynically to manipulate an audience, we presuppose an arguer whose position is based on reasoned investigation of the evidence and on consistent and communicable values and beliefs. Our goal is to help you create arguments that are responsible, rationally sound, and persuasive.

STARTING FROM YOUR READERS' BELIEFS: THE POWER OF AUDIENCE-BASED REASONS

Whenever you ask if an argument is persuasive, the immediate rejoinder should be, "Persuasive to whom?" What seems a good reason to you may not be a good reason to others. The force of a logical argument, as Aristotle showed in his explanation of enthymemes, depends on the audience's acceptance of underlying assumptions, values, or beliefs (see pp. 74-75). Finding audience-based reasons means creating arguments that are effectively rooted in your audience's values.

Difference Between Writer- and Audience-Based Reasons

To illustrate the difference between writer- and audience-based reasons, consider the following hypothetical case. Suppose you believed that the government should build a dam on the nearby Rapid River—a project bitterly opposed by several environmental groups. Which of the following two arguments might you use to address environmentalists?

1. The government should build a dam on the Rapid River because the only alternative power sources are coal-fired or nuclear plants, both of which pose greater risk to the environment than a hydroelectric dam.

2. The government should build a hydroelectric dam on the Rapid River because this area needs cheap power to attract heavy industry.

Clearly, the warrant of Argument 1 ("Choose the source of power that poses least risk to the environment") is rooted in the values and beliefs of environmentalists, whereas the warrant of Argument 2 ("Growth of industry is good") is likely to make them wince. To environmentalists, new industry means more congestion, more smokestacks, and more pollution. However, Argument 2 may appeal to out-of-work laborers or to the business community, to whom new industry means more jobs and a booming economy.

From the perspective of *logos* alone, Arguments 1 and 2 are both sound. They are internally consistent and proceed from reasonable premises. But they will affect different audiences very differently. Neither argument proves that the government should build the dam; both are open to objection. Passionate environmentalists, for example, might counter Argument 1 by asking why the government needs to build any power plant at all. They could argue that energy conservation would obviate the need for a new power plant. Or they might argue that building a dam hurts the environment in ways unforeseen by dam supporters. Our point, then, isn't that Argument 1 will persuade environmentalists. Rather, our point is that Argument 1 will be more persuasive than Argument 2 because it is rooted in beliefs and values the intended audience shares.

❖ FOR CLASS DISCUSSION

Working in groups, decide which of the two reasons offered in each instance would be more persuasive to the specified audience. Be prepared to explain your reasoning to the class. Write out the implied warrant for each *because* clause and decide whether the specific audience would likely grant it.

1. Audience: a beleaguered parent
   a. I should be allowed to stay out until 2 A.M. because all my friends do.
   b. I should be allowed to stay out until 2 A.M. because only if I'm free to make my own decisions will I mature.
2. Audience: people who oppose the present grading system on the grounds that it is too competitive
   a. We should keep the present grading system because it prepares people for the dog-eat-dog pressures of the business world.
   b. We should keep the present grading system because it tells students that certain standards of excellence must be met if individuals are to reach their full potential.
3. Audience: young people aged fifteen to twenty-five
   a. You should become a vegetarian because an all-vegetable diet is better for your heart than a meaty diet.
   b. You should become a vegetarian because that will help eliminate the suffering of animals raised in factory farms.
4. Audience: conservative proponents of "family values"
   a. Same-sex marriages should be legalized because doing so will promote public acceptance of homosexuality.
   b. Same-sex marriages should be legalized because doing so will make it easier for gay people to establish and sustain long-term stable relationships.

Finding Audience-Based Reasons: Asking Questions about Your Audience

As the preceding exercise makes clear, reasons are most persuasive when linked to your audience's values. This principle seems simple enough, yet it is easy to forget. For example, employers frequently complain about job interviewees whose first concern is what the company will do for them, not what they might do for the company. Conversely, job search experts agree that most successful job candidates do extensive background research on a prospective company so that in an interview they can relate their own skills to the company's problems and needs. Successful arguments typically grow out of similar attention to audience needs.

To find out all you can about an audience, we recommend that you explore the following questions:

1. Who is your audience? Your audience might be a single, identifiable person. For example, you might write a letter to a professor arguing for a change in a course grade, or your audience might be a decision-making body such as an influential committee. At other times your audience might be the general readership of a newspaper, church bulletin, magazine, or journal, or you might produce a flier to be handed out on street corners.

2. How much does your audience know or care about your issue? Are they currently part of the conversation on this issue, or do they need considerable background information? If you are writing to specific decision makers (for example, the administration at your college about restructuring the intramural program), are they currently aware of the problem or issue you are addressing and do they care about it? If not, how can you get their attention? Your answers to these questions will especially affect your introduction and conclusion.

3. What is your audience's current attitude toward your issue? Are they supportive of your position on the issue? Neutral or undecided? Skeptical? Strongly opposed? What other points of view besides your own will your audience be weighing? In Chapter 8 we will explain how your answers to these questions can help you decide the structure, content, and tone of your argument.

4. What objections is your audience likely to make to your argument? What weaknesses will they find? What aspects of your position will be most threatening to them and why? How are your basic assumptions, values, or beliefs different from your audience's? Your answers here will help determine the content of your argument and will alert you to extra research you may need to do to bolster your response to audience objections.

5. Finally, what values, beliefs, or assumptions about the world do you and your audience share? Despite differences of view on this issue, where can you find common links with your audience? How might you use these links to build bridges to your audience?

Suppose, for example, that you support universal mandatory testing for the HIV virus. It's important from the start that you understand and acknowledge the interests of those opposed to your position. Who are they and what are their concerns? Gays and others in high-risk categories may fear discrimination from being publicly identified as HIV carriers. Moreover, gays may see mandatory AIDS testing as part of an ongoing attempt by homophobes to stigmatize the gay community. Liberals, meanwhile, will question the necessity of invading people's privacy and compromising their civil liberties in the name of public health.

What shared values might you use to build bridges to those opposed to mandatory testing? At a minimum, you share a desire to find a cure for AIDS and a fear of the horrors of an epidemic. Moreover, you also share a respect for the dignity and humanity of those afflicted with AIDS and do not see yourself as part of a backlash against gays.

Given all that, you begin to develop a strategy to reduce your audience's fears and to link your reasons to their values. Your thinking might go something like this:

PROBLEM: How can I create an argument rooted in shared values?

POSSIBLE SOLUTIONS:	I can try to reduce the audience's fear that mandatory AIDS testing implies a criticism of gays. I must assure that my plan ensures confidentiality. I must make clear that my first priority is stopping the spread of the disease and that this concern is shared by the gay community.
PROBLEM:	How can I reduce fear that mandatory HIV testing will violate civil liberties?
POSSIBLE SOLUTIONS:	I must show that the enemy here is the HIV virus, not victims of the disease. Also, I might cite precedents for how we fight other infectious diseases. For example, many states require marriage license applicants to take a test for sexually transmitted diseases, and many communities have imposed quarantines to halt the spread of epidemics. I could also argue that the right of everyone to be free from this disease outweighs the right to privacy, especially when confidentiality is assured.

The preceding example shows how a writer's focus on audience can shape the actual invention of the argument.

 FOR CLASS DISCUSSION

Working individually or in small groups, plan an audience-based argumentative strategy for one or more of the following cases. Follow the thinking process used by the writer of the mandatory HIV-testing argument: (1) State several problems that the writer must solve to reach the audience, and (2) develop possible solutions to those problems.

1. An argument for the right of software companies to continue making and selling violent video games: Aim the argument at parents who oppose their children's playing these games.
2. An argument limiting the number of terms that can be served by members of Congress: Aim the argument at supporters of an influential incumbent who would no longer be eligible to hold office.
3. An argument supporting a $1-per-gallon increase in gasoline taxes as an energy conservation measure: Aim your argument at business leaders who oppose the tax for fear it will raise the cost of consumer goods.
4. An argument supporting the legalization of cocaine: Aim your argument at readers of *Reader's Digest*, a conservative magazine that supports the current war on drugs.

ETHOS AND *PATHOS* AS PERSUASIVE APPEALS: AN OVERVIEW

The previous section focused on audience-based reasons as a means of moving an audience. In terms of the rhetorical triangle introduced in Chapter 4, searching for audience-based reasons can be seen primarily as a function of *logos*—finding the best structure of reasons and evidence to sway an audience— although, as we shall see, it also affects the other points of the triangle. In what follows, we turn to the power of *ethos* (the appeal to credibility) and *pathos* (the appeal to an audience's sympathies) as further means of making your arguments more effective.

It's tempting to think of these three kinds of appeals as "ingredients" in an essay, like spices you add to a casserole. Succumbing to this metaphor, you might say to yourself something like this: "Just enough *logos* to give the dish body; but for more piquancy it needs a pinch of *pathos*. And for the back of the palate, a tad more *ethos*."

But this metaphor is misleading because *logos, ethos,* and *pathos* are not substances; they are ways of seeing rather than objects of sight. A better metaphor might be that of different lamps and filters used on theater spotlights to vary lighting effects on a stage. Thus, if you switch on a *pathos* lamp (possibly through using more concrete language or vivid examples), the resulting image will engage the audience's sympathy and emotions more deeply. If you overlay an *ethos* filter (perhaps by adopting a different tone toward your audience), the projected image of the writer as a person will be subtly altered. If you switch on a *logos* lamp (by adding, say, more data for evidence), you will draw the reader's attention to the logical appeal of the argument. Depending on how you modulate the lamps and filters, you shape and color your readers' perception of the issue.

Our metaphor is imperfect, of course, but our point is that *logos, ethos,* and *pathos* work together to create an impact on the reader. Consider, for example, the different impacts of the following arguments, all having roughly the same logical appeal.

1. People should adopt a vegetarian diet because only through vegetarianism can we prevent the cruelty to animals that results from factory farming.

2. I hope you enjoyed your fried chicken this evening. You know, of course, how much that chicken suffered just so you could have a tender and juicy meal. Commercial growers cram the chickens so tightly together into cages that their beaks are cut off to keep them from pecking each other's eyes out. The only way to end the torture is to adopt a vegetarian diet.

3. People who eat meat are no better than sadists who torture other sentient creatures to enhance their own pleasure. Unless you enjoy sadistic tyranny over others, you have only one choice: Become a vegetarian.

4. People committed to justice might consider the extent to which our love of eating meat requires the agony of animals. A visit to a modern chicken

factory—where chickens live their entire lives in tiny darkened coops without room to spread their wings—might raise doubts about our right to inflict such suffering on sentient creatures. Indeed, such a visit might persuade us that vegetarianism is a juster alternative.

Each argument has roughly the same logical core:

CLAIM:	People should adopt a vegetarian diet.
STATED REASON:	because only vegetarianism will end the suffering of animals subjected to factory farming
GROUNDS:	the evidence of suffering in commercial chicken farms, where chickens peck each other's eyes out; evidence that only widespread adoption of vegetarianism will end factory farming
WARRANT:	If we have an alternative to making animals suffer, we should adopt it.

But the impact of each argument varies. The difference between Arguments 1 and 2, most of our students report, is the greater emotional power of 2. Whereas Argument 1 refers only to the abstraction "cruelty to animals," Argument 2 paints a vivid picture of chickens with their beaks cut off to prevent their pecking each other blind. Argument 2 makes a stronger appeal to *pathos* (not necessarily a stronger argument), stirring feelings by appealing simultaneously to the heart and to the head.

The difference between Arguments 1 and 3 concerns both *ethos* and *pathos*. Argument 3 appeals to the emotions through highly charged words like "torture," "sadist," and "tyranny." But Argument 3 also draws attention to its writer, and most of our students report not liking that writer very much. His stance is self-righteous and insulting. In contrast, Argument 4's author establishes a more positive *ethos*. He establishes rapport with his audience by assuming they are committed to justice and by qualifying his argument with conditional terms such as *might* and *perhaps*. He also invites sympathy for his problem—an appeal to *pathos*—by offering a specific description of chickens crammed into tiny coops.

Which of these arguments is best? They all have appropriate uses. Arguments 1 and 4 seem aimed at receptive audiences reasonably open to exploration of the issue, whereas Arguments 2 and 3 seem designed to shock complacent audiences or to rally a group of True Believers. Even Argument 3, which is too abusive to be effective in most instances, might work as a rallying speech at a convention of animal liberation activists.

Our point thus far is that *logos, ethos,* and *pathos* are different aspects of the same whole, different lenses for intensifying or softening the light beam you project onto the screen. Every choice you make as a writer affects in some way each of the three appeals. The rest of this chapter examines these choices in more detail.

HOW TO CREATE AN EFFECTIVE
ETHOS: THE APPEAL TO CREDIBILITY

The ancient Greek and Roman rhetoricians recognized that an argument would be more persuasive if the audience trusted the speaker. Aristotle argued that such trust resides within the speech itself, not in the prior reputation of the speaker. In the speaker's manner and delivery, in his tone, word choice, and arrangement of reasons, in the sympathy with which he treats alternative views, a speaker creates a trustworthy persona. Aristotle called the impact of the speaker's credibility the appeal from *ethos.* How does a writer create credibility? We will suggest three ways.

Be Knowledgeable about Your Issue

The first way to gain credibility is to *be* credible; that is, to argue from a strong base of knowledge, to have at hand the examples, personal experiences, statistics, and other empirical data needed to make a sound case. If you have done your homework, you will command the attention of most audiences.

Be Fair

Besides being knowledgeable about your issue, you need to demonstrate fairness and courtesy to alternative views. Because true argument can occur only where persons may reasonably disagree with one another, your *ethos* will be strengthened if you demonstrate that you understand and empathize with other points of view. There are times, of course, when you may appropriately scorn an opposing view. But these times are rare, and they mostly occur when you address audiences predisposed to your view. Demonstrating empathy to alternative views is generally the best strategy.

Build a Bridge to Your Audience

A third means of establishing credibility—building a bridge to your audience—has been treated at length in our earlier discussion of audience-based reasons. By grounding your argument in shared values and assumptions, you demonstrate your goodwill and enhance your image as a trustworthy person respectful of your audience's views. We mention audience-based reasons here to show how this aspect of *logos*—finding the reasons that are most rooted in the audience's values—also affects your *ethos* as a person respectful of your readers' views.

HOW TO CREATE *PATHOS:* THE
APPEAL TO BELIEFS AND EMOTIONS

At the height of the Vietnam protest movement, a group of demonstrators "napalmed" a puppy by dousing it with gasoline and setting it on fire, thereby outraging people all across the country. Many sent indignant letters to their local newspapers, provoking the following response from the demonstrators: "Why are you outraged by the napalming of a single puppy when you are not outraged by the daily napalming of human babies in Vietnam?"

From the demonstrators' view, napalming the puppy constituted an appeal from *pathos*. *Logos*-centered arguments, the protesters felt, numbed the mind to human suffering; in napalming the puppy, they intended to reawaken in their audience a capacity for gut-level revulsion that had been dulled by too many statistics, too many abstract moral appeals, and too much superficial TV coverage of the war.

Of course, the napalmed puppy was a real-life event, a street theater protest, not a written argument. But writers often use similar strategies. Anti-abortion proponents use it whenever they graphically describe the dismemberment of a fetus during abortion; euthanasia proponents use it when they describe the prolonged suffering of a terminally ill patient hooked hopelessly to machines. And a student uses it when he argues that a professor ought to raise his grade from a C to a B, lest he lose his scholarship and leave college, shattering the dreams of his dear old grandmother.

Are such appeals legitimate? Our answer is yes, if they intensify our response to an issue rather than divert our attention from it. Because understanding is a matter of feeling as well as perceiving, *pathos* can give access to nonlogical, but not necessarily nonrational, ways of knowing. Used effectively, pathetic appeals reveal the fullest human meaning of an issue, helping us walk in the writer's shoes. That is why arguments are often improved through the use of sensory details that allow us to see the reality of a problem or through stories that make specific cases and instances come alive.

Appeals to *pathos* become illegitimate, we believe, when they confuse an issue rather than clarify it. To the extent that students' grades should be based on performance or effort, the student's image of the dear old grandmother is an illegitimate appeal to *pathos,* for it diverts the reader from rational to irrational criteria. The weeping grandmother may provide a legitimate motive for the student to study harder, but not for the professor to change a grade.

Although it is difficult to classify all the ways that writers can create appeals from *pathos*, we will focus on four strategies: concrete language; specific examples and illustrations; narratives; and connotations of words, metaphors, and analogies.

Use Concrete Language

Concrete language—one of the chief ways that writers achieve voice—can increase the liveliness, interest level, and personality of a writer's prose. When used in argument, concrete language typically heightens *pathos*. For example, consider the differences between the first and second drafts of the following student argument:

First draft: People who prefer driving a car to taking a bus think that taking the bus will increase the stress of the daily commute. Just the opposite is true. Not being able to find a parking spot when in a hurry to work or school can cause a person stress. Taking the bus gives a person time to read or sleep, etc. It could be used as a mental break.

Second draft: Taking the bus can be more relaxing than driving a car. Having someone else behind the wheel gives people time to chat with friends or cram for an exam. They can balance their checkbooks, do homework, doze off, read the daily newspaper, or get lost in a novel rather than foaming at the mouth looking for a parking space.

In this revision, specific details enliven the prose by creating images that trigger positive feelings—who wouldn't want some free time to doze off or to get lost in a novel?

Use Specific Examples and Illustrations

Specific examples and illustrations serve two purposes in an argument: They provide evidence that supports your reasons; simultaneously, they give your argument presence and emotional resonance. Note the flatness of the following draft arguing for the value of multicultural studies in a university core curriculum:

Early draft: Another advantage of a multicultural education is that it will help us see our own culture in a broader perspective. If all we know is our own heritage, we might not be inclined to see anything bad about this heritage because we won't know anything else. But if we study other heritages, we can see the costs and benefits of our own heritage.

Now note the increase in "presence" when the writer adds a specific example.

Revised draft: Another advantage of multicultural education is that it raises questions about traditional Western values. For example, owning private property (such as buying your own home) is part of the American dream and is a basic right guaranteed in our Constitution. However, in studying the beliefs of American Indians, students are confronted with a very different view of private property. When the U.S. Government sought to buy land in the Pacific Northwest from Chief Sealth, he replied:

> The president in Washington sends words that he wishes to buy our land. But how can you buy or sell the sky? The land? The idea is strange to us. If we do not own the freshness of the air and the sparkle of the water, how can you buy them? . . . We are part of the earth and it is part of us. . . . This we know: the earth does not belong to man, man belongs to the earth.

Our class was shocked by the contrast between traditional Western views of property and Chief Sealth's views. One of our best class discussions was initiated by this quotation from Chief Sealth. Had we not been exposed to a view from another culture, we would have never been led to question the "rightness" of Western values.

The writer begins his revision by evoking a traditional Western view of private property, which he then questions by shifting to Chief Sealth's vision of land as open, endless, and unobtainable as the sky. Through the use of a specific example, the writer brings to life his previously abstract point about the benefit of multicultural education.

Use Narratives

A particularly powerful way to evoke *pathos* is to tell a story that embodies your thesis implicitly and appeals directly to the reader's feelings and imagination. Brief narratives—whether real or hypothetical—are particularly effective as opening attention grabbers for an argument. To illustrate how an introductory narrative (either a story or a brief scene) can create pathetic appeals, consider the following vignettes from two different arguments about the homeless. The first argument, in support of legislation to help the poor, aims to create sympathy for homeless people. It opens this way:

It hurts the most when you come home from the theater on a cold January night. As you pull your scarf tighter around your neck and push your gloved hands deeper into the pockets of your wool overcoat, you notice the man huddled over the sewer grate, his feet wrapped in newspapers. He blows on his hands, then tucks them under his armpits and lies down on the sidewalk with his shoulders over the grate, his bed for the night. There are hundreds like him downtown, and their numbers are growing. How can we help?

The second argument, supporting an antiloitering law to keep the homeless out of posh shopping areas, aims to create sympathy not for the homeless but for the shoppers. It opens like this:

Panhandlers used to sit on corners with tin cups that they rattled politely. Not any more. Today we are besieged by ratty woe mongers who scuttle up behind you, clutching bottles of Mad Dog 20/20 in a sack, breathe their foul fumes down your neck, tap your arm or grab your sleeve, and demand your money. If you ignore them, they try to embarrass or threaten you.

Each of these brief narratives makes a case for a particular point of view toward the homeless. They help us see a problem through the eyes of the person making the argument. Although each makes a powerful appeal to *pathos*, both can face resistance in some quarters. The first narrative may strike some as sentimental; the second may strike others as flippant and callous. The emotional charge set by an introductory narrative can sometimes work against you as well as for you. If you have doubts about an opening narrative, test it out on other readers before using it in your final draft.

❧ FOR CLASS DISCUSSION

Suppose that you want to write arguments on the following issues. Working individually or in groups, think of an introductory scene or brief story that would create a pathetic appeal favorable to your argument.

1. a. an argument supporting the use of animals for biomedical research
   b. an argument opposing the use of animals for biomedical research
   [Note that the purpose of the first narrative is to create sympathy for the use of animals in medical research; perhaps you could describe the happy home-coming of a child cured by a medical procedure developed through testing on animals. The second narrative, aimed at evoking sympathy for abolishing animal research, might describe a lab rabbit's suffering.]
2. a. an argument for a program to restore a national park to its natural condition
   b. an argument for creating more camping places and overnight sites for recreational vehicles in national parks
3. a. an argument favoring legalization of drugs
   b. an argument opposing legalization of drugs

❧

Choose Words, Metaphors, and Analogies with Appropriate Connotations

Another way of appealing to *pathos* is to select words, metaphors, or analogies with connotations that match your aim. Thus, a rapidly made decision by a city council might be called "haughty and autocratic" or "bold and decisive," depending on whether you oppose or support the council. Similarly, writers can use favorable or unfavorable metaphors and analogies to evoke different imaginative or emotional responses. Thus, a tax bill might be viewed as a "potentially fatal poison pill" or as "unpleasant but necessary economic medicine."

The writer's control over word selection raises the problem of slant or bias. Some contemporary philosophers argue that a bias-free, perfectly transparent language is impossible because all language is a lens. Thus, when we choose word A rather than word B, when we put this sentence in the passive voice rather than the active, when we select this detail and omit that detail, we create bias.

Let's illustrate. When you see an unshaven man sitting on a city sidewalk with his back up against a doorway, wearing old, slovenly clothes, and drinking from a bottle hidden in a sack, what is the objective, "true" word for this person?

a person on welfare?	a welfare leech?	a beggar?
a panhandler?	a bum?	a hobo?
a wino?	a drunk?	an alcoholic
a crazy guy?	a homeless person?	a transient?

None of these words can be called "true" or perfectly objective because each creates its own slant. Each word causes us to view the person through that word's lens. If we call the person a beggar, for example, we evoke connotations of helpless poverty and of the biblical call to give alms to the poor. *Beggar,* then, is slightly more favorable than *panhandler,* which conjures up the image of someone pestering you for money. Calling the person "homeless," on the other hand, shifts the focus away from the person's behavior and onto a faulty economic system that fails to provide sufficient housing. The word *wino,* meanwhile, identifies a different cause for the person's condition—alcoholism rather than economics.

Our point, then, is that a purely objective language may be impossible. But the absence of pure objectivity doesn't mean that all language is equally slanted or that truth can never be discerned. Readers can recognize degrees of bias in someone's language and distinguish between a reasonably trustworthy passage and a highly distortive one. By being on the lookout for slanted language—without claiming that any language can be totally objective—we can defend ourselves from distortive appeals to *pathos* while recognizing that responsible use of connotation can give powerful presence to an argument.

CONCLUSION

In this chapter, we have explored ways that writers can strengthen the persuasiveness of their arguments by using audience-based reasons and by creating appeals to *ethos* and *pathos.* Arguments are more persuasive if they are rooted in the underlying assumptions, beliefs, and values of the intended audience. Similarly, arguments are more persuasive if readers trust the credibility of the writer and if the argument appeals to readers' hearts and imaginations as well as their intellects.

chapter 8

Accommodating Your Audience

Treating Differing Views

In the previous chapter we discussed ways of moving an audience. In this chapter we discuss a writer's options for accommodating differing views on an issue—whether to omit them, refute them, concede to them, or incorporate them through compromise and conciliation. In particular, we show you how your choices about structure, content, and tone may differ depending on whether your audience is sympathetic, neutral, or strongly resistant to your views. The strategies explained in this chapter will increase your flexibility as an arguer and enhance your chance of persuading a wide variety of audiences.

ONE-SIDED VERSUS MULTISIDED ARGUMENTS

Arguments are sometimes said to be one-sided or multisided. A one-sided argument presents only the writer's position on the issue without summarizing and responding to opposing viewpoints. A multisided argument presents the writer's position but also summarizes and responds to possible objections that an audience might raise. Which kind of argument is more persuasive to an audience?

According to some researchers, if people already agree with a writer's thesis, they usually find one-sided arguments more persuasive. A multisided argument appears wishy-washy, making the writer seem less decisive. On the other hand, if people initially disagree with a writer's thesis, a multisided argument often seems more persuasive because it shows that the writer has listened to other views and thus seems more open-minded and fair. An especially interesting effect has been documented for neutral audiences. In the short run, one-sided arguments seem more persuasive to neutral audiences, but in the long run multisided arguments seem to have more staying power. Neutral audiences who've heard only one side of an issue tend to change their minds when they hear alternative arguments. By anticipating and in some cases refuting opposing views, the multisided argument diminishes the surprise and force of subsequent counterarguments and also exposes their weaknesses.

In the rest of this chapter we will show you how your choice of writing one-sided or multisided arguments is a function of how you perceive your audience's resistance to your views.

DETERMINING YOUR AUDIENCE'S RESISTANCE TO YOUR VIEWS

When you write an argument, you must always consider your audience's point of view. One way to imagine your relationship to your audience is to place them on a scale of resistance from strong support of your position to strong opposition (see Figure 8.1). At the accord end of this scale are likeminded people who basically agree with your position on the issue. At the resistance end are those who strongly disagree with you, perhaps unconditionally, because their values, beliefs, or assumptions sharply differ from your own. In between the accord and resistance ends of the scale lies a range of opinions. Close to your position will be those leaning in your direction but with less conviction than you. Close to the resistance position will be those basically opposed to your view but willing to listen to your argument and perhaps willing to acknowledge some of its strengths. In the middle are those undecided people who are still sorting out their feelings, seeking additional information, and weighing the strengths and weaknesses of alternative views.

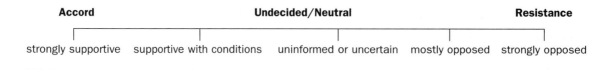

FIGURE 8.1   Scale of resistance

Seldom, however, will you encounter an issue in which the range of disagreement follows a simple line from accord to resistance. Often resistant views fall into different categories so that no single line of argument appeals to all those whose views are different from your own. You have to identify not only your audience's resistance to your ideas but also the causes of that resistance.

Consider, for example, an issue that divided the state of Washington when the Seattle Mariners baseball team demanded a new stadium. A ballot initiative asked

Accord	Undecided/Neutral	Resistance
strong support for initiative	uninformed or uncertain	opposition 1 [no interest in sports] opposition 2 [opposed to public funding of sports] opposition 3 [opposed to raising taxes] opposition 4 [opposed to retractable roof]

FIGURE 8.2   Scale of resistance, baseball stadium issue

citizens to raise taxes to build a new retractable roof stadium for the Mariners. Supporters of the initiative faced a complex array of resisting views (see Figure 8.2). Opponents of the initiative could be placed into four different categories. Some simply had no interest in sports, cared nothing about baseball, and saw no benefit in building a huge sports facility in downtown Seattle. Another group loved baseball, perhaps followed the Mariners passionately, but were philosophically opposed to subsidizing rich players and owners with taxpayer money. They argued that the whole sports industry needed to be restructured so that stadiums were paid for out of sports revenues. Still another group was opposed to tax hikes in general. They focused on the principle of reducing the size of government and of using tax revenues only for essential services. Finally, another powerful group supported baseball and supported the notion of public funding of a new stadium, but they opposed the kind of retractable roof stadium specified in the initiative. They wanted an old-fashioned, open-air stadium like Baltimore's Camden Yards or Cleveland's Jacobs Field.

Writers supporting the initiative found it impossible to address all these resisting audiences at once. If a supporter of the initiative wanted to aim an argument at sports haters, he or she could stress the spinoff benefits of a new ballpark (for example, the new ball park would attract tourist revenue, renovate the deteriorating Pioneer Square neighborhood, create jobs, make sports lovers more apt to vote for public subsidies of the arts, and so forth). But these arguments were irrelevant to those who wanted an open-air stadium, who opposed tax hikes categorically, or who objected to public subsidy of millionaires.

The Mariners example illustrates that it is not always easy to adapt your argument to your audience's position on the scale of resistance. Yet identifying your audience is important because writers need a stable vision of audience before they can determine an effective content, structure, and tone for an argument. Sometimes as a writer you will simply need to "invent" your audience—that is, to assume that a certain category of readers will be your primary audience. Making this decision gives you a stable base from which to create audience-based reasons and to craft an appropriate tone and structure. The next sections show how you can adjust your arguing strategy depending on whether you imagine your audience as supportive, neutral, or hostile.

APPEALING TO A SUPPORTIVE AUDIENCE: ONE-SIDED ARGUMENT

Although arguing to a supportive audience might seem like preaching to the choir, such arguments are common. Usually, the arguer's goal is to convert belief into action—to inspire a party member to contribute to a senator's campaign or a bored office worker to sign up for a change-your-life weekend seminar.

Typically, appeals to a supportive audience are structured as one-sided arguments that either ignore opposing views or reduce them to "enemy" stereotypes. Filled with motivational language, these arguments list the benefits that will ensue from your donations to the cause and the horrors just around the corner if the other side wins. One of the authors of this text recently received a fundraising letter from an environmental lobbying group declaring, "It's crunch time for the polluters and their pals on Capitol Hill." The "corporate polluters" and "anti-environment politicians," the letter continues, have "stepped up efforts to roll back our environmental protections—relying on large campaign contributions, slick PR firms and well-heeled lobbyists to get the job done before November's election." This letter makes the reader feel part of an in-group of good guys fighting the big business "polluters." Nothing in the letter examines environmental issues from business's perspective or attempts to examine alternative views fairly. Since the intended audience already believes in the cause, nothing in the letter invites readers to consider the issues more complexly. Rather, the goal is to solidify support, increase the fervor of belief, and inspire action. Most appeal arguments make it easy to act, ending with an 800 phone number to call, a tear-out postcard to send in, or a congressperson's address to write to.

APPEALING TO A NEUTRAL OR UNDECIDED AUDIENCE: CLASSICAL ARGUMENT

The in-group appeals that motivate an already supportive audience can repel a neutral or undecided audience. Because undecided audiences are like jurors weighing all sides of an issue, they distrust one-sided arguments that caricature other views. Generally the best strategy for appealing to undecided audiences is the classical argument described in Chapter 3 (pp. 50–51).

What characterizes the classical argument is the writer's willingness to summarize opposing views fairly and to respond to them openly—either by trying to refute them or by conceding to their strengths and then shifting to a different field of values. Let's look at these strategies in more depth.

Summarizing Opposing Views

The first step toward responding to opposing views in a classical argument is to summarize them fairly. Follow the *principle of charity*, which obliges you to avoid loaded, biased, or "strawman" summaries that oversimplify or distort opposing arguments, making them easy to knock over.

Consider the differences between an unfair and a fair summary of Charles Murray's "The Coming White Underclass" (pp. 20–25), which we examined in Chapter 2.

UNFAIR SUMMARY

Right-wing critic Charles Murray, writing in the October 29, 1993 *Wall Street Journal,* parrots the wealthy class party line that all the troubles of modern America can be blamed on unmarried welfare mothers. Murray wants to end all welfare payments to single moms, forcing them deeper into poverty, and placing their kids in state-run orphanages. Caring nothing for the suffering of those affected, Murray treats poor people like trash and believes everything would be fine if we returned to *Leave It to Beaver* values.

This summary both distorts and oversimplifies Murray's position. By using loaded phrases (such as "right-wing," "parrots the wealthy class party line," and so forth), the writer reveals a bias against Murray that neutral readers will distrust. By claiming that Murray blames *all* America's troubles on welfare moms or that he wants to put *all* poor kids in orphanages, the writer oversimplifies Murray's argument. Most damagingly, by omitting Murray's use of rising illegitimacy rates as an index of social breakdown, the writer prevents readers from understanding Murray's reasoning. The writer thus sets up a strawman that is easier to knock down than is Murray's original argument.

For an example of fair summaries of Murray, see the versions we have written in Chapter 2 (pp. 26–28). In those examples we follow the principle of charity by summarizing Murray's views as justly and accurately as possible.

Refuting Opposing Views

Once you have summarized an opposing view, you can either refute it or concede to its strengths. In refuting an opposing view, you attempt to convince readers that its argument is logically flawed, inadequately supported, or based on erroneous assumptions or wrong values. In Toulmin's terms, you can refute (1) the writer's stated reason and grounds, or (2) the writer's warrant and backing, or (3) both.

For example, suppose you wanted to refute the following argument: "We shouldn't elect Joe as chairperson because he is too bossy." Displayed in Toulmin terms, the argument looks like this:

CLAIM:	We shouldn't elect Joe as chairperson.
STATED REASON:	because he is too bossy
GROUNDS:	evidence that Joe is bossy
WARRANT:	Bossy people make bad chairpersons.

One way to refute this argument is to rebut the stated reason and grounds.

> I disagree with you that Joe is bossy. In fact, Joe is very non-bossy. He's a good listener who's willing to compromise, and he involves others in decisions. The example you cite for his being bossy wasn't typical. It was a one-time circumstance that doesn't represent his normal behavior. [The writer could then provide examples of Joe's cooperative nature.]

Or you could concede that Joe is bossy but rebut the argument's warrant that bossiness is a bad trait.

> I agree that Joe is bossy, but in this circumstance bossiness is just the trait we need. This committee hasn't gotten anything done for six months and time is running out. We need a decisive person who can come in, get the committee organized, assign tasks, and get the job done.

Let's now illustrate these strategies in a more complex situation. For an example, we'll look at the issue of whether recycling is an effective strategy for saving the environment. A controversial subissue of recycling is whether the United States is running out of space for sanitary landfills. Here is how one environmental writer argues that there are no places left to dump our garbage.

> Because the United States is running out of landfill space, Americans will simply not be able to put the 180 million tons of solid waste they generate each year into landfills, where 70 percent of it now goes. Since 1979, the United States has exhausted more than two-thirds of its landfills; projections indicate that another one-fifth will close over the next five years. Between 1983 and 1987, for example, New York closed 200 of its 500 landfills; this year Connecticut will exhaust its landfill capacity. If the problem seemed abstract to Americans, it became odiously real in the summer of 1989 as most of the nation watched the notorious garbage barge from Islip, New York wander 6,000 miles, searching for a place to dump its rancid 3,100-ton load.*

This passage tries to persuade us that the U.S. is running out of landfill space. Now watch how writer John Tierney attempts to refute this argument in an influential 1996 *New York Times Magazine* article entitled "Recycling Is Garbage."

> [Proponents of recycling believe that] our garbage will bury us. The Mobro's† saga was presented as a grim harbinger of future landfill scarcity, but it actually repre-

---

*Lodge, George C. and Jeffrey F. Rayport. "Knee-deep and Rising: America's Recycling Crisis," *Harvard Business Review* (Sept./Oct. 1991) 132.

†The *Mobro* is the name of the notorious garbage barge from Islip, New York, referred to at the end of the previous quotation.

sented a short-lived scare caused by new environmental regulations. As old municipal dumps were forced to close in the 1980's, towns had to send their garbage elsewhere and pay higher prices for scarce landfill space. But the higher prices predictably encouraged companies to open huge new landfills, in some regions creating a glut that set off price-cutting wars. Over the past few years, landfills in the South and Middle West have been vying for garbage from the New York area, and it has become cheaper to ship garbage there than to bury it locally.

America has a good deal more landfill space available than it did 10 years ago. . . . A. Clark Wiseman, an economist at Gonzaga University in Spokane, Wash., has calculated that if Americans keep generating garbage at current rates for 1,000 years, and if all their garbage is put in a landfill 100 yards deep, by the year 3000 this national garbage heap will fill a square piece of land 35 miles on each side.

This doesn't seem a huge imposition in a country the size of America. The garbage would occupy only 5 percent of the area needed for the national array of solar panels proposed by environmentalists. The millennial landfill would fit on one-tenth of 1 percent of the range land now available for grazing in the continental United States.*

In this case, Tierney uses counterevidence to rebut the reason and grounds of the original enthymeme: "Recycling is needed because the United States is running out of landfill space." Tierney attacks this argument by disagreeing with the stated reason that the United States is running out of landfill space.

But writers are also apt to question the underlying assumptions (warrants) of an opposing view. For an example, consider another recycling controversy: From an economic perspective, is recycling cost effective? In criticizing recycling, Tierney argues that recycling wastes money; he provides evidence that "every time a sanitation department crew picks up a load of bottles and cans from the curb, New York City loses money." The warrant of this argument is that "we should dispose of garbage in the most cost-effective way."

In rebutting Tierney's argument, proponents of recycling typically accepted Tierney's figures on recycling costs in New York City (that is, they agreed that in New York City recycling was more expensive than burying garbage). But in various ways they attacked his warrant. Typically, proponents of recycling said that even if the costs of recycling were higher than burying wastes in a landfill, recycling still benefited the environment by reducing the amount of virgin materials taken from nature. This argument says, in effect, that saving virgin resources takes precedence over economic costs.

These examples show how a refutation can focus on either the stated reasons and grounds of an argument or upon the warrants and backing.

---

*John Tierney, "Recycling Is Garbage," *New York Times Magazine* 30 June 1996: 28.

❦ **FOR CLASS DISCUSSION** ▬▬▬▬▬▬▬▬▬▬▬▬▬▬▬

Imagine how each of the following arguments might be fleshed out with grounds and backing. Then attempt to refute each argument by suggesting ways to rebut the reason and grounds, or the warrant and backing, or both.

1. Writing courses should be pass/fail because the pass/fail system would encourage more creativity.

2. The government should make cigarettes illegal because cigarettes cause cancer and heart disease.

3. Majoring in engineering is better than majoring in music because engineers make more money than musicians.

4. People should not eat meat because doing so causes needless pain and suffering to animals.

5. The endangered species law is too stringent because it seriously hampers the economy.

▬▬▬▬▬▬▬▬▬▬▬▬▬▬▬▬▬▬▬▬▬▬▬▬▬▬ ❦

Strategies for Rebutting Evidence

Whether you are rebutting an argument's reasons and grounds or its warrant and backing, you will frequently need to question a writer's use of evidence. Here are some strategies that you can use:

Deny the Facticity of the Data

What one writer considers a fact another may consider a case of wrong information. If you have reason to doubt a writer's facts, then call them into question.

Cite Counterexamples or Countertestimony

One of the most effective ways to counter an argument based on examples is to cite a counterexample. The effect of counterexamples is to deny the conclusiveness of the original data. Similarly, citing an authority whose testimony counters other expert testimony is a good way to begin refuting an argument based on testimony.

Cast Doubt on the Representativeness or Sufficiency of Examples

Examples are powerful only if the audience feels them to be representative and sufficient. Many environmentalists complained that John Tierney's attack on recycling was based too largely on data from New York City and that it didn't accurately take into account the more positive experiences of other cities and states.

When data from outside New York City were examined, the cost-effectiveness and positive environmental impact of recycling seemed more apparent.

Cast Doubt on the Relevance or Recency of the Examples, Statistics, or Testimony

The best evidence is up to date. In a rapidly changing universe, data that are even a few years out of date are often ineffective. For example, as the demand for recycled goods increases, the cost of recycling will be reduced. Out-of-date statistics will skew any argument about the cost of recycling. Another problem with data is their occasional lack of relevance. For example, in arguing that an adequate ozone layer is necessary for preventing skin cancers, it is not relevant to cite statistics on the alarming rise of lung cancers.

Call into Question the Credibility of an Authority

If an opposing argument is based on testimony, you can undermine its persuasiveness if you show that a person being cited lacks up-to-date or relevant expertise in the field. (This procedure is different from the *ad hominem* fallacy discussed in Appendix 1 because it doesn't attack the personal character of the authority but only the authority's expertise on a specific matter.)

Question the Accuracy or Context of Quotations

Evidence based on testimony is frequently distorted by being either misquoted or taken out of context. Often scientists will qualify their findings heavily, but these qualifications will be omitted by the popular media. You can thus attack the use of a quotation by putting it in its original context or by restoring the qualifications accompanying the quotation in its original source.

Question the Way Statistical Data Were Produced or Interpreted

Chapter 6 provides fuller treatment of how to question statistics. In general, you can rebut statistical evidence by calling into account how the data were gathered, treated mathematically, or interpreted. It can make a big difference, for example, whether you cite raw numbers or percentages or whether you choose large or small increments for the axes of graphs.

Conceding to Opposing Views

In writing a classical argument, a writer must sometimes concede to an opposing argument rather than refute it. Sometimes you encounter portions of an argument that you simply can't refute. For example, suppose you support the legalization of hard drugs such as cocaine and heroin. Adversaries argue that legalizing hard drugs will increase the number of drug users and addicts. You might dispute the size of their numbers, but you reluctantly agree that they are right. Your strategy in this case is not to refute the opposing argument, but to concede to it by admitting that legalization of hard drugs will promote heroin and cocaine addiction. Having made that concession, your task is then to show that the benefits of drug legalization still outweigh the costs you've just conceded.

As this example shows, the strategy of a concession argument is to switch from the field of values employed by the writer you disagree with to a different field of values more favorable to your position. You don't try to refute the writer's stated reason and grounds (by arguing that legalization will *not* lead to increased drug usage and addiction), nor his warrant (by arguing that increased drug use and addiction is not a problem). Rather, you shift the argument to a new field of values by introducing a new warrant, one that you think your audience can share (that the benefits of legalization—eliminating the black market and ending the crime and violence associated with procurement of drugs—outweigh the costs of increased addiction). To the extent that opponents of legalization share your desire to stop drug-related crime, shifting to this new field of values is a good strategy. Although it may seem that you weaken your own position by conceding to an opposing argument, you may actually strengthen it by increasing your credibility and gaining your audience's goodwill. Moreover, conceding to one part of an opposing argument doesn't mean that you won't refute other parts of that argument.

APPEALING TO A RESISTANT AUDIENCE: DELAYED THESIS OR ROGERIAN ARGUMENT

Whereas classical argument is effective for neutral or undecided audiences, it is often less effective for audiences strongly opposed to the writer's position. Because resisting audiences often hold values, assumptions, or beliefs widely different from the writer's, they are unswayed by classical argument, which attacks their world view too directly. On many values-laden issues such as abortion, gun control, gay rights, and welfare reform the distance between a writer and a resisting audience can be so great that dialog hardly seems possible.

Because of these wide differences in basic beliefs and values, a writer's goal is seldom to convert resistant readers to the writer's position. The best that the writer can hope for is to reduce somewhat the level of resistance, perhaps by opening up a channel of conversation, increasing the reader's willingness to listen, and preparing the way for future dialog. If you can get a resistant audience to say, "Well, I still don't agree with you, but I now understand you better and respect your views more," you will have been highly successful.

Delayed Thesis Argument

In many cases you can reach a resistant audience by using a *delayed thesis* structure in which you wait until the end of your argument to reveal your thesis. Classical argument asks you to state your thesis in the introduction, support it with reasons and evidence, and then summarize and refute opposing views. Rhetorically, however, it is not always advantageous to tell your readers where you stand at the start of your argument or to separate yourself so definitively from alternative views. For resistant audiences, it may be better to keep the issue open, delaying the revelation of your own position until the end of the essay.

To illustrate the different effects of classical versus delayed thesis arguments, we invite you to read a delayed thesis argument by nationally syndicated columnist Ellen Goodman. The article appeared shortly after the nation was shocked by a brutal gang rape in New Bedford, Massachusetts, in which a woman was raped on a pool table by patrons of a local bar.*

Minneapolis Pornography Ordinance

Ellen Goodman

Just a couple of months before the pool-table gang rape in New Bedford, Mass., *Hustler* magazine printed a photo feature that reads like a blueprint for the actual crime. There were just two differences between *Hustler* and real life. In *Hustler,* the woman enjoyed it. In real life, the woman charged rape.   1

There is no evidence that the four men charged with this crime had actually read the magazine. Nor is there evidence that the spectators who yelled encouragement for two hours had held previous ringside seats at pornographic events. But there is a growing sense that the violent pornography being peddled in this country helps to create an atmosphere in which such events occur.   2

As recently as last month, a study done by two University of Wisconsin researchers suggested that even "normal" men, prescreened college students, were changed by their exposure to violent pornography. After just ten hours of viewing, reported researcher Edward Donnerstein, "the men were less likely to convict in a rape trial, less likely to see injury to a victim, more likely to see the victim as responsible." Pornography may not cause rape directly, he said, "but it maintains a lot of very callous attitudes. It justifies aggression. It even says you are doing a favor to the victim."   3

If we can prove that pornography is harmful, then shouldn't the victims have legal rights? This, in any case, is the theory behind a city ordinance that recently passed the Minneapolis City Council. Vetoed by the mayor last week, it is likely to be back before the Council for an overriding vote, likely to appear in other cities, other towns. What is unique about the Minneapolis approach is that for the first time it attacks pornography, not because of nudity or sexual explicitness, but because it degrades and harms women. It opposes pornography on the basis of sex discrimination.   4

University of Minnesota Law Professor Catherine MacKinnon, who co-authored the ordinance with feminist writer Andrea Dworkin, says that they chose this tactic because they   5

---

*The rape occurred in 1985 and was later made into an Academy Award–winning movie, *The Accused,* starring Jody Foster.

believe that pornography is central to "creating and maintaining the inequality of the sexes. . . . Just being a woman means you are injured by pornography."

6   They defined pornography carefully as, "the sexually explicit subordination of women, graphically depicted, whether in pictures or in words." To fit their legal definition it must also include one of nine conditions that show this subordination, like presenting women who "experience sexual pleasure in being raped or . . . mutilated. . . ." Under this law, it would be possible for a pool-table rape victim to sue *Hustler.* It would be possible for a woman to sue if she were forced to act in a pornographic movie. Indeed, since the law describes pornography as oppressive to all women, it would be possible for any woman to sue those who traffic in the stuff for violating her civil rights.

7   In many ways, the Minneapolis ordinance is an appealing attack on an appalling problem. The authors have tried to resolve a long and bubbling conflict among those who have both a deep aversion to pornography and a deep loyalty to the value of free speech. "To date," says Professor MacKinnon, "people have identified the pornographer's freedom with everybody's freedom. But we're saying that the freedom of the pornographer is the subordination of women. It means one has to take a side."

8   But the sides are not quite as clear as Professor MacKinnon describes them. Nor is the ordinance.

9   Even if we accept the argument that pornography is harmful to women—and I do—then we must also recognize that anti-Semitic literature is harmful to Jews and racist literature is harmful to blacks. For that matter, Marxist literature may be harmful to government policy. It isn't just women versus pornographers. If women win the right to sue publishers and producers, then so could Jews, blacks, and a long list of people who may be able to prove they have been harmed by books, movies, speeches or even records. The Manson murders, you may recall, were reportedly inspired by the Beatles.

10   We might prefer a library or book store or lecture hall without Mein Kampf or the Grand Whoever of the Ku Klux Klan. But a growing list of harmful expressions would inevitably strangle freedom of speech.

11   This ordinance was carefully written to avoid problems of banning and prior restraint, but the right of any woman to claim damages from pornography is just too broad. It seems destined to lead to censorship.

12   What the Minneapolis City Council has before it is a very attractive theory. What MacKinnon and Dworkin have written is a very persuasive and useful definition of pornography. But they haven't yet resolved the conflict between the harm of pornography and the value of free speech. In its present form, this is still a shaky piece of law.

Consider now how this argument's rhetorical effect would be different if Ellen Goodman had revealed her thesis in the introduction using the classical argument form. Here is how this introduction might have looked:

GOODMAN'S INTRODUCTION REWRITTEN IN CLASSICAL FORM

Just a couple of months before the pool-table gang rape in New Bedford, Mass., *Hustler* magazine printed a photo feature that reads like a blueprint for the actual crime. There were just two differences between *Hustler* and real life. In *Hustler,* the woman enjoyed it. In real life, the woman charged rape. Of course, there is no evidence that the four men charged with this crime had actually read the magazine. Nor is there evidence that the spectators who yelled encouragement for two hours had held previous ringside seats at pornographic events.

But there is a growing sense that the violent pornography being peddled in this country helps to create an atmosphere in which such events occur. One city is taking a unique approach to attack this problem. An ordinance recently passed by the Minneapolis City Council outlaws pornography not because it contains nudity or sexually explicit acts, but because it degrades and harms women. Unfortunately, despite the proponents' good intentions, the Minneapolis ordinance is a bad law because it has potentially dangerous consequences.

Even though Goodman's position can be grasped more quickly in this classical form, our students generally find the original delayed thesis version more effective. Why is this?

Most people point to the greater sense of complexity and surprise in the delayed-thesis version, a sense that comes largely from the delayed discovery of the writer's position. Whereas the classical version immediately labels the ordinance a "bad law," the original version withholds judgment, inviting the reader to examine the law more sympathetically and to identify with the position of those who drafted it. Rather than distancing herself from those who see pornography as a violation of women's rights, Goodman shares with her readers her own struggles to think through these issues, thereby persuading us of her genuine sympathy for the ordinance and for its feminist proponents. In the end, her delayed thesis renders her final rejection of the ordinance not only more surprising but more convincing.

Clearly, then, a writer's decision about when to reveal her thesis is critical. Revealing the thesis early makes the writer seem more hardnosed, more sure of her position, more confident about how to divide the ground into friendly and hostile camps, more in control. Delaying the thesis, in contrast, complicates the issues, increases reader sympathy for more than one view, and heightens interest in the tension among alternative views and in the writer's struggle for clarity.

Rogerian Argument

An even more powerful strategy for addressing resistant audiences is a conciliatory strategy often called *Rogerian argument*, named after psychologist Carl Rogers, who used this strategy to help people resolve differences.* Rogerian argument emphasizes "empathic listening," which Rogers defined as the ability to see an issue sympathetically from another person's perspective. He trained people

---

*See Carl Rogers' essay "Communication: Its Blocking and Its Facilitation" in his book *On Becoming a Person* (Boston: Houghton Mifflin, 1961) 329–37. For a fuller discussion of Rogerian argument, see Richard Young, Alton Becker, and Kenneth Pike, *Rhetoric: Discovery and Change* (New York: Harcourt Brace, 1972).

to withhold judgment of another person's ideas until after they listened attentively to the other person, understood that person's reasoning, appreciated that person's values, respected that person's humanity—in short, walked in that person's shoes. Before disagreeing with another person, Rogers would tell his clients, you must be able to summarize that person's argument so accurately that he or she will say, "Yes, you understand my position."

What Carl Rogers understood is that traditional methods of argumentation are threatening. When you try to persuade people to change their minds on an issue, Rogers claimed, you are actually demanding a change in their worldview—to get other people, in a sense, to quit being their kind of person and start being your kind of person. Research psychologists have shown that persons are often not swayed by a logical argument if it somehow threatens their own view of the world. Carl Rogers was therefore interested in finding ways to make arguments less threatening. In Rogerian argument the writer typically waits until the end of the essay to present his position, and that position is often a compromise between the writer's original views and those of the resisting audience. Because Rogerian argument stresses the psychological as well as logical dimensions of argument, and because it emphasizes reducing threat and building bridges rather than winning an argument, it is particularly effective when dealing with emotionally laden issues.

Under Rogerian strategy, the writer reduces the sense of threat in her argument by showing that *both writer and resistant audience share many basic values.* Instead of attacking the audience as wrongheaded, the Rogerian writer respects her audience's intelligence and humanity and demonstrates an understanding of the audience's position before presenting her own position. Finally, the Rogerian writer never asks the audience to capitulate entirely to the writer's side—just to shift somewhat toward the writer's views. By acknowledging that he or she has already shifted toward the audience's views, the writer makes it easier for the audience to accept compromise. All of this negotiation ideally leads to a compromise between—or better, a synthesis of—the opposing positions.

The key to successful Rogerian argument, besides the art of listening, is the ability to point out areas of agreement between the writer's and reader's positions. For example, if you support a woman's right to choose abortion and you are arguing with someone completely opposed to abortion, you're unlikely to convert your reader, but you might reduce the level of resistance. You begin this process by summarizing your reader's position sympathetically, stressing your shared values. You might say, for example, that you also value babies; that you also are appalled by people who treat abortion as a form of birth control; that you also worry that the easy acceptance of abortion diminishes the value society places on human life; and that you also agree that accepting abortion lightly can lead to lack of sexual responsibility. Building bridges like these between you and your readers makes it more likely that they will listen to you when you present your own position.

In its emphasis on establishing common ground, Rogerian argument has much in common with recent feminist theories of argument. Many feminists criticize classical argument as rooted in a male value system and tainted by metaphors of war and combat. Thus, classical arguments, with their emphasis on assertion and refutation, are typically praised for being "powerful," "forceful," or "disarming." The writer "defends" his position and "attacks" his "opponent's" position using facts and data as "ammunition" and reasons as "big guns" to "blow away" his opponent's claim. According to some feminists, viewing argument as war can lead to inauthenticity, posturing, and game playing. The traditional pro-con debate—defined in one of our desk dictionaries as "a formal contest of argumentation in which two opposing teams defend and attack a given proposition"—treats argument as verbal jousting, more concerned to determine a winner than to clarify an issue.

One of our woman students, who excelled as a debater in high school and received straight As in argument classes, recently explained in an essay her growing alienation from male rhetoric. "Although women students are just as likely to excel in 'male' writing . . . we are less likely to feel as if we were saying something authentic and true." Later the student elaborated on her distrust of "persuasion":

> What many writing teachers have told me is that "the most important writing/speaking you will ever do will be to persuade someone." My experience as a person who has great difficulty naming and expressing emotions is that the most important communication in my life is far more likely to be simply telling someone how I feel. To say "I love you," or "I'm angry with you," will be far more valuable in most relationship contexts than to say "These are the three reasons why you shouldn't have done what you did. . . ."*

Writers who share this woman's distrust of classical argumentation often find Rogerian argument appealing because it stresses self-examination, clarification, and accommodation rather than refutation. Rogerian argument is more in tune with win-win negotiation than with win-lose debate.

To illustrate a conciliatory or Rogerian approach to an issue, here is how one student wrote a letter to her boss recommending a change in the kind of merchandise stocked in a small town music store.

Letter to Beth Downey

Ms. Beth Downey, Owner/Manager
Downey's Music
Grayfish

Dear Ms. Downey:

I would just like to comment on the success of "Downey's Music" in Grayfish and say that,   1
as owner and manager, you have done a wonderful job. I'm sure that you have the most

---

*Our thanks to Catherine Brown in an unpublished paper written at Seattle University.

extensive classical music, music teaching books, piano and acoustic guitar inventory of any store in a 100-square-mile area. After working for you for three years, I have encountered music teachers and classical music lovers coming as far as 70 miles to buy their music from Downey's. All have had nothing but compliments for you and for the store. However, I would once again like to bring up the subject of introducing an inventory of electronic music equipment to the store. Since Grayfish is mainly a tourist town, many times a week I have people from touring bands, visiting Canadians, and also locals coming into the store looking for such things as electronic keyboards, electric guitars, and amplifiers. I know that you have qualms about this idea, but I believe that I have a suggestion that we could both agree on.

2   First, let me restate your reasons for objecting to such a move. You have already stated that if a change will benefit the store, the initial investment is well worth the expense in the long run (e.g., when pianos were added to the inventory). Therefore, I assume that cost is not a factor at this time. However, you feel that the "kind of people" that electronics may draw could possibly offend our present clientele. You feel, as well as others, that the people who are drawn by electronics are often long haired, dirty, and give a bad impression. This would in effect change the store's image. Also, you are afraid that the noise caused by these instruments could turn classical music lovers away from the store. The sounds of electronic instruments are not always pleasing, and since most of our clientele are older, more refined persons, you feel that these sounds will force some to go to other stores. Mainly, however, you are worried about the result that the change in the store's image could have upon a community the size of Grayfish. Many people in this area, I realize, feel that electronic music means heavy rock music, while this in turn means alcohol and drugs.

3   Basically, I agree with you that Grayfish needs a "classical" music store and that the culture that your store brings to Grayfish greatly enhances the area. I also love classical music and want to see it growing and alive. I also have some of the same fears about adding electronic music to the inventory. I enjoy the atmosphere of Downey's, and I have always enjoyed working there, so I don't want to see anything adverse happen to it, either. On the other hand, I feel that if a large electronic music section were added to the store with sound-proof rooms, a "sit and try it" atmosphere, and a catalog inventory large enough to special order anything that a customer might want that is not in the store, it would help immensely in the success of the store. With the way that Downey's is built, on two levels, it would be very easy to accommodate the needs of both departments. Even now we are only using about half the floor space available, while the rest is empty storage area. By building sound-proof rooms on the lower level, we could easily double the in-use floor area, increase our tourist clientele, have the music business in *all* areas cornered for approximately 60 square miles, and also add practice rooms for our present customers to use when they are choosing music.

4   I know that you are wrestling with this idea of such a drastic changeover, so I would like to propose a nonthreatening, easy-to-reverse first step. My solution is to start slowly, on a trial basis, and see how it works. I suggest that we start with a few small electronic keyboards, a few electric guitars, and one or two amps. In this way, we could begin to collect the information and literature on other electronic equipment that may be added later on, see how the community responds to such a move, find out how our present clientele

reacts, get a feel for the demand in this field, and yet still be a small hometown music store without a great investment in this electronic area. I still feel that a large addition would be more successful, but I also believe that this little test may help prove to you, or disprove to me, that electronic music instruments in this area are in high demand. I honestly feel that electronics could produce fantastic profits for the people who get in the business first. I would love it if these "people" could be the owners and workers at Downey's Music.

Sincerely,

Mary Doe

 FOR CLASS DISCUSSION

1. In this letter, what shared values between writer and audience does the writer stress?

2. Imagine the letter rewritten as a classical argument. How would it be different?

CONCLUSION

This chapter has shown you the difference between one- and multisided arguments and explained why multisided arguments are apt to be more persuasive to neutral or resisting audiences. A multisided argument generally includes a fair summary of differing views, followed by either refutation, concession, or Rogerian synthesis. The strategies you use for treating resistant views depend on the audience you are trying to reach and your purpose. We explained how audiences can be placed on a scale of resistance ranging from strongly supportive to strongly resistant. In addressing supportive audiences, writers typically compose one-sided arguments with strong motivational appeals to action. Neutral or undecided audiences generally respond most favorably to classical arguments that set out strong reasons in support of the writer's position and yet openly address alternative views, which are first summarized and then either rebutted or conceded to. When the audience is strongly resistant, a delayed thesis or Rogerian strategy is most effective at reducing resistance and helping move the audience slightly toward the writer's views.

 WRITING ASSIGNMENTS FOR CHAPTERS 7 AND 8

The writing options for Chapters 7 and 8 require careful attention to your audience's views.

OPTION 1: *Write a classical argument*   This assignment asks you to write an argument, aimed at neutral or undecided audiences, in the classical format. It asks you to adopt an *ethos* of confident self-assurance about the rightness of your own position. Choose an issue where there are clear opposing views that you disagree with. The purpose of this assignment is to support your own position with reasons and evidence while also summarizing and refuting opposing views. Before drafting this essay, reread pages 116–122 on "Appealing to Neutral or Undecided Audiences." Also read the explanation of classical argument on pages 50–52.

A classical argument has a self-announcing structure. The introduction presents your issue, provides needed background, and announces your thesis. It may also include a brief forecasting passage to help the reader anticipate the shape of your essay. (See pp. 69–71.) The body of your essay summarizes and refutes opposing views as well as presents your own reasons and evidence in support of your position. It is your choice whether you summarize and refute opposing views before or after you have made your own case. Generally, try to end your essay with your strongest arguments.

OPTION 2: *Rogerian strategy*   This assignment asks you to practice a Rogerian strategy aimed at reducing the psychological distance between you and a strongly resisting audience. Choose a topic in which you address an audience that has strong psychological or emotional resistance to your position.

Write a multiparagraph essay that refrains from presenting your position until the conclusion. The opening section introduces the issue and provides background. The second section sympathetically summarizes the resistant view. The third section creates a bridge between writer and resistant audience by pointing out major areas of agreement. After examining this common ground, the third section then points out areas of disagreement but stresses that these are minor compared with the major areas of agreement already discussed. Finally, the last section presents the writer's position, which, if possible, should be a compromise or synthesis indicating that the writer has shifted his original position (or at least his sympathies) toward the resistant view and is now asking the opposition to make a similar shift toward the writer's new position. Your goal here, through tone, arrangement, and examination of common values, is to reduce the threat of your argument in the eyes of your audience. Before drafting this essay, reread pages 125–127, where we discuss Rogerian argument.

The student letter to Beth Downey (pp. 127–129) illustrates this strategy.

part three

Arguments in Depth

Five Categories of Claims

chapter 9

Using the Categories of Claims to Generate Ideas

In Parts One and Two, we discussed the arguing process, the basic structure of arguments, and the relation of arguments to audience. In Part Three, our goal is to help you understand the different patterns of thought called for by different kinds of argument claims. Once you learn the patterns of organization and thought characteristic of each claim category, you can use those patterns to develop your argument.

In particular, Part Three introduces you to five different categories of argument: definitional arguments, cause/consequence arguments, analogy/resemblance arguments, evaluation arguments, and proposal arguments. The first three of these categories concern questions of truth; the last two concern questions of value.

The five-category schema is not primarily a tool for classifying arguments; in fact, you will come across many arguments that resist and some that defy ready classification. Rather, the five-category schema is mainly an invention tool. By understanding how certain categories of claims are typically developed, you can confidently generate reasons and support for your position and evaluate the strengths and weaknesses of alternative views.

The present chapter introduces you to the five-category schema and explains a simple three-step strategy for generating ideas for values arguments. The remaining chapters of Part Three treat each of the categories in more detail.

WHAT IS A TRUTH ARGUMENT?

The first three categories in our schema—sometimes called *truth arguments*—involve disputes about the way reality is (or was or will be). Unlike factual claims, which can be confirmed or disconfirmed by using agreed-on empirical measures, truth claims involve interpretation of facts that must be supported by reasons.

Determining the point at which factual claims turn into truth claims, however, is tricky. The French mathematician Poincaré said that a fact is something that is "common to several thinking beings and could be common to all." Water freezes at 32 degrees; Chicago is in Illinois; the state of Illinois did not ratify the Equal Rights Amendment. These are all factual claims insofar as few people would question them in the first place; if they were questioned, we could refer to a common source (e.g., an almanac or science textbook) that would affirm the claim to the skeptic's satisfaction.

But what about an apparently factual claim such as "Joe is literate." Does that mean Joe can read a newspaper? A traffic sign? A fourth-grade reader? A novel? Or does it mean that Joe has read a number of books that we've agreed are essential for all educated members of our culture to have read? Any time an apparent statement of fact requires interpretation (in this case, the meaning of *literate*), any time there is less than universal agreement about the meaning of a given term and no common source has the authority to settle that difference, we are in the realm of truth claims. Here are some examples of the kinds of truth claims we'll be examining:

Bill Clinton is/is not a liberal. (X is a Y—definitional argument)

Gun control laws will/will not reduce the violent crime rate in the United States. (X causes Y—causal argument)

Investing in the stock market is/is not like gambling. (X is like Y—resemblance argument)

WHAT IS A VALUES ARGUMENT?

For many people, arguments over claims of truth are the only legitimate arguments we can have. Values, after all, are personal, whereas truth can be looked at "objectively." But the notion that values are purely personal is a dangerous one. If for no other reason, it's dangerous because every day we encounter values issues that must be resolved. If you think, for example, that you deserve a promotion and your boss disagrees, your own sense of self-worth won't let you ignore the resulting values conflict.

Although it's true that one's values often begin as feelings founded on personal experience, they must be articulated and justified if they are to be influential in the public sphere. Values incapable of being justified are vulnerable to every sort of questioning. They are reduced to mere "opinions" or "tastes" in your own private collection of likes and dislikes. But values can be justified with reasons and evidence; they are transpersonal and shareable. We can articulate criteria for our values that others would agree are significant and coherent and we can apply those criteria to situations, people, and things to create a reasoned argument.

Here are some examples of the kinds of values claims we'll be examining:

Dr. Choplogic is/is not a good teacher. (X is a good/bad Y—evaluation claim)

Congress should/should not pass a bill protecting speech on the Internet. (We should/should not do X—proposal claim)

Dr. Kervorkian is/is not a good person. (special case of evaluation claim—moral argument)

THREE-STEP STRATEGY FOR DEVELOPING VALUES ARGUMENTS

The five-category schema is an especially powerful invention tool for any argument making a good/bad claim (evaluation) or a should claim (proposal) because the supporting reasons for values claims are often truth claims. For example, consider the arguments used in the early 1990s to protest government funding for an exhibition of homoerotic photographs by Robert Mapplethorpe. Those opposed to the exhibit used all three sorts of truth claims to support their central values claim.

> Taxpayer funding for the Mapplethorpe exhibits ought to be withdrawn [*proposal claim*] because the photographs are pornographic [*definitional claim*], because they promote community acceptance of homosexuality [*cause/consequence claim*], and because the photographs are more like political statements than art [*analogy/resemblance claim*].

Whatever you might think of the argument, the example shows how the *because* clauses in support of the proposal claim are truth claims of definition, cause/consequence, and analogy/resemblance. The example suggests how the three truth claims can be used as a strategy to help you think of ways to support value arguments. The rest of this chapter explains this three-step strategy in more detail.

The three-step strategy works by focusing your attention on three different approaches to developing a values argument:

1. An *argument from definition,* in which you argue that doing X is right (wrong) according to some value, assumption, principle, or belief that you share with your audience. (This strategy is also called by various other names, such as an "argument from principle" or an "argument from genus or category.")
2. An *argument from consequence,* in which you argue that doing X is right (wrong) because doing X will lead to consequences that you and your audience believe are good (bad).

3. An *argument from resemblance,* in which you argue that doing X is right (wrong) because doing X is like doing Y, which you and your audience agree is right (wrong).

Let's now illustrate the strategy in more detail. In a recent college course, the instructor asked students whether they would report a classmate for plagiarizing a paper. To the instructor's dismay, the majority of students said "No." How might the teacher support her claim that students should report plagiarists?

An Argument from Definition or Principle

One strategy she could use is to argue as follows: "A student should report a classmate for plagiarizing a paper because plagiarism is fraud." We can call this an *argument from principle* because it is based on the assumption that the audience opposes fraud categorically, no matter what form it takes. Such an argument can also be called an argument from definition because it places the term X (plagiarizing a paper) inside the class or category Y (fraud).

Argument from Definition/Principle

To discover reasons using this strategy, you conduct the following kind of search:

   We should (should not) do X because X is _____.

Try to fill in the blank with an appropriate adjective or noun (*good, just, ethical, criminal, ugly, violent, peaceful, wrong, inflationary, healing; an act of kindness, terrorism, murder, true art, political suicide,* and so forth). The point is to try to fill in the blank with a noun or adjective that appeals in some way to your audience's values. Your goal is to show that X belongs to the chosen class or category.

In saying that plagiarism is fraud, the teacher assumes that students would report classmates for other kinds of fraud (for example, for counterfeiting a signature on a check, for entering the university's computer system to alter grades, and so forth). In other words, she knows that the term *fraud* has force on the audience because most people will agree that instances of fraud should be reported. Her task is to define *fraud* and show how plagiarism fits that definition. She could show that fraud is an act of deception to obtain a benefit that doesn't rightly belong to a person. She could then argue that plagiarism is such an act in that it uses deception to procure the benefits of a grade that the plagiarizer has not earned. Although the person whose work is plagiarized may not be directly damaged, the reputation and stature of the university is damaged whenever it grants credentials that have been fraudulently earned. The degree earned by a plagiarizer is fraudulent. Although convincing students that plagiarism is fraud won't guarantee that students will report it, putting plagiarism inside the category of seriously bad things does make such whistle blowing more likely.

An Argument from Consequence

Besides arguing from principle, the teacher could argue from consequence: "A student should report a classmate for plagiarizing a paper because the consequences of plagiarism are bad for everyone." An argument of this type shows first that X causes Y and then that Y is bad.

Argument from Consequence

To discover reasons for using this strategy, conduct the following kind of search:

We should (should not) do X because X leads to these consequences: _____, _____, _____, _____.

Then think of consequences that your audience will agree are good or bad, as your argument requires.

Using this strategy, the teacher now focuses on the ill effects of plagiarism. She might argue that plagiarism raises the grading curve to the disadvantage of honest students or that it can lead to ill-trained people getting into critical professions. How would you like to have your eyes operated on by someone who plagiarized her work in medical school? She might argue that accepting plagiarism leads to acceptance of moral laxity throughout society, thus making tax dodging, bogus repair charges, and petty theft at work more widespread. She might argue that plagiarism hurts the plagiarist by preventing that person from developing skills needed for later success. She could further argue that plagiarism scandals weaken the reputation of the university and dilute the worth of its degrees. Finally, she could argue that reporting plagiarism will reduce its incidence. All the preceding are arguments from consequence.

An Argument from Resemblance

There is a third strategy the teacher might employ. She could say, "You should report someone for plagiarizing an essay just as you should report someone for entering someone else's painting in an art show." Although similar to an argument from definition, this argument from resemblance employs very different sorts of reasoning.

In using this strategy, the teacher encourages her audience to recognize that an essay is a piece of property like a painting. Once her audience accepts an essay as a piece of property, it's easier for that audience to see its unauthorized use as an act of theft. Whenever we deal with new ways of understanding, analogies are a valuable bridge from old to new ways. But beware—argument from analogy can be very persuasive but also vulnerable to the charge of *false analogy*. Chapter 12 treats resemblance arguments in depth.

Argument from Resemblance

To discover supporting reasons using this strategy, conduct the following kind of search:

We should (should not) do X because doing X is like _____.

Then think of analogies or precedents that are similar to doing X but that currently have more force for your audience. Your task is then to transfer your audience's attitude toward X to the precedent or analogy.

These three strategies—trying to support a values claim from the perspectives of principle, consequence, and resemblance—are powerful means of invention. In selecting among these reasons, choose those most likely to appeal to your audience's assumptions, beliefs, and values.

 FOR CLASS DISCUSSION

1. Working individually or in small groups, use the strategies of principle, consequence, and resemblance to create *because* clauses that support each of the following claims. Try to have at least one *because* clause from each of the strategies, but generate as many reasons as possible. Don't worry about whether any individual reason exactly fits the strategy. The purpose is to stimulate thinking, not to fill in the slots.

   EXAMPLE:

CLAIM:	Pit bulls make bad pets
PRINCIPLE:	because they are vicious
CONSEQUENCE:	because owning a pit bull leads to conflicts with neighbors
RESEMBLANCE:	because owning a pit bull is like having a shell-shocked roommate—mostly they're lovely companions but they can turn violent if startled

  a. Marijuana should be legalized.
  b. Division I college athletes should receive salaries.
  c. Couples should live together before they marry.
  d. The United States should end its energy dependence on other nations.
  e–i. Repeat the exercise, taking a different position on each issue. You might try beginning with the claim: "Pit bulls make good pets."

2. Working individually or in groups, use the principle/consequences/resemblance strategy to explore arguments on both sides of the following issues.
  a. Should spanking be made illegal?
  b. Has affirmative action been good or bad for the nation?
  c. Should all eighteen-year-old American citizens be required to perform some sort of public service?
  d. Should high schools pass out free contraceptives?
  e. Should writing students be graded on the basis of effort rather than performance?

chapter 10

❖ | Definition Arguments
X Is (Is Not) a Y

EXAMPLE CASE

Economist Isabella Sawhill believes that the current distinctions among "poor," "middle income," and "rich" don't help us understand the real problem of poverty in America. She proposes a new term, *underclass*. According to her definition, the defining characteristic of the underclass is "dysfunctional behavior," which means failure to follow four major norms of middle-class society: (1) Children are supposed to study hard in school, (2) no one is supposed to become a parent until able to afford a child, (3) adults are supposed to hold regular jobs, and (4) everyone is supposed to obey laws. If we use this definition instead of income level, a rich drug dealer may be a member of the underclass while a poor widow might not be. Sawhill believes society can improve the lives of the underclass by changing these dysfunctional characteristics rather than by relieving poverty directly. Thus a new definition of "the poor," based on behaviors rather than income, aims at changing social policy.[*]

OVERVIEW OF DEFINITIONAL ARGUMENTS

Many arguments require a definition of key terms. If you argue, for example, that euthanasia should be illegal, you will need to define what you mean by *euthanasia*. (Do you distinguish between active and passive euthanasia? Does your definition include the removal of life support systems for the terminally ill as well as Dr. Kervorkian's suicide machines?) Writers regularly define key terms as a preliminary move in an argument.

---

[*]Spenser Rich, "Economist: Behavior Draws Lines Between the Classes," *Seattle Times* 13 Sept. 1989: A4.

However, the main focus of this chapter is not on occasional explanatory definitions but on those arguments where the central issue is a definitional problem. Definitional arguments occur whenever people disagree about the actual definition of a term or about the match or fit between an agreed-on definition and a specific case. For example, an argument about whether or not *Penthouse* magazine is pornographic is a definitional argument; as such it will involve two related issues: (1) What do we mean by "pornographic" (the definition issue)? and (2) Does *Penthouse* fit that definition (the match issue)?

Definitional arguments thus arise whenever an arguer is concerned to show that a specific case X belongs (or does not belong) to category Y. Consider, for example, the environmental controversy over the definition of "wetlands." Section 404 of the federal Clean Water Act provides for federal protection of wetlands, but it leaves the task of defining wetlands to administrative agencies and the courts. Currently about 5 percent of the land surface of the contiguous forty-eight states is potentially affected by the wetlands provision, and 75 percent of this land is privately owned. Efforts to define wetlands have created a battleground between pro-environment and pro-development (or pro–private property rights) groups. Farmers, homeowners, and developers often want a narrow definition of wetlands so that more property is available for commercial or private use. Environmentalists favor a broad definition in order to protect different habitat types and maintain the environmental safeguards that wetlands provide (control of water pollution, spawning grounds for aquatic species, floodwater containment, and so forth). The problem is that defining wetlands is tricky. For example, one federal regulation defines a wetland as any area that has a saturated ground surface for 21 consecutive days during the year. How would you apply this law to a pine flatwood ecosystem that was wet for ten days this year but thirty days last year? And how should the courts react to lawsuits claiming that the regulation itself is either too broad or too narrow? One can see why the wetlands controversy provides hefty incomes for lawyers and congressional lobbyists.

THE CRITERIA-MATCH STRUCTURE OF DEFINITIONAL ARGUMENTS

As the wetlands example suggests, definitional arguments usually have a two-part structure: (1) How should the controversial term be defined? and (2) Does this particular case fit that definition? We use the term *criteria match* to describe this structure, which occurs regularly not only in definitional arguments but also in evaluation arguments of the type "X is a good (bad) Y" (see Chapter 13). The criteria part of the structure defines the Y term by setting forth the criteria that must be met for something to be considered a Y. (In Toulmin terms, these criteria are the warrants for the argument.) The match part examines whether the X term meets these criteria. (In Toulmin terms, evidence that X meets the criteria constitutes the grounds for the argument.)

Let's consider another example. Suppose you work for a consumer information group that wishes to encourage patronage of socially responsible companies while boycotting irresponsible ones. Your group's first task is to define a "socially responsible company." After much discussion and research, your group establishes three criteria that a company must meet to be considered socially responsible:

Your definition: A company is socially responsible if it (1) avoids polluting the environment, (2) sells goods or services that contribute to the well-being of the community, and (3) treats its workers justly.

The criteria section of your argument would explain and illustrate these criteria, providing more detailed definitions of such key terms as "pollution of the environment," "well-being of the community," and "just treatment of workers" and illustrating the criteria with positive and negative examples.

The match part of the argument would then try to persuade readers that a specific company does or does not meet the criteria. A typical thesis statement might be as follows:

Your thesis statement: Although the Hercules Shoe Company is nonpolluting and provides a socially useful product, it is *not* a socially responsible company because it treats workers unjustly.

Here is how the core of the argument could be displayed in Toulmin terms:

INITIAL ENTHYMEME:	The Hercules Shoe Company is not a socially responsible company because it treats workers unjustly.
CLAIM:	The Hercules Shoe Company is *not* a socially responsible company.
STATED REASON:	because it treats workers unjustly
GROUNDS:	evidence that the company manufactures its shoes in East Asian sweat shops; evidence of the inhumane conditions in these shops; evidence of hardships imposed on displaced American workers
WARRANT:	Socially responsible companies treat workers justly.
BACKING:	arguments showing that just treatment of workers is right in principle and also benefits society; arguments that capitalism helps society as a whole only if workers achieve a reasonable standard of living, have time for leisure, and are not exploited

POSSIBLE CONDITIONS OF REBUTTAL	Opponents of this thesis might argue that justice needs to be considered from an emerging nation's standpoint: The wages paid workers are low by American standards but are above average by East Asian standards. Displacement of American workers is part of the necessary adjustment of adapting to a global economy and does not mean that a company is unjust.

As this Toulmin frame illustrates, the writer's argument needs to contain a criteria section (warrant and backing) showing that just treatment of workers is a criterion for social responsibility and a match section (stated reason and grounds) showing that the Hercules Shoe Company does not treat its workers justly. The conditions of rebuttal help the writer imagine alternative views and see places where opposing views need to be acknowledged and rebutted.

 FOR CLASS DISCUSSION ▬▬▬▬▬▬▬▬▬▬▬▬▬▬▬▬▬▬▬▬▬▬▬▬

Consider the following definitional claims. Working as individuals or in small groups, identify the criteria issue and the match issue for each of the following claims.

EXAMPLE: A Honda assembled in Ohio is (is not) an American-made car.

CRITERIA PART: What criteria have to be met before a car can be called "American made"?

MATCH PART: Does a Honda assembled in Ohio meet these criteria?

1. Accounting is (is not) a creative profession.

2. Writing graffiti on subways is (is not) vandalism.

3. American Sign Language is (is not) a "foreign language" for purposes of a college graduation requirement.

4. Beauty contests are (are not) sexist events.

5. Bungee jumping from a crane is (is not) a "carnival amusement ride" subject to state safety inspections.

CONCEPTUAL PROBLEMS OF DEFINITION

Before moving on to discuss ways of defining the Y term in a definitional argument, we should explore briefly some of the conceptual difficulties of definition. Language, for all its wonderful powers, is an arbitrary system that requires agreement among its users before it can work. And it's not always easy to get that agreement. In fact, the task of defining something can be devilishly complex.

Why Can't We Just Look in the Dictionary?

What's so hard about defining? you might ask. Why not just look in a dictionary? To get a sense of the complexity of defining something, consider again the word *wetland*. A dictionary can tell us the ordinary meaning of a word (the way it is commonly used), but it can't resolve a debate between competing definitions when different parties have interests in defining the word in different ways. For example, the *Webster's Seventh New Collegiate Dictionary* defines *wetland* as "land containing much soil moisture"—a definition that is hardly helpful in determining whether the federal government can prevent the development of a beach resort on some landowner's private property. Moreover, dictionary definitions rarely tell us such things as *to what degree* a given condition must be met before it qualifies for class membership. How wet does a wetland have to be before it is *legally* a wetland? How long does this wetness have to last? When is a wetland a mere swamp that ought to be drained rather than protected?

Definitions and the Rule of Justice: At What Point Does X Quit Being a Y?

For some people, all this concern about definition may seem misplaced. How often, after all, have you heard people accuse each other of getting bogged down in "mere semantics"? But how we define a given word can have significant implications for people who must either use the word or have the word used on them. Take, for example, what some philosophers refer to as the *rule of justice*. According to this rule, "beings in the same essential category should be treated in the same way." Should an insurance company, for example, treat anorexia nervosa as a physical illness like diabetes (in which case treatment is paid for by the insurance company) or as a mental illness like paranoia (in which case insurance payments are minimal)? Or, to take another example, if a company gives "new baby" leave to a mother, should it also give "new baby" leave to a father? In other words, is this kind of leave "new mother" leave or is it "new parent" leave? And what if a couple adopts an infant? Should "new mother" or "new parent" leave be available to them also? These questions are all definitional issues involving arguments about what class of beings an individual belongs to and about what actions to take to comply with the "rule of justice," which demands that all members of that class be treated equally.

The rule of justice becomes even harder to apply when we consider Xs that grow, evolve, or otherwise change through time. When Young Person back in Chapter 1 argued that she could set her own curfew because she was mature, she raised the question "What are the attributes or criteria of a 'mature' person?" In this case, a categorical distinction between two separate kinds of things ("mature" versus "not mature") evolves into a distinction of degree ("mature enough"). So perhaps we should not ask whether Young Person is mature, but whether she is "mature enough." At what point does a child become an adult? (When does a fetus become a human person? When does a social drinker become an alcoholic?)

Although we may be able arbitrarily to choose a particular point and declare, through stipulation, that "mature" means eighteen years old or that "human person" includes a fetus at conception, or at three months, or at birth, in the everyday world the distinction between child and adult, between egg and person, between social drinking and alcoholism seems an evolution, not a sudden and definitive step. Nevertheless, our language requires an abrupt shift between classes. In short, applying the rule of justice often requires us to adopt a digital approach to reality (switches are either on or off, either a fetus is a human person or it is not), whereas our sense of life is more analogical (there are numerous gradations between on and off, there are countless shades of gray between black and white).

As we can see by the preceding examples, the promise of language to fix what psychologist William James called "the buzz and confusion of the world" into an orderly set of categories turns out to be elusive. In most definitional debates, an argument, not a quick trip to the dictionary, is required to settle the matter.

KINDS OF DEFINITIONS

In this section we discuss two methods of definition commonly used in definitional arguments: Aristotelian and operational.

Aristotelian Definition

Aristotelian definitions, regularly used in dictionaries, define a term by placing it within the next larger class or category and then showing the specific attributes that distinguish the term from other terms within the same category. For example, a *pencil* is a "writing implement" (next larger category) that differs from other writing implements in that it makes marks with lead or graphite rather than ink. You could elaborate this definition by saying, "Usually the lead or graphite is a long, thin column embedded in a slightly thicker column of wood with an eraser on one end and a sharpened point, exposing the graphite, on the other." You could even distinguish a wooden pencil from a mechanical pencil, thereby indicating again that the crucial identifying attribute is the graphite, not the wooden column.

As you can see, an Aristotelian definition of a term identifies specific attributes or criteria that enable you to distinguish it from other members of the next larger class. We created an Aristotelian definition in our example about socially responsible companies. A socially responsible company, we said, is any company (next larger class) that meets three criteria: (1) It doesn't pollute the environment, (2) it creates goods/services that promote the well-being of the community, and (3) it treats its workers justly.

In constructing Aristotelian definitions, you may find it useful to employ the concepts of accidental, necessary, and sufficient criteria. An *accidental criterion* is a usual but not essential feature of a concept. For example, "made out of wood" is an accidental feature of a pencil. Most pencils are made out of wood, but something can still be a pencil even if it isn't made out of wood (a mechanical pencil). In our example about socially responsible companies, "makes regular contributions to charities" might be an accidental criterion; most socially responsible companies contribute to charities, but some do not. And many socially irresponsible companies also contribute to charities—often as a public relations ploy.

A *necessary criterion* is an attribute that *must* be present for something to belong to the category being defined. For example, "is a writing implement" is a necessary criterion for a pencil; "marks with graphite or lead" is also a necessary criterion. However, neither of these criteria by itself is a sufficient criterion for a pencil. Many writing implements aren't pencils (for example, pens); also, many things that mark with lead or graphite aren't pencils (for example, a lead paperweight will make pencil-like marks on paper). Because a pencil must possess both these criteria together, we say that these two criteria together are *sufficient criteria* for the concept "pencil." In our example of socially responsible companies, all three criteria are necessary, but none of them alone is sufficient.

 ## FOR CLASS DISCUSSION

Working individually or in small groups, try to determine whether each of the following is a necessary criterion, a sufficient criterion, an accidental criterion, or no criterion for defining the indicated concept. Be prepared to explain your reasoning and to account for differences in points of view.

CRITERION	CONCEPT TO BE DEFINED
presence of gills	fish
yellow hair on head	blond
birthplace inside the United States	American citizen
Age of 65 or older	senior citizen
line endings that form a rhyming pattern	poem
spanking child for discipline	child abuse
diet that excludes meat	vegetarian
killing another human being	murder
good sex life	happy marriage

Operational Definitions

In some rhetorical situations, particularly those arising in the physical and social sciences, writers need precise definitions that can be measured empirically and are not subject to problems of context and disputed criteria. Consider, for example, an argument involving the concept "aggression": "Do violent television programs increase the incidence of aggression in children?" To do research on this issue, a scientist needs a precise, measurable definition of *aggression*. Typically, a scientist might measure "aggression" by counting the number of blows or kicks a child gives to an inflatable bozo doll over a fifteen-minute period when other play options are available. The scientist might then define "aggressive behavior" as six or more blows to the bozo doll. In our wetlands example, a federal authority created an operational definition of a wetlands: A wetlands is a parcel of land that has a saturated ground surface for twenty-one consecutive days during the year. Such definitions are useful because they are precisely measurable, but they are also limited because they omit criteria that may be unmeasurable but important. Many scientists, for example, object to definitions of wetlands based on consecutive days of wetness. What is more relevant, they argue, is not the duration of wetness in any parcel of land, but the kind of plants and animals that depend on the wetland as a habitat. As another example, we might ask whether it is adequate to define a "superior student" as someone with a 3.5 GPA or higher or a "successful sex education program" as one that results in a 25 percent reduction in teenage pregnancies. What important aspects of a superior student or a successful sex education program are not considered in these operational definitions?

STRATEGIES FOR DEFINING THE CONTESTED TERM IN A DEFINITIONAL ARGUMENT

In constructing criteria to define your contested term, you can take two basic approaches—what rhetoricians call reportive and stipulative definitions. A *reportive definition* cites how others have used the term, whereas a *stipulative definition* cites how you define the term. To put it another way, you can take a reportive approach by turning to standard or specialized dictionaries, judicial opinions, or expert testimony to establish a definition based on the authority of others. A lawyer defining a wetlands based on twenty-one consecutive days of saturated ground surface would be using a reportive definition with a federal regulation as her source. The other approach is to use your own critical thinking to stipulate a definition, thereby defining the contested term yourself. Our definition of a socially responsible company, specifying three criteria, is an example of a stipulative definition. This section explains these approaches in more detail.

Reportive Approach: Research How Others Have Used the Term

When you take a reportive approach, you research how others have used the term, searching for authoritative definitions acceptable to your audience, yet favorable to your case. Student writer Kathy Sullivan uses this approach in her argument that photographs displayed at the Oncore Bar are not obscene (see pp. 154–155). To define "obscenity," she turns to *Black's Law Dictionary* and Pember's *Mass Media Laws.* (Specialized dictionaries are a standard part of the reference section of any library—see your reference librarian for assistance.) Other sources of specialized definitions are state and federal appellate court decisions, legislative and administrative statutes, and scholarly articles examining a given definitional conflict. Lawyers use this research strategy exhaustively in preparing court briefs. They begin by looking at the actual text of laws as passed by legislatures or written by administrative authorities. Then they look at all the court cases in which the laws have been tested and examine the ways courts have refined legal definitions and applied them to specific cases. Using these refined and elaborated definitions, lawyers then apply them to their own case at hand.

When research fails to uncover a definition favorable to the arguer's case, the arguer can sometimes adopt an *original intentions* strategy. For example, if a scientist is dissatisfied with definitions of wetlands based on consecutive days of saturated ground surface, she might proceed as follows: "The original intention of the Congress in passing the Clean Water Act was to preserve the environment." What they intended, she could then claim, was to prevent development of those wetland areas that provide crucial habitat for wildlife or that inhibit water pollution. She could then propose an alternative definition (either a stipulative one that she develops herself or a reportive one that she uncovers in research) based on criteria other than consecutive days of ground saturation. (Of course, original intentions arguments can often be refuted by a "times have changed" strategy or by a "we can't know what they originally intended; we can only know what they wrote" strategy.)

Another way to make a reportive definition is to employ a strategy based on etymology or *earlier meaning* strategy. Using an etymological dictionary or the *Oxford English Dictionary* (which traces the historical evolution of a word's meaning), an arguer can often unveil insights favorable to the writer's case. For example, if you wanted to argue that portrayal of violence in films is obscene, you could point to the etymology of the word, which literally means "offstage." The word derives from the practice of classical Greek tragedy, where violent acts occurred offstage and were only reported by a messenger. This strategy allows you to show how the word originally applied to violence rather than to sexual explicitness.

Stipulative Approach: Create Your Own Definition Based on Positive, Contrastive, and Borderline Cases

Often, however, you need to create your own definition of the contested term. An effective strategy for developing your own definition is to brainstorm examples of positive, contrastive, and borderline cases. Suppose, for example, you wanted to argue the claim that "accounting is (is not) a creative profession." Your first goal is to establish criteria for creativity. You could begin by thinking of examples of obvious creative behaviors, then of contrastive behaviors that seem similar to the previous behaviors but yet are clearly not creative, and then finally of borderline behaviors that may or may not be creative. Your list might look like this:

EXAMPLES OF CREATIVE BEHAVIORS

> Beethoven composes a violin concerto.
>
> An architect designs a house.
>
> Edison invents the light bulb.
>
> An engineer designs a machine that will make widgets in a new way.
>
> A poet writes a poem. (Later revised to "A poet writes a poem that poetry experts say is beautiful"—see following discussion.)

CONTRASTIVE EXAMPLES OF NONCREATIVE BEHAVIORS

> A conductor transposes Beethoven's concerto into a different key.
>
> A carpenter builds a house from the architect's plan.
>
> I change a lightbulb in my house.
>
> A factory worker uses the new machine to stamp out widgets.
>
> A graduate student writes sentimental "love/dove" verses for greeting cards.

EXAMPLES OF BORDERLINE CASES

> A woman gives birth to a child.
>
> An accountant figures out your income tax.
>
> A violinist plays Beethoven's concerto with great skill.
>
> A monkey paints an oil painting by smearing paint on canvas; a group of art critics, not knowing a monkey was the artist, call the painting beautiful.

Next you can begin developing your criteria by determining what features the "clearly creative" examples have in common and what features the "clearly noncreative" examples lack. Then refine your criteria by deciding on what grounds you might include or eliminate your borderline cases from the category "creative." For example, you might begin with the following criterion:

DEFINITION: FIRST TRY

> For an act to be creative, it must result in an end product that is significantly different from other products.

But then, by looking at some of the examples in your creative and noncreative columns, you decide that just producing a different end product isn't enough. A bad poem might be different from other poems, but you don't want to call a bad poet creative. So you refine your criteria.

DEFINITION: SECOND TRY

> For an act to be creative, it must result in an end product that is significantly different from other products and is yet useful or beautiful.

This definition would allow you to include all the acts in your creative column but eliminate the acts in the noncreative column.

Your next step is to refine your criteria by deciding whether to include or reject items in your borderline list. You decide to reject the childbirth case by arguing that creativity must be a mental or intellectual activity, not a natural process. You reject the monkey as painter example on similar grounds, arguing that although the end product may be both original and beautiful, it is not creative because it is not a product of the monkey's intellect. Finally, you reject the example of the violinist playing Beethoven's violin concerto. Like the carpenter who builds the house, the violinist possesses great skill but doesn't design a new product; rather, he or she follows the instructions of the designer.

A music major in your group reacts bitterly, arguing that musicians "interpret" music and that such behavior is creative. She notes that the music department is housed in a building called the "Creative Arts Complex." Your group, however, can't figure out a way to reword the definition to include performance rather than production. If you call performing musicians creative, the rest of the group argues, then the rule of justice forces you to call carpenters creative also, because both kinds of craftspeople reproduce the creative intentions of others. Once we call performers creative, they argue, the concept of creativity will get so broad that it will no longer be useful.

Your group's final definition, then, looks like this (with the music major dissenting):

DEFINITION: THIRD TRY

> For an act to be creative, it must be produced by intellectual design, and it must result in an end product that is significantly different from other products and is yet useful or beautiful.

Having established these criteria, you are ready for your final borderline case, your original issue of whether or not accounting is a creative profession. Based on your criteria, you might decide that accounting is not generally a creative profession because the final products are not significantly new or different. For the most part, accountants perform elaborately complex calculations, but they generally follow established procedures in doing so. However, the profession can sometimes offer creative opportunities when an accountant, for example, develops a new kind of computer program or develops new, improved procedures for handling routine business. (Accounting majors may argue that accounting is creative in other ways.)

This strategy produces a systematic procedure for developing criteria for a definitional argument. Moreover, it provides a strategy for writing the criteria part of your argument because it produces the examples you will need to illustrate your criteria and explain your reasoning.

FOR CLASS DISCUSSION

1. Suppose you wanted to define the concept "courage." Working in groups, try to decide whether each of the following cases is an example of courage:

   a. A neighbor rushes into a burning house to rescue a child from certain death and emerges, coughing and choking, with the child in his arms. Is the neighbor courageous?

   b. A fireman rushes into a burning house to rescue a child from certain death and emerges with the child in his arms. The fireman is wearing protective clothing and a gas mask. When a newspaper reporter calls him courageous, he says, "Hey, this is my job." Is the fireman courageous?

   c. A teenager rushes into a burning house to recover a memento given to him by his girlfriend, the first love of his life. Is the teenager courageous?

   d. A parent rushes into a burning house to save a trapped child. The fire marshal tells the parent to wait because there is no chance the child can be reached from the first floor. The fire marshal wants to try cutting a hole in the roof to reach the child. The parent rushes into the house anyway and is burned to death. Was the parent courageous?

2. As you make your decisions on each of these cases, create and refine the criteria you use.

3. Make up your own series of controversial cases, like those above for "courage," for one or more of the following concepts:

   a. cruelty to animals
   b. child abuse
   c. true athlete
   d. sexual harassment
   e. free speech protected by the First Amendment

Then, using the strategy of positive, contrastive, and borderline cases, construct a definition of your chosen term.

CONDUCTING THE MATCH PART OF A DEFINITIONAL ARGUMENT

In conducting a match argument, you need to show that your contested case does (or does not) meet the criteria you established in your definition. Generally you do so by comparing your case to each criterion in your definition, supplying evidence and examples (or chains of reasons) showing why the case meets (or does not) meet the criterion.

For example, if you were developing the argument that the Hercules Shoe Company is not socially responsible because it treats its workers unjustly, your match section would provide evidence of this injustice. You might supply data about the percentage of shoes produced in East Asia, about the low wages paid these workers, and about the working conditions in these factories. You might also describe the suffering of displaced American workers when Hercules closed its American factories and moved operations to Asia, where the labor was nonunion and cheap. The match section should also summarize and respond to opposing views (see "conditions of rebuttal" in the Toulmin scheme on p. 143).

ORGANIZING A DEFINITIONAL ARGUMENT

As you compose a first draft of your essay, you may find it helpful to know a prototypical structure for definitional arguments. Here are several possible plans.

Plan 1 (Criteria and Match in Separate Sections)

- Introduce the issue by showing disagreements about the definition of a key term or about its application to a problematic case.
- State your claim.
- Present your definition of the key term.
  State and develop Criterion 1.
  State and develop Criterion 2.
  Continue with rest of criteria.
- Summarize and respond to possible objections to your definition.
- Restate your claim about the contested case (it does/does not meet your definition).
  Apply Criterion 1 to your case.
  Apply Criterion 2 to your case.
  Continue the match argument.
- Summarize and respond to possible objections to your match argument.
- Conclude your argument.

Plan 2 (Criteria and Match Interwoven)

- Introduce the issue by showing disagreements about the definition of a key term or about its application to a problematic case.
- Present your claim.
  State Criterion 1 and argue that contested case meets (does not meet) criterion.
  State Criterion 2 and argue that contested case meets (does not meet) criterion.

Continue with criteria-match sections for additional criteria.

- Summarize opposing views.
- Refute or concede to opposing views.
- Conclude your argument.

CONDITIONS FOR REBUTTAL: TESTING A DEFINITIONAL ARGUMENT

In refuting a definitional argument, you need to appreciate its criteria-match structure. Your refutation can attack either the argument's criteria or its match, or both.

Attacking the Criteria

Might a skeptic claim that your criteria are not the right ones? This is the most common way to attack a definitional argument. Opponents might say that one or more of your argument's criteria are only accidental criteria, not necessary or sufficient ones. Or they might argue for different criteria or point out crucial missing criteria.

Might a skeptic point out possible bad consequences of accepting your argument's criteria? Here a skeptic could raise doubts about your definition by showing how it would lead to unintended bad consequences.

Might a skeptic cite extraordinary circumstances that weaken your argument's criteria? Opponents might argue that your criteria are perfectly acceptable in ordinary circumstances but are rendered unacceptable by extraordinary circumstances.

Might a skeptic point out a bias or slant in your definition? Writers create definitions favorable to their case. By making this slant visible, an opponent may be able to weaken the persuasiveness of your definition.

Attacking the Match

A match argument usually uses examples and other evidence to show that the contested case meets or does not meet the criteria in the definition. The standard methods of refuting evidence thus apply (see pp. 120–121). Thus skeptics might ask one or more of the following questions:

Are your examples out of date or too narrow and unrepresentative?

Are your examples inaccurate?

Are your examples too extreme?

The following essay was written by student writer Kathy Sullivan in response to the assignment at the end of this chapter.

Oncore, Obscenity, and the
Liquor Control Board
Kathy Sullivan (student)

1   In early May, Geoff Menasee, a Seattle artist, exhibited a series of photographs with the theme of "safe sex" on the walls of an inner city, predominantly homosexual restaurant and lounge called the Oncore. Before hanging the photographs, Menasee had to consult with the Washington State Liquor Control Board because, under the current state law, art work containing material that may be considered indecent has to be approved by the board before it can be exhibited. Of the almost thirty photographs, six were rejected by the board because they partially exposed "private parts" of the male anatomy. Menasee went ahead and displayed the entire series of photographs, placing bandaids over the "indecent" areas, but the customers continually removed the bandaids.

2   The liquor control board's ruling on this issue has caused controversy in the Seattle community. The *Seattle Times* has provided news coverage, and a "Town Meeting" segment was filmed at the restaurant. The central question is this: Should an establishment that caters to a predominantly homosexual clientele be enjoined from displaying pictures promoting "safe sex" on the grounds that the photographs are obscene?

3   Before I can answer this question, I must first determine whether the art work should truly be classified as obscene. To make that determination, I will use the definition of obscenity in *Black's Law Dictionary:*

> Material is "obscene" if to the average person, applying contemporary community standards, the dominant theme of material taken as a whole appeals to prurient interest, if it is utterly without redeeming social importance, if it goes substantially beyond customary limits of candor in description or representation, if it is characterized by patent offensiveness, and if it is hard core pornography.

An additional criterion is provided by Pember's *Mass Media Laws:* "A work is obscene if it has a tendency to deprave and corrupt those whose minds are open to such immoral influences (children for example) and into whose hands it might happen to fall" (394). The art work in question should not be prohibited from display at predominantly homosexual establishments like the Oncore because it does not meet the above criteria for obscenity.

4   First of all, to the average person applying contemporary community standards, the predominant theme of Menasee's photographs is not an appeal to prurient interests. The first element in this criterion is "average person." According to Rocky Breckner, manager of the Oncore, 90 percent of the clientele at the Oncore is made up of young white homosexual males. This group therefore constitutes the "average person" viewing the exhibit. "Contemporary community standards" would ordinarily be the standards of the Seattle community. However, this art work is aimed at a particular group of people—the homosexual community. Therefore, the "community standards" involved here are those of the gay community rather than the city at large. Since the Oncore is not an art museum or gallery, which

attracts a broad spectrum of people, it is appropriate to restrict the scope of "community standards" to that group who voluntarily patronize the Oncore.

Second, the predominant theme of the photographs is not "prurient interest" nor do   5 the photographs go "substantially beyond public limits of candor." There are no explicit sexual acts found in the photographs; instead, their theme is the prevention of AIDS through the practice of safe sex. Homosexual displays of affection could be viewed as "prurient interest" by the larger community, but same-sex relationships are the norm for the group at whom the exhibit is aimed. If the exhibit were displayed at McDonalds or even the Red Robin it might go "substantially beyond customary limits of candor," but it is unlikely that the clientele of the Oncore would find the art work offensive. The manager stated that he received very few complaints about the exhibit and its contents.

Nor is the material pornographic. The liquor control board prohibited the six pho-   6 tographs based on their visible display of body parts such as pubic hair and naked buttocks, not on the basis of sexual acts or homosexual orientation. The board admitted that the photographs depicted no explicit sexual acts. Hence, it can be concluded that they did not consider the suggestion of same-sex affection to be hard-core pornography. Their sole objection was that body parts were visible. But visible genitalia in art work are not necessarily pornographic. Since other art work, such as Michelangelo's sculptures, explicitly depict both male and female genitalia, it is arguable that pubic hair and buttocks are not patently offensive.

It must be conceded that the art work has the potential of being viewed by children, which would violate Pember's criterion. But once again the incidence of minors frequenting this establishment is very small.

But the most important reason for saying these photographs are not obscene is that   7 they serve an important social purpose. One of Black's criteria is that obscene material is "utterly without redeeming social importance." But these photographs have the explicit purpose of promoting safe sex as a defense against AIDS. Recent statistics reported in the *Seattle Times* show that AIDS is now the leading cause of death of men under forty in the Seattle area. Any methods that can promote the message of safe sex in today's society have strong redeeming social significance.

Those who believe that all art containing "indecent" material should be banned or cov-   8 ered from public view would most likely believe that Menasee's work is obscene. They would disagree that the environment and the clientele should be the major determining factor when using criteria to evaluate art. However, in the case of this exhibit I feel that the audience and the environment of the display are factors of overriding importance. Therefore, the exhibit should have been allowed to be displayed because it is not obscene.

❧ WRITING ASSIGNMENT FOR CHAPTER 10

Extended Definition/Borderline Case: Is This X a Y?   This assignment asks you to solve a definitional problem. In your essay, you must argue whether or not a given X (a borderline case) belongs to concept Y, which you must define.[*] You will need to write an extended definition of a concept such as "police brutality," "courageous action," "child abuse," "cruelty to animals," "free speech," or another, similar concept that is both familiar yet tricky to define precisely. After you have established your definition, you will need to apply it to a borderline case, arguing whether the borderline case fits or does not fit the definition. For example:

1. Is a daring bank robbery an "act of courage"?
2. Are highly skilled videogame players "true athletes"?
3. Is a case like the following an instance of "cruelty to animals"?

A bunch of starlings build nests in the attic of a family's house, gaining access to the attic through a torn vent screen. Soon the eggs hatch, and every morning at sunrise the family is awakened by the sounds of birds squawking and wings beating against rafters as the starlings fly in and out of the house to feed the hatchlings. After losing considerable early morning sleep, the family repairs the screen. Unable to get in and out, the parent birds are unable to feed their young. The birds die within a day.

---

[*]The writing assignment for this chapter is based on the work of George Hillocks and his research associates at the University of Chicago. See George Hillocks, Jr., Elizabeth A. Kahn, and Larry R. Johannessen, "Teaching Defining Strategies as a Mode of Inquiry: Some Effects on Student Writing," *Research in the Teaching of English*, 17 (October 1983): 275–84. See also Larry R. Johannessen, Elizabeth A. Kahn, and Carolyn Calhoun Walter, *Designing and Sequencing Prewriting Activities* (Urbana, IL; NCTE, 1982).

chapter 11

Causal Arguments

X Causes/Does Not Cause Y

EXAMPLE CASE

Many U.S. citizens wonder why it is so difficult to stop illegal immigration into the United States from Mexico. They want more intensive patrolling of the borders, and some have even advocated building a wall along the entire Mexican-American border. A number of economists, however, have shown that manufacturing companies and agribusinesses profit from illegal immigration, which supplies cheap, mobile, nonunion labor. While taking a public stand against illegal immigration—thus winning lots of votes—many legislators and government officials are beholden to under-the-table corporate interests that want illegal immigration to continue. "Illegal immigration," says analyst Wade Gordon, "is only epiphenomenally a law-enforcement issue; it is at root a labor-market event."[*] To understand the phenomenon of illegal immigration, says Gordon, we must understand the complex causal forces that drive it.

THE FREQUENCY OF CAUSAL ARGUMENTS

We encounter causal issues all the time. What are the causes of illegal immigration and of the United States' failure to stem it? Where should people invest

---

[*]Masters of the Game: How the U.S. Protects the Traffic in Cheap Mexican Labor," *Harper's* July 1996: 36.

157

their savings in periods of high inflation? Will legalization of drugs cause an increase or decrease in drug addicts? What caused the death rate of infants in Washington to rise by 235 percent in July and August 1986? (One proposed answer to this last question: the Chernobyl nuclear reactor meltdown in the Ukraine.)

Some arguments are devoted entirely to causal issues; just as frequently, causal arguments support proposal arguments in which the writer argues that we should or should not do X *because X will lead to specified consequences.* Convincing readers how X will lead to these consequences—a causal argument—thus bears on the success of many proposal arguments.

THE NATURE OF CAUSAL ARGUING

Typically, causal arguments try to show how one event brings about another. On the surface, causal arguments may seem a fairly straightforward matter—more concrete, to be sure, than the larger moral issues in which they are often embedded. But consider for a moment the classic illustration of causality—one billiard ball striking another on a pool table. Surely we are safe in saying that the movement of the second ball was "caused" by a transfer of energy from the first ball at the moment of contact. Well, yes and no. British philosopher David Hume (among others) argued long ago that we don't really perceive "causality"; what we perceive is one ball moving and then another ball moving. We infer the notion of causality, which is a human construct, not a property of billiard balls.

When humans become the focus of a causal argument, the very definition of causality is immediately vexed. When we say, for example, that a given factor X "caused" a person to do Y, we might mean that X "forced her to do Y," thereby negating her free will (for example, the presence of a brain tumor caused my erratic behavior, which caused me to lose my job); on the other hand, we might simply mean that factor X "motivated" her to do Y, in such a way that doing Y is still an expression of freedom (for example, my allergic reaction to polyester caused me to give up my job as a Wal-Mart greeter and become a roadie for Hootie and the Blowfish).

When we argue about causality in human beings, we must guard against confusing these two senses of "cause" or assuming that human behavior can be predicted or controlled in the same way that nonhuman behavior can. A rock dropped from a roof will always fall to the ground at 32 feet per second squared; and a rat zapped for making left turns in a maze will always quit making left turns. But if we raise interest rates, will consumers save more? If so, how much? This is the sort of question we debate endlessly.

Fortunately, most causal arguments can avoid the worst of these scientific and philosophic quagmires. As human beings, we share a number of assumptions about what causes events in the observable world, and we can depend on the goodwill of our audiences to grant us most of these assumptions. Most of us, for example, would be satisfied with the following explanation for why a car went into a skid: "In a panic the driver locked the brakes of his car, causing the car to go into a skid."

panic → slamming brake pedal → locking brakes → skid

We probably do not need to defend this simple causal chain because the audience will grant the causal connections between events A, B, C, and D. The sequence seems reasonable according to our shared assumptions about psychological causality (panic leads to slamming brake pedal) and physical causality (locked brakes lead to skid).

But if you are an attorney defending a client whose skidding car caused considerable damage to an upscale boutique, you might see all sorts of additional causal factors. ("Because the stop sign at that corner was obscured by an untrimmed willow tree, my client innocently entered what he assumed was an open intersection only to find a speeding beer truck bearing down on him. When my client took immediate decelerating corrective action, the improperly maintained, oil-slicked roadway sent his car into its near-fatal skid and into the boutique's bow windows—windows that extrude into the walkway 11 full inches beyond the limit allowed by city code.") Okay, now what's the cause of the crash and who's at fault?

DESCRIBING THE LOGICAL STRUCTURE OF A CAUSAL ARGUMENT: *BECAUSE* CLAUSES AND THE TOULMIN SCHEMA

Causal arguments can usually be stated using *because* clauses. Typically, a causal because clause pinpoints one or two key elements in the causal chain rather than trying to summarize every link. For example, if we wished to argue that a series of tobacco ads featuring a raffish young rebel named Nick O. Teen influenced teenage males to buy smokeless tobacco, one of our lines of reasoning might be nutshelled this way:

ENTHYMEME: The Nick O. Teen ads influenced teenage males to buy smokeless tobacco because the ads created a subconscious link between chewing snuff and being cool like Nick.

Like other kinds of arguments, causal arguments can be analyzed using the Toulmin schema. (It is easiest to apply Toulmin's schema to causal arguments if you think of the grounds as the observable phenomena at any point in the causal chain and the warrants as the shareable assumptions about causality that join links together.) Here is how the preceding argument could be displayed in Toulmin terms.

CLAIM:	The Nick O. Teen ads influenced teenage males to buy smokeless tobacco.
STATED REASON:	because the ads created a subconscious link between chewing snuff and being cool like Nick
GROUNDS:	arguments and evidence showing how the Nick O. Teen character created an image of being cool, tough, and rebellious; arguments and evidence that these are subconscious desires of teenage males
WARRANT:	Consumers will buy products that make subconscious links to their desires.
BACKING:	studies of how contemporary advertising works; testimony of psychologists who study advertising; comparisons to other successful ad campaigns
CONDITIONS OF REBUTTAL:	*Attacking the grounds:* unless Nick O. Teen doesn't portray a tough, rebellious character at all (Tobacco execs might say: "You pointy-headed intellectual types are reading too much into this innocent cartoon character; Nick O. Teen is just a humorous drawing"); unless the ad makes no subliminal appeal ("I don't know what psychological problems you senators have, but this ad isn't making any kind of subconscious appeal to anything")
	Attacking the warrant: unless ad campaigns work entirely on name recognition and not on psychological appeals; unless this campaign isn't similar to other campaigns
QUALIFIER:	This is a likely explanation for how the ads work.

 FOR CLASS DISCUSSION

1. Working individually or in small groups, create a causal chain to show how the first-mentioned item could help lead to the second one.

   a. invention of the automobile   redesign of cities

   b. invention of the automobile   changes in sexual mores

   c. Elvis Presley arrives   rise of the drug culture in the 1960s

d. invention of the telephone   loss of a sense of community in
                                      neighborhoods

e. development of the "pill"   rise in the divorce rate

f. development of way to prevent   liberalization of euthanasia laws
   rejections in transplant operations

2. For each of your causal chains, compose a claim with an attached *because* clause summarizing one or two key links in the causal chain. For example, "The invention of the automobile helped cause the redesign of cities because automobiles made it possible for people to live farther away from their places of work."

THREE METHODS FOR ARGUING THAT ONE EVENT CAUSES ANOTHER

One of the first things you need to do when preparing a causal argument is to note just what sort of causal relationship you're dealing with. Are you concerned with the causes of a specific event or phenomenon such as the increase in homelessness in the 1980s, the crash of TWA flight 800, or the shift of President Clinton toward the political right? Or are you planning to write about the cause of some recurring phenomenon such as cancer, laughter, math anxiety among females, or teen suicide?

With recurring phenomena, you have the luxury of being able to study multiple cases over long periods of time and establishing correlations between suspected causal factors and effects. In some cases you can even intervene in the process and test for yourself whether diminishing a suspected causal factor results in a lessening of the effect or whether increasing the causal factor results in a corresponding increase in the effect. Additionally, you can spend a good deal of time exploring just how the mechanics of causation might work.

But with a one-time occurrence your focus is on the details of the event and specific causal chains that may have contributed to the event. Sometimes evidence has disappeared or changed its nature. You often end up in the position more of a detective than of a scientific researcher and your conclusion will have to be more tentative as a result.

Having briefly stated these words of caution, let's turn now to the various ways you can argue that one event causes another.

First Method: Explain the Causal Mechanism Directly

The most convincing kind of causal argument identifies every link in the causal chain, showing how X causes A, which causes B, which in turn causes C, which finally causes Y. In some cases, all you have to do is fill in the missing links; in other cases—when your assumptions about causality may seem questionable to your audience—you have to argue for the causal connection with more vigor.

A careful spelling out of each step in the causal chain is the technique used by astronomer Carl Sagan in "The Warming of the World" (pp. 171–175), in which he explains the greenhouse effect and predicts its consequences. His causal chain looks like this:

Starting Point A	Starting Point B
Cutting down of forests lead to fewer plants on Earth's land surface.	Burning of fossil fuels produces carbon dioxide.
Fewer plants lead to more carbon dioxide in the atmosphere.	Production of carbon dioxide leads to more carbon dioxide in the atmosphere.

LINK 2

More carbon dioxide in atmosphere reduces amount of infrared light radiated into space. (*Warrant:* Carbon dioxide absorbs infrared radiation; Sagan backs this warrant with further explanation)

LINK 3

Earth heats up. (*Warrant:* Earth stays cool by reflecting heat back into space through infrared radiation)

LINK 4

Land will become parched; seas will rise. (*Warrant:* Heat causes changes in precipitation patterns causing land to parch; also heat causes glacial ice to melt)

LINK 5

Massive global danger (*Warrant:* Parched farmland and rising seas will cause social and economic upheaval)

Sagan concludes his essay with a proposal based on this causal argument. Placed into a claim with a *because* clause, Sagan's proposal argument looks like this:

Nations should initiate worldwide efforts to find alternative energy sources because the continued burning of fossil fuels will lead to global catastrophe.

Thus, in Sagan's essay, a lengthy causal argument in the beginning supports a final proposal argument.

This causal chain method is also used by student writer Mary Lou Torpey in predicting the consequences of mandatory drug testing (pp. 175–177). Her argument shows the links of the chain, beginning with a mandatory drug-testing program and culminating in prejudice against employees with certain treatable disorders such as narcolepsy.

Second Method: Use Various Inductive Methods to Establish a High Probability of a Causal Link

Informal Induction

Although few of us are scientists, all of us practice the scientific method informally through *induction.* Induction is a form of reasoning by which we make generalizations based on a limited number of specific cases. For example, if on several occasions you got a headache after drinking red wine but not after drinking white wine, you would be apt to conclude inductively that red wine causes you to get headaches. However, because there are almost always exceptions to rules arrived at inductively and because we can't be certain that the future will always be like the past, inductive reasoning gives only probable truths, not certain ones.

When your brain thinks inductively, it sorts through data looking for patterns of similarity and difference. Toddlers are thinking inductively when they learn the connection between flipping a wall switch and watching the ceiling light come on. Like scientists, they are holding all variables constant except the position of the switch. But the inductive process does not explain the causal mechanism itself. Thus, through induction you know that red wine gives you a headache, but you don't know how the wine actually works on your nervous system—the causal chain itself.

Largely because of its power, the process of induction often can lead you to wrong conclusions. You should be aware of two common fallacies of inductive reasoning that can tempt you into erroneous assumptions about causality. (Both fallacies are treated more fully in Appendix 1.)

The *post hoc, ergo propter hoc* fallacy ("after this, therefore because of this") mistakes precedence for cause. Just because event A regularly precedes event B doesn't mean that event A causes event B. The same reasoning that tells us that flipping a switch causes the light to go on can make us believe that low levels of radioactive fallout from the Chernobyl nuclear disaster caused a sudden rise in infant death rates in the state of Washington. The nuclear disaster clearly preceded the rise in death rates. But did it clearly *cause* it? Our point is that precedence alone is no proof of causality and that we are guilty of this fallacy whenever we are swayed to believe that X causes Y primarily because X precedes Y. We can guard against this fallacy by seeking plausible link-by-link connections showing how X causes Y.

The *hasty generalization* fallacy occurs when you make a generalization based on too few cases or too little consideration of alternative explanations: You flip the switch, but the light bulb doesn't go on. You conclude—too hastily—that the power has gone off. (Perhaps the light bulb has burned out or the switch is broken.) How many trials does it take before you can make a justified generalization rather than a hasty generalization? It is difficult to say, for sure. Both the *post hoc* fallacy and the hasty generalization fallacy remind us that induction requires a leap from individual cases to a general principle and that it is always possible to leap too soon.

Scientific Experimentation

One way to avoid inductive fallacies is to examine our causal hypotheses as carefully as possible. When we deal with a recurring phenomenon such as cancer, we can create scientific experiments that give us inductive evidence of causality with a fairly high degree of certainty. If, for example, we were concerned that a particular food source such as spinach might contain cancer-causing chemicals, we could test our hypothesis experimentally. We could take two groups of rats and control their environment carefully so that the only difference between them (in theory, anyway) was that one group ate large quantities of spinach and the other group ate none. Spinach eating, then, is the one variable between the two groups that we are testing. After a specified period of time, we would check to see what percentage of rats in each group developed cancer. If twice as many spinach-eating rats contracted cancer, we could probably conclude that our hypothesis had held up.

Correlation

Still another method of induction is *correlation*, which expresses a statistical relationship between X and Y. A correlation between X and Y means that when X occurs, Y is likely to occur also, and vice versa. To put it another way, correlation establishes a possibility that an observed link between an X and a Y is a causal one rather than a mere coincidence. The existence of a correlation, however, does not tell us whether X causes Y, whether Y causes X, or whether both are caused by some third phenomenon. For example, there is a fairly strong correlation between nearsightedness and intelligence. (That is, in a given sample of nearsighted people and people with normal eyesight, a higher percentage of the nearsighted people will be highly intelligent. Similarly, in a sample of high-intelligence people and people with normal intelligence, a higher percentage of the high-intelligence group will be nearsighted.) But the direction of causality isn't clear. It could be that high intelligence causes people to read more, thus ruining their eyes (high intelligence causes nearsightedness). Or it could be that nearsightedness causes people to read more, thus raising their intelligence (nearsightedness causes high intelligence). Or it could be that some unknown phenomenon inside the brain causes both nearsightedness and high intelligence.

In recent years, correlation studies have been made stunningly sophisticated through the power of computerized analyses. For example, we could attempt to do the spinach-cancer study without resorting to a scientific experiment. If we identified a given group that ate lots of spinach (for example, vegetarians) and another group that ate little if any spinach (Inuits) and then checked to see if their rates of cancer correlated to their rates of spinach consumption, we would have the beginnings of a correlation study. But it would have no scientific validity until we factored out all the other variables between vegetarians and Inuits that might skew the findings—variables such as lifestyle, climate, genetic inheritance, differences in diet other than spinach, and so forth. Factoring out such variables is one of the complex feats that modern statistical analyses attempt to accomplish. But the fact remains that the most sophisticated correlation studies still cannot tell us the direction of causality or even for certain that there is causality.

Conclusion about Inductive Methods

Induction, then, can tell us within varying degrees of certainty whether or not X causes Y. It does not, however, explain the causal mechanism itself. Typically, the *because* clause structure of an inductive argument would take one of the following three shapes: (1) "Although we cannot explain the causal mechanism directly, we believe that X and Y are very probably causally linked because we have repeatedly observed their conjunction"; (2) " . . . because we have demonstrated the linkage through controlled scientific experiments"; or (3) " . . . because we have shown that they are statistically correlated and have provided a plausible hypothesis concerning the causal direction."

❧ FOR CLASS DISCUSSION

Working individually or in small groups, develop plausible causal chains that might explain the correlations between the following pairs of phenomena:

a. A person registers low stress level on electrochemical stress meter.   Does daily meditation.

b. A person regularly consumes frozen dinners.   Is likely to vote for improved rapid transit.

c. High achiever   Is first-born child.

d. Member of the National Rifle Association   Favors tough treatment of criminals.

Third Method: Argue by Analogy or Precedent

Another common method of causal arguing is through analogy or precedent. (See also Chapter 12, which deals in more depth with the strengths and weaknesses of this kind of arguing.) When you argue through resemblance, you try to find a case that is similar to the one you are arguing about but is better known and less controversial to the reader. If the reader agrees with your view of causality in the similar case, you then try to transfer this understanding to the case at issue. Causal arguments by analogy and precedent are logically weaker than arguments based on causal chains or on induction and will typically be used in cases where empirical evidence is weak. Here are two examples of this method in causal arguing:

1. If you wanted to argue that overcrowding in high-density apartment houses causes dangerous stress in humans, you could compare humans to mice, which develop symptoms of high stress when they are crowded together in cages. (This argument depends on the warrant that humans and mice will respond similarly to the condition of crowding.)

2. If you want to argue that doing regular thinking skills exercises will result in improved thinking ability, you could compare the mind to a muscle and the thinking skills exercises to daily weight training. (Because the audience will probably accept the causal chain of weight training leading to improved physical strength, you hope to transfer that acceptance to the field of mental activity. This argument depends on the warrant that the mind is like a muscle.)

Both arguments have a persuasive power. However, any two things that are alike in some ways (analogous) are different in others (disanalogous), and these differences are apt to be ignored in arguments from analogy. You should realize, then, that the warrant that says X is like Y is almost always vulnerable. Psychologists, for example, have pretty much demonstrated that the mind is not like a muscle, and we can all think of ways that humans are not like mice. *All* resemblance arguments, therefore, are in some sense "false analogies." But some analogies are so misleading that logicians have labeled them as fallacious—the fallacy of *false analogy.* The false analogy fallacy covers those truly blatant cases where the differences between X and Y are too great for the analogy to hold. An example might be the following: "Putting red marks all over students' papers causes great emotional distress just as putting knife marks over their palms would cause great physical distress." It is impossible to draw a precise line, however, between an analogy that has true clarifying and persuasive power and one that is fallacious.

GLOSSARY OF TERMS ENCOUNTERED IN CAUSAL ARGUMENTS

Because causal arguments are often easier to conduct if writer and reader share a few specialized terms, we offer the following glossary for your convenience.

Fallacy of Oversimplified Cause: One of the greatest temptations when establishing causal relationships is to fall into the habit of looking for *the* cause of something. Most phenomena, especially the ones we argue about, have multiple causes. For example, few presidents have won elections on the basis of one characteristic or event. Usually elections result from a combination of abilities, stances on key issues, personal characteristics, mistakes on the part of the competition, events in the world, and so forth. Similarly, scientists know that a number of different causes must work together to create a disease such as cancer. But though we know all this, we still long to make the world less complex by attributing a single cause to puzzling effects.

Immediate/Remote Causes: Every causal chain links backward indefinitely into the past. An immediate cause is the closest in time to the event being examined. If a normally passive man goes on a killing rampage, the *immediate cause* may be a brain tumor or a recent argument with his wife that was the "last straw" in a long chain of events. A number of earlier events may have led up to the present—failure to get medical attention for headaches or failure to get counseling when a marriage began to disintegrate. Such causes going further back into the past are considered *remote causes.* It's sometimes difficult to determine the relative significance of remote causes insofar as immediate causes are so obviously linked to the event whereas remote causes often have to be dug out or inferred. It's difficult to know, for example, just how seriously to take serial murderer Ted Bundy's defense that he was "traumatized" at age twelve by the discovery that he was illegitimate. How big a role are we willing to grant a causal factor so remote in time and so apparently minor in relation to the murder of thirty-five young women?

Precipitating/Contributing Causes: These terms are similar to *immediate* and *remote* causes but don't designate a temporal linking going into the past. Rather, they refer to a main cause emerging out of a background of subsidiary causes. The *contributing causes* are a set of conditions that give rise to the *precipitating cause,* which triggers the effect. If, for example, a husband and wife decide to separate, the precipitating cause may be a stormy fight over money, which itself is a symptom of their inability to communicate with each other any longer. All the factors that contribute to that inability to communicate—preoccupation with their respective careers, anxieties about money, in-law problems— may be considered contributing causes. Note that the contributing causes and precipitating cause all coexist simultaneously in time—none is temporally more remote than another. But the marriage might have continued had the contributing causes not finally resulted in frequent angry fighting, which doomed the marriage.

Constraints: Sometimes an effect occurs, not because X happened, but because another factor—a *constraint*—was removed. At other times a possible effect will not occur because a given constraint prevents it from happening. A constraint is a kind of negative cause that limits choices and possibilities. As soon as the constraint is removed, a given effect may occur. For example, in the marriage we have been discussing, the presence of children in the home might have been a constraint against divorce; as soon as the children graduate from high school and leave home, the marriage may well dissolve.

Necessary/Sufficient Causes: We speak of *necessary causes* as those that must be present when a given effect takes place. If a necessary cause is absent, the effect cannot take place. Thus the presence of a spark is a necessary cause for the operation of a gasoline engine. A *sufficient cause,* on the other hand, is one that guarantees a given effect. An electric spark is thus a necessary cause for the operation of a gasoline engine but not a sufficient cause since other causes must also be present to make the engine work (fuel, etc.). Few causes are ever both necessary and sufficient to bring about a given effect.

❧ FOR CLASS DISCUSSION

The terms in the preceding glossary can be effective brainstorming tools for thinking of possible causes of an event. For the following events, try to think of as many causes as possible by brainstorming possible *immediate causes, remote causes, precipitating causes, contributing causes,* and *constraints*:

1. Working individually, make a list of different kinds of causes/constraints for one of the following:
   a. your decision to attend your present college
   b. an important event in your life or your family (a divorce, a major move, etc.)
   c. a personal opinion you hold that is not widely shared

2. Working as a group, make a list of different kinds of causes/constraints for one of the following:
   a. why women's fashion and beauty magazines are the most frequently purchased magazines in college bookstores
   b. why the majority of teenagers don't listen to classical music
   c. why the number of babies born out of wedlock has increased dramatically in the last thirty years

ORGANIZING A CAUSAL ARGUMENT

At the outset, it is useful to know some of the standard ways that a causal argument can be organized. Later, you may decide on a different organizational pattern, but these standard ways will help you get started. .

Plan 1

When your purpose is to describe and explain all the links in a causal chain:

- Introduce phenomenon to be explained and show why it is problematical.
- Present your thesis in summary form.
- Describe and explain each link in the causal chain.

Carl Sagan's essay on the greenhouse effect (pp. 171–175) follows this format.

Plan 2

When your purpose is to explore the relative contribution of all causes to a phenomenon or to explore all possible consequences of a phenomenon:

- Introduce the phenomenon to be explained and suggest how or why it is controversial.
- Devote one section to each possible cause/consequence and decide whether it is necessary, sufficient, contributory, remote, and so forth. (Arrange sections so that those causes most familiar to the audience come first and the most surprising ones come last.)

Plan 3

When your purpose is to argue for a cause or consequence that is surprising or unexpected to your audience:

- Introduce a phenomenon to be explained and show why it is controversial.
- One by one, examine and reject the causes or consequences your audience would normally assume or expect.
- Introduce your unexpected or surprising cause or consequence and argue for it.

Plans 2 and 3 are similar in that they examine numerous possible causes or consequences. Plan 2, however, tries to establish the relative importance of each cause or consequence, whereas plan 3 aims at rejecting the causes or consequences normally assumed by the audience and argues for an unexpected surprising cause or consequence. Plan 3 is the strategy used by Mary Lou Torpey (pp. 175–177) in arguing for an unexpected consequence of drug testing.

Plan 4

When your purpose is to change your audience's mind about a cause or consequence:

- Introduce the issue and show why it is controversial.
- Summarize your opponent's causal argument and then refute it.
- Present your own causal argument.

Plan 4 is a standard structure for all kinds of arguments. This is the structure you would use if you were the attorney for the person whose car skidded into the boutique (p. 159). The opposing attorney would blame your client's reckless driving. You would lay blame on a poorly signed intersection, a speeding beer truck, and violation of building codes.

CONDITIONS FOR REBUTTAL: TESTING A CAUSAL ARGUMENT

Because of the strenuous conditions that must be met before causality can be proven, causal arguments are vulnerable at many points. The following strategies will generally be helpful.

If you described every link in a causal chain, would skeptics point out weaknesses in any of the links? Describing a causal chain can be a complex business. A skeptic can raise doubts about an entire argument simply by undercutting one of the links. Your best defense is to make a diagram of the linkages and role play a skeptic trying to refute each link in turn. Whenever you find possible arguments against your position, see how you can strengthen your own argument at that point.

If your argument is based on a scientific experiment, could skeptics question the validity of the experiment? The scientific method attempts to demonstrate causality experimentally. If the experiment isn't well designed, however, the demonstration is less likely to be acceptable to skeptical audiences. Here are ways to critique a scientific argument:

- *Question the findings.* Skeptics may have reason to believe that the data collected were not accurate or representative. They might provide alternative data or simply point out flaws in the way the data were collected.

- *Question the interpretation of the data.* Many research studies are divided into a "findings" and a "discussion" section. In the discussion section the researcher analyzes and interprets the data. A skeptic might provide an alternative interpretation of the data or otherwise argue that the data don't support what the original writer claims.

- *Question the design of the experiment.* A detailed explanation of research design is beyond the scope of this text, but we can give a brief example of how a typical experiment did go wrong. Graduate students recently completed an experiment to test the effect of word processors on students' writing in junior high school. They reported that students who used the word processors for revising all their essays did significantly better on a final essay than a control group of students who didn't use word processors.

It turned out, however, that there were at least two major design flaws in the experiment. First, the researchers allowed students to volunteer for the experimental group. Perhaps these students were already better writers than the control group from the start. (Can you think of a causal explanation of why the better students might volunteer to use the computers?) Second, when the teachers graded essays from both the computer group and the control group, the essays were not retyped uniformly. Thus the computer group's essays were typed with "computer perfection," whereas the control group's essays were handwritten or typed on ordinary typewriters. Perhaps the readers were affected by the pleasing appearance of the computer-typed essays. More significantly, perhaps the graders were biased in favor of the computer project and unconsciously scored the computer-typed papers higher.

This example illustrates just a few of the ways a scientific study can be flawed. Our point is that skeptics might not automatically accept your citation of a scientific study as a proof of causality. By considering opposing views in advance, you may be able to strengthen your argument.

If you have used correlation data, could skeptics argue that the correlation is much weaker than you claim or that you haven't sufficiently demonstrated causality? As we discussed earlier, correlation data tell us only that two or more phenomena are likely to occur together. They don't tell us that one caused the other. Thus, correlation arguments are usually accompanied by hypotheses about causal connections between the phenomena. Correlation arguments can often be refuted as follows:

- Find problems in the statistical methods used to determine the correlation.
- Weaken the correlation by pointing out exceptions.
- Provide an alternative hypothesis about causality.

If you have used an analogy argument, could skeptics point out disanalogies? Although among the most persuasive of argumentative strategies, analogy arguments are also among the easiest to refute. The standard procedure is to counter your argument that X is like Y by pointing out all the ways that X is *not* like Y. Once again, by role playing an opposing view you may be able to strengthen your own analogy argument.

Could a skeptic cast doubt on your argument by reordering your priority of causes? Up to this point we've focused on refuting the claim that X causes Y. However, another approach is to concede that X helps cause Y but that X is only one of several contributing causes and not the most significant one at that.

The Warming of the World
Carl Sagan

When humans first evolved—in the savannahs of East Africa a few million years ago—   1
our numbers were few and our powers feeble. We knew almost nothing about controlling our environment—even clothing had yet to be invented. We were creatures of the climate, utterly dependent upon it.

A few degrees hotter or colder on average, and our ancestors were in trouble. The toll   2
taken much later by the ice ages, in which average land temperatures dropped some 8° C (centigrade, or Celsius), must have been horrific. And yet, it is exactly such climatic change

that pushed our ancestors to develop tools and technology, science and civilization. Certainly, skills in hunting, skinning, tanning, building shelters and refurbishing caves must owe much to the terrors of the deep ice age.

3   Today, we live in a balmy epoch, 10,000 years after the last major glaciation. In this climatic spring, our species has flourished; we now cover the entire planet and are altering the very appearance of our world. Lately—within the last century or so—humans have acquired, in more ways than one, the ability to make major changes in that climate upon which we are so dependent. The Nuclear Winter findings are one dramatic indication that we can change the climate—in this case, in the spasm of nuclear war. But I wish here to describe a different kind of climatic danger, this one slower, more subtle and arising from intentions that are wholly benign.

4   It is warm down here on Earth because the Sun shines. If the Sun were somehow turned off, the Earth would rapidly cool. The oceans would freeze, and eventually the atmosphere itself would condense out and our planet would be covered everywhere by snowbanks of solid oxygen and nitrogen 10 meters (about 30 feet) high. Only the tiny trickle of heat from the Earth's interior and the faint starlight would save our world from a temperature of absolute zero.

5   We know how bright the Sun is; we know how far from it we are; and we know what fraction of the sunlight reaching the Earth is reflected back to space (about 30 percent). So we can calculate—with a simple mathematical equation—what the average temperature of the Earth should be. But when we do the calculation, we find that the Earth's temperature should be about 20° C below the freezing point of water, in stark contradiction to our everyday experience. What have we done wrong?

6   As in many such cases in science, what we've done wrong is to forget something—in this case, the atmosphere. Every object in the universe radiates some kind of light to space; the colder the object, the longer the wavelength of radiation it emits. The Earth—much colder than the Sun—radiates to space mainly in the infrared part of the spectrum, not the visible. Were the Sun turned off, the Earth would soon be indetectable in ordinary visible light, though it would be brilliantly illuminated in infrared light.

7   When sunlight strikes the Earth, part is reflected back into the sky; much of the rest is absorbed by the ground and heats it—the darker the ground, the greater the heating. The ground radiates back upward in the infrared. Thus, for an airless Earth, the temperature would be set solely by a balance between the incoming sunlight absorbed by the surface and the infrared radiation that the surface emits back to space.

8   When you put air on a planet, the situation changes. The Earth's atmosphere is, generally, still transparent to visible light. That's why we can see each other when we talk, glimpse distant mountains and view the stars.

9   But in the infrared, all that is different. While the oxygen and nitrogen in the air are transparent in both the infrared and the visible, minor constituents such as water vapor (H_2O) and carbon dioxide (CO_2) tend to be much more opaque in the infrared. It would be useless for us to have eyes that could see at a wavelength, say, of 15 microns in the infrared, because the air is murky black there.

10   Accordingly, if you add air to a world, you heat it: The surface now has difficulty when it tries to radiate back to space in the infrared. The atmosphere tends to absorb the infrared

radiation, keeping heat near the surface and providing an infrared blanket for the world. There is very little CO_2 in the Earth's atmosphere—only 0.03 percent. But that small amount is enough to make the Earth's atmosphere opaque in important regions of the infrared spectrum. CO_2 and H_2O are the reason the global temperature is not well below freezing. We owe our comfort—indeed, our very existence—to the fact that these gases are present and are much more transparent in the visible than in the infrared. Our lives depend on a delicate balance of invisible gases. Too much blanket, or too little, and we're in trouble.

This property of many gases to absorb strongly in the infrared but not in the visible, and thereby to heat their surroundings, is called the "greenhouse effect." A florist's greenhouse keeps its planty inhabitants warm. The phrase "greenhouse effect" is widely used and has an instructive ring to it, reminding us that we live in a planetary-scale greenhouse and recalling the admonition about living in glass houses and throwing stones. But, in fact, florists' greenhouses do not keep warm by the greenhouse effect; they work mainly by inhibiting the movement of air inside, another matter altogether. 11

We need look only as far as the nearest planet to see an example of an atmospheric greenhouse effect gone wild. Venus has in its atmosphere an enormous quantity of carbon dioxide (roughly as much as is buried as carbonates in all the rocks of the Earth's crust). There is an atmosphere of CO_2 on Venus 90 times thicker than the atmosphere on the Earth and containing some 200,000 times more CO_2 than in our air. With water vapor and other minor atmospheric constituents, this is enough to make a greenhouse effect that keeps the surface of Venus around 470° C (900° F)—enough to melt tin or lead. 12

When humans burn wood or "fossil fuels" (coal, oil, natural gas, etc.), they put carbon dioxide into the air. One carbon atom (C) combines with a molecule of oxygen (O_2) to produce CO_2. The development of agriculture, the conversion of dense forest to comparatively sparsely vegetated farms, has moved carbon atoms from plants on the ground to carbon dioxide in the air. About half of this new CO_2 is removed by plants or by the layering down of carbonates in the oceans. On human time-scales, these changes are irreversible: Once the CO_2 is in the atmosphere, human technology is helpless to remove it. So the overall amount of CO_2 in the air has been growing—at least since the industrial revolution. If no other factors operate, and if enough CO_2 is put into the atmosphere, eventually the average surface temperature will increase perceptibly. 13

There are other greenhouse gases that are increasingly abundant in the Earth's atmosphere—halocarbons, such as the freon used in refrigerator cooling systems; or nitrous oxide (N_2O), produced by automobile exhausts and nitrogenous fertilizers; or methane (CH_4), produced partly in the intestines of cows and other ruminants. 14

But let's for the moment concentrate on carbon dioxide: How long, at the present rates of burning wood and fossil fuels, before the global climate becomes significantly warmer? And what would the consequences be? 15

It is relatively simple to calculate the immediate warming from a given increase in the CO_2 abundance, and all competent calculations seem to be in good agreement. More difficult to estimate are (1) the rate at which carbon dioxide will continue to be put into the atmosphere (it depends on population growth rates, economic styles, alternative energy sources and the like) and (2) feedbacks—ways in which a slight warming might produce other, more drastic, effects. 16

17   The recent increase in atmospheric CO_2 is well documented. Over the last century, this CO_2 buildup should have resulted in a few tenths of a degree of global warming, and there is some evidence that such a warming has occurred.

18   The National Academy of Sciences estimates that the present atmospheric abundance of CO_2 is likely to double by the year 2065, although experts at the academy predict a one-in-20 chance that it will double before 2035—when an infant born today becomes 50 years old. Such a doubling would warm the air near the surface of the Earth by 2° C or 3° C—maybe by as much as 4° C. These are average temperature values; there would naturally be considerable local variation. High latitudes would be warmed much more, although a baked Alaska will be some time coming.

19   There would be precipitation changes. The annual discharge of rivers would be altered. Some scientists believe that central North America—including much of the area that is now the breadbasket of the world—would be parched in summer if the global temperature increases by a few degrees. There would be some mitigating effects; for example, where plant growth is not otherwise limited, more CO_2 should aid photosynthesis and make more luxuriant growth (of weeds as well as crops). If the present CO_2 injection into the atmosphere continued over a few centuries, the warming would be greater than from all other causes over the last 100,000 years.

20   As the climate warms, glacial ice melts. Over the last 100 years, the level of the world's oceans has risen by 15 centimeters (6 inches). A global warming of 3° C or 4° C over the next century is likely to bring a further rise in the average sea level of about 70 centimeters (28 inches). An increase of this magnitude could produce major damage to ports all over the world and induce fundamental change in the patterns of land development. A serious speculation is that greenhouse temperature increases of 3° C or 4° C could, in addition, trigger the disintegration of the West Antarctic Ice Sheet, with huge quantities of polar ice falling into the ocean. This would raise sea level by some 6 meters (20 feet) over a period of centuries, with the eventual inundation of all coastal cities on the planet.

21   There are many other possibilities that are poorly understood, including the release of other greenhouse gases (for example, methane from peat bogs) accelerated by the warming climate. The circulation of the oceans might be an important aspect of the problem. The scientific community is attempting to make an environmental-impact statement for the entire planet on the consequences of continued burning of fossil fuels. Despite the uncertainties, a kind of consensus is in: Over the next century or more, with projected rates of burning coal, oil and gas, there is trouble ahead.

22   The problem is difficult for at least three different reasons:
    (1) We do not yet fully understand how severe the greenhouse consequences will be.
    (2) Although the effects are not yet strikingly noticeable in everyday life, to deal with the problem, the present generation might have to make sacrifices for the next.
    (3) The problem cannot be solved except on an international scale: The atmosphere is ignorant of national boundaries. South African carbon dioxide warms Taiwan, and Soviet coal-burning practices effect productivity in America. The largest coal resources in the world are found in the Soviet Union, the United States and China, in that order. What incentives are there for a nation such as China, with vast coal reserves and a commitment to rapid economic development, to hold back on the burning of fossil fuels because the result

might, decades later, be a parched American sunbelt or still more ghastly starvation in sub-Saharan Africa? Would countries that might benefit from a warmer climate be as vigorous in restraining the burning of fossil fuels as nations likely to suffer greatly?

Fortunately, we have a little time. A great deal can be done in decades. Some argue 23 that government subsidies lower the price of fossil fuels, inviting waste; more efficient usage, besides its economic advantage, could greatly ameliorate the CO_2 greenhouse problem. Parts of the solution might involve alternative energy sources, where appropriate: solar power, for example, or safer nuclear fission reactors, which, whatever their other dangers, produce no greenhouse gases of importance. Conceivably, the long-awaited advent of commercial nuclear fusion power might happen before the middle of the next century.

However, any technological solution to the looming greenhouse problem must be 24 worldwide. It would not be sufficient for the United States or the Soviet Union, say, to develop safe and commercially feasible fusion power plants: That technology would have to be diffused worldwide, on terms of cost and reliability that would be more attractive to developing nations than a reliance on fossil fuel reserves or imports. A serious, very high-level look at patterns of U.S. and world energy development in light of the greenhouse problem seems overdue.

During the last few million years, human technology, spurred in part by climatic 25 change, has made our species a force to be reckoned with on a planetary scale. We now find, to our astonishment, that we pose a danger to ourselves. The present world order is, unfortunately, not designed to deal with global-scale dangers. Nations tend to be concerned about themselves, not about the planet; they tend to have short-term rather than long-term objectives. In problems such as the increasing greenhouse effect, one nation or region might benefit while another suffers. In other global environmental issues, such as nuclear war, all nations lose. The problems are connected: Constructive international efforts to understand and resolve one will benefit the others.

Further study and better public understanding are needed, of course. But what is essential is a global consciousness—a view that transcends our exclusive identification with the generational and political groupings into which, by accident, we have been born. The solution to these problems requires a perspective that embraces the planet and the future. We are all in this greenhouse together.

The following essay by student writer Mary Lou Torpey was written in response to the assignment on page 177.

What Drugs I Take Is None of Your Business— The Consequences of Drug Testing

Mary Lou Torpey (student)

So you have a job interview with a new company tomorrow? Well my advice is to go 1 home, get some rest, and drink plenty of fluids, because chances are you'll have to leave more than just a good impression with your prospective employer. You may have to leave a full specimen bottle to check you out for drug use, too. Imagine having to stand in a line in your business suit with your application in one hand and a steaming cup of urine in the other, waiting to turn each of them in, wondering which one is really more important in the job selection process. Some companies and every branch of the Armed Forces require a witness present during the test so the person being tested doesn't try to switch specimens with someone who is drug or alcohol free. As one can imagine, having to be witnessed during a drug test could give a whole new meaning to the term "stage fright." The embarrassing situation of being drug tested is a real possibility, since mandatory drug testing is becoming more and more prevalent in today's workplaces.

2   Despite the embarrassment, many employers, including western Washington's largest, Boeing, believe the consequences of mandatory drug testing would be beneficial. By trying to ensure safe work environments by cutting down on drug abusers who could create potential hazards for other employees, such companies believe that quality in workmanship will improve. They also believe that their employees will operate at peak performance levels to keep productivity up. However, there is a consequence of mandatory drug testing that is not being considered by the employers who have instituted it, a consequence that will be devastating for hundreds of thousands of people.

3   Perhaps the most potentially damaging result of mandatory drug testing lies with people who have legitimate uses for controlled substance drugs—people like me. I have narcolepsy, a serious lifelong disorder that causes crippling sleepiness without the help of controlled substance drugs, similar to the way a mobility impaired person would be crippled without crutches, a walker, or a wheelchair. In other words, I, as a narcoleptic, must have a controlled substance drug to maintain any sort of normal lifestyle at all. Without amphetamines, I could not drive a car, go to college, read, or even hold a decent conversation without falling asleep.

4   The damaging consequence of mandatory drug testing here is that if I, or others with a myriad of other chronic disorders requiring the use of controlled substance drugs, such as epilepsy, depression due to chemical imbalance, or a number of other seizure disorders, were seeking employment where a drug test is administered, we would be forced to divulge information about the illness. It should be every person's choice whether or not they will inform their employer, especially if their medications manage their illness adequately.

5   Having to inform a prospective employer about an illness would open the way for prejudice. In all honesty, why would an employer hire a "sick" person when there are so many "normal" ones on the job market? This prejudice is ironic since people like me with narcolepsy or other "silent disabilities" try so hard to compensate that they make exemplary employees. The way I think of it is like that commercial for "Scrubbing Bubbles." That's the commercial where the little bubbles go down the bathtub drain after making it sparkling clean, shouting "we work hard so you don't have to." When it comes to my job, I work hard so my employer doesn't have to think about making special exceptions for me.

6   In the case of a random test for employees already with a company, those individuals would be forced to explain why a controlled substance is coming up on their test results. When this happens to an employee who has not previously told his employer about an illness or medication he must take, that employee runs the strong chance of being terminated

or prejudiced against in the promotion process. After all, what would make an employer believe an employee's explanation about a necessary drug if the employer already showed so little trust as to administer a test at all?

In addition, the emphasis in drug testing for the abuse of drugs such as Ritalin® and   7
Dexedrine® is making them increasingly difficult to purchase in pharmacies. Quotas are now being put on their production, and some states are working on banning them or making them more and more difficult to get. For example, many times I have taken a prescription to be filled into a pharmacy only to find that they had run out of their allotment and would not have any for a few days. A few days is like a lifetime for most narcoleptics without medication, some of whom can be virtually housebound without it. Imagine, in the hysteria over these drugs caused by being targeted in mandatory drug testing, what would happen if a few days turned into weeks or maybe even a month?

There is no denying the need for programs to address drug and alcohol abuse. The ben-   8
eficial causes the employers are seeking are reasonable in themselves, but just won't happen through mandatory drug testing. Instead, why can't employers take a positive approach to dealing with substance abuse within the workplace? Employers could set up counseling programs and encourage people with problems to step forward and get help. Employers who show trust and respect for their employees will get trust and respect in return. A positive, caring approach would be better for everyone, considering the far-reaching negative consequences of mandatory drug testing. After all, one should never forget that disorders requiring the use of controlled substance drugs have no prejudice. They can strike anyone at anytime. Believe me, I know.

❧ WRITING ASSIGNMENT FOR CHAPTER 11

An Argument Involving Surprising or Disputed Causes: Choose an issue question about the causes (or consequences) of a trend, event, or other phenomenon. Write an argument that persuades an audience to accept your explanation of the causes (or consequences) of your chosen phenomenon. Within your essay you should examine alternative hypotheses or opposing views and explain your reasons for rejecting them.

You can imagine your issue either as a puzzle or as a disagreement. If a puzzle, your task will be informational as well as persuasive because your role will be that of an analyst explaining causes or consequences of an event to an audience that doesn't have an answer already in mind. If you see your issue as a disagreement, your task will be more directly persuasive since your goal will be to change your audience's views so as to align more closely with your own

chapter 12

Resemblance Arguments
X Is/Is Not Like Y

EXAMPLE CASE

In May 1987, a controversy arose between Israeli and West German historians over the reinterpretation of the Holocaust, the Nazi attempt to destroy the Jews. According to one West German historian, the Nazi annihilation of the Jews was comparable to Stalin's massacre of the Russian peasants and Pol Pot's murder of his opponents in Cambodia. The effect of this comparison, in the eyes of many Israeli historians, was to diminish the horror of the Holocaust by denying its uniqueness. Israeli historian Shaul Friedlander responded that while the scale and criminality of the murders might be compared, "there is no other example to my knowledge of a government deciding that an entire race of millions of people spread all over a continent is to be brought together by all means at the disposal of the state and eliminated."*

OVERVIEW OF RESEMBLANCE ARGUMENTS

Resemblance arguments use analogies or precedents to support a claim. Although sometimes an entire argument makes a resemblance claim, more often writers use resemblance in the service of other claims. Thus lawyer Charles

---

*From Karen Winkler, "German Scholars Sharply Divided over Place of Holocaust in History," *Chronicle of Higher Education* 27 May 1987: 4–5

178

Rembar, in attacking the American Civil Liberties Union (ACLU) for its opposition to mandatory reporting of AIDS cases, compared the ACLU's desire to protect the privacy of individuals to out-of-date war tactics:

> [The ACLU] clings to once useful concepts that are inappropriate to current problems. Like the French military, which prepared for World War II by building the Maginot Line, which was nicely adapted to the trench warfare of World War I, the ACLU sometimes hauls up legal arguments effective to old libertarian battles but irrelevant to those at hand.*

The strategy of resemblance arguments is to take the audience's attitude toward the claim made in the analogy (it is inappropriate to fight World War II with the out-of-date strategies of World War I) and transfer it to the issue being debated (it is inappropriate to fight the battle against AIDS with an out-of-date libertarian philosophy).

As we will explain in this chapter, resemblance arguments have enormous persuasive power because they can clarify an audience's conception of contested issues while conveying powerful emotions. Resemblance arguments typically take the form X is (is not) like Y. Resemblance arguments work best when the audience has a clear (and sometimes emotionally charged) understanding of the Y term. The writer then hopes to transfer this understanding, along with accompanying emotions, to the X term. The danger of resemblance arguments, as we shall see, is that the differences between the X and Y terms are often so significant that the resemblance argument collapses under close examination.

Like most other argument types, resemblance arguments can be analyzed using the Toulmin schema. Suppose, for example, that you wanted to write an argument favoring a balanced federal budget. In one section of your argument you might develop the following claim of resemblance: "Just as a family will go bankrupt if it continually spends more than it makes, so the federal government will go bankrupt if its expenses exceed its revenues." This claim depends on the resemblance between the fiscal problems of the federal government and the fiscal problems of a private family. The argument can be displayed in Toulmin terms as follows:

ENTHYMEME:	If the Fed doesn't balance its budget, it will go bankrupt because the Fed is like a family that goes bankrupt when it fails to balance its budget.
CLAIM:	If the Fed doesn't balance its debt, it will go bankrupt.
STATED REASON:	because the fed is like a family that goes bankrupt when it fails to balance its budget

---

*Charles Rembar. *New York Times* 15 May 1987: I, 31:2

GROUNDS:	evidence that the Fed is like a family; evidence showing that families that overspend their budgets go bankrupt
WARRANT:	The economic laws that apply to families apply also to governments.
BACKING:	evidence that when governments and families behave in economically similar ways, they suffer similar consequences
CONDITIONS OF REBUTTAL:	all cases in which governments and families behaved in similar ways and did not suffer similar consequences; all the ways that families and governments differ
QUALIFIER:	The claim is supported by the analogy only to the extent that family and government economics resemble each other.

For many audiences, this comparison of the government to a family might be persuasive: It uses an area of experience familiar to almost everyone (the problem of balancing the family budget) to help make sense of a more complex area of experience (the problem of balancing the federal budget). At its root is the warrant that what works for the family will work for the Fed.

But this example also illustrates the dangers of resemblance arguments, which often ignore important differences or *disanalogies* between the terms of comparison. One can think, for instance, of many differences between the economics of a family and that of the federal government. For example, unlike a private family, the federal government prints its own money and does most of its borrowing from its own members. Perhaps these differences negate the claim that family debt and federal debt are similar in their effects. Thus, an argument based on resemblance is usually open to refutation if a skeptic points out important disanalogies.

We turn now to the two types of resemblance arguments: analogy and precedent.

ARGUMENTS BY ANALOGY

The use of *analogies* can constitute the most imaginative form of argument. If you don't like your new boss, you can say that she's like a marine drill sergeant, a drowning swimmer, a mother hen, or a poster child for dysfunctional authorities. Each of these analogies suggests a different management style, clarifying the nature of your dislike while conveying an emotional charge. The ubiquity of analogies undoubtedly stems from their power to clarify the writer's understanding of an issue through comparisons that grip the audience.

Of course, this power to make things clear comes at a price. Analogies often clarify one aspect of a relationship at the expense of other aspects. Thus, for example, in nineteenth-century America many commentators were fond of justifying certain negative effects of capitalism (for example, the squalor of the poor) by comparing social and economic processes to Darwinian evolution—the survival of the fittest. In particular, they fastened on one aspect of evolution, competition, and spoke darkly of life as a cutthroat struggle for survival. Clearly the analogy clarified one aspect of human interaction: People and institutions do indeed compete for limited resources, markets, and territory. Moreover, the consequences of failure are often dire (the weak get eaten by the strong).

But competition is only one aspect of evolution—albeit a particularly dramatic one. The ability to dominate an environment is less important to long-term survival of a species than the ability to adapt to that environment. Thus, the mighty dinosaur disappeared while the lowly cockroach continues to flourish because of the latter's uncanny ability to adjust to circumstance.

The use of the evolutionary analogies to stress the competitive nature of human existence fit the world view (and served the interests) of those who were most fond of invoking them, in particular the so-called robber barons and conservative social Darwinists. But in overlooking other dimensions of evolution, especially the importance of adaptation and cooperation to survival, the analogy created a great deal of mischief.

So analogies have the power to get an audience's attention like virtually no other persuasive strategy. But seldom are they sufficient in themselves to provide full understanding. At some point with every analogy you need to ask yourself, "How far can I legitimately go with this? At what point are the similarities between the two things I am comparing going to be overwhelmed by their dissimilarities?" They are useful attention-getting devices; used carefully and cautiously, they can be extended to shape an audience's understanding of a complex situation. But they can conceal and distort as well as clarify.

With this caveat, let's look at the uses of both undeveloped and extended analogies.

Using Undeveloped Analogies

Typically, writers will use short, *undeveloped analogies* to drive home a point (and evoke an accompanying emotion) and then quickly abandon the analogy before the reader's awareness of disanalogies begins to set in. Thus one writer, arguing against the complexities of recent tax legislation, showed his disgust by drawing an analogy between tax laws and rotting plants or festering wounds.

> It does not take a deep or broadly informed analysis to sense the reek of economic decay and social fester that such irresponsible legislation cultivates.*

---

*From C. Thomas Higgins. "New Tax Law Is a Roll of the Dice." *Seattle Times,* 21 Sept. 1986: A21.

Later this writer went on to compare recent tax legislation to an infection by a new virus. Through his use of the analogy, the writer hoped to transfer to the new tax law the audience's already existing revulsion to disease-producing virus.

Using Extended Analogies

Sometimes writers elaborate an analogy so that it takes on a major role in the argument. As an example of a claim based on an extended analogy, consider the following excerpt from a professor's argument opposing a proposal to require a writing proficiency exam for graduation. In the following portion of his argument, the professor compares development of writing skills to the development of physical fitness.

> A writing proficiency exam gives the wrong symbolic messages about writing. It suggests that writing is simply a skill, rather than an active way of thinking and learning. It suggests that once a student demonstrates proficiency then he or she doesn't need to do any more writing.
>
> Imagine two universities concerned with the physical fitness of their students. One university requires a junior-level physical fitness exam in which students must run a mile in less than 10 minutes, a fitness level it considers minimally competent. Students at this university see the physical fitness exam as a one-time hurdle. As many as 70 percent of them can pass the exam with no practice; another 10–20 percent need a few months' training; and a few hopeless couch potatoes must go through exhaustive remediation. After passing the exam, any student can settle back into a routine of TV and potato chips having been certified as "physically fit."
>
> The second university, however, believing in true physical fitness for its students, is not interested in minimal competency. Consequently, it creates programs in which its students exercise 30 minutes every day for the entire four years of the undergraduate curriculum. There is little doubt which university will have the most physically fit students. At the second university, fitness becomes a way of life with everyone developing his or her full potential.

If you choose to write an extended analogy such as this, you will focus on the points of comparison that serve your purposes. The writer's purpose in the preceding case is to support the achievement of mastery rather than minimalist standards as the goal of the university's writing program. Whatever other disanalogous elements are involved (for example, writing requires the use of intellect, which may or may not be strengthened by repetition), the comparison reveals vividly that a commitment to mastery involves more than a minimalist test. The analogy serves primarily to underscore this one crucial point. In reviewing the different groups of students as they "prepare" for the fitness exam, the author makes clear just how irrelevant such an exam is to the whole question of mastery.

Typically, then, in developing your analogy you are not developing all possible points of comparison so much as you are bringing out those similarities consistent with the point you are trying to make.

❧ FOR CLASS DISCUSSION ▬▬▬▬▬▬▬▬▬▬▬▬▬▬▬▬▬▬▬▬▬▬

The following is a two-part exercise to help you clarify for yourself how analogies function in the context of arguments. Part 1 is to be done outside class; part 2 is to be done in class. This exercise is an excellent "Starting Point" task for the Option 1 writing assignment for this chapter.

PART 1 Think of an analogy that accurately expresses your feeling toward each of the following topics. Then write your analogy in the following one-sentence format:

> X is like Y: A, B, C . . . (where X is the main topic being discussed; Y is the analogy; and A, B, and C are the points of comparison).

EXAMPLES:

Cramming for an exam to get better grades is like pumping iron for 10 hours straight to prepare for a weightlifting contest: exhausting and counterproductive.

A right-to-lifer bombing an abortion clinic is like a vegetarian bombing a cattle barn: futile and contradictory.

a. Spanking a child to teach obedience is like . . .
b. Building low-cost housing for poor people is like . . .
c. The use of steroids by college athletes is like . . .
d. Mandatory AIDS testing for all U.S. residents is like . . .
e. A legislative proposal to eliminate all federally subsidized student loans is like . . .
f. The effect of American fast food on our health is like . . .
g. The personal gain realized by people who have committed questionable or even illegal acts and then made money by selling book and movie rights is like . . .

In each case, begin by asking yourself how you feel about the subject. If you have negative feelings about a topic, then begin by calling up negative pictures that express those feelings (or if you have positive feelings, call up positive comparisons). As they emerge, test each one to see if it will work as an analogy. An effective analogy will convey both the feeling you have toward your topic and your understanding of the topic. For instance, the writer in the "cramming for an exam" example obviously believes that pumping iron for 10 hours before a weightlifting match is stupid. This feeling of stupidity is then transferred to the original topic—cramming for an exam. But the analogy also clarifies understanding. The writer imagines the mind as a muscle (which gets exhausted after too much exercise and which is better developed through some exercise every day rather than a lot all at once) rather than as a large container (into which lots of stuff can be "crammed").

PART 2   Now, bring your analogies to class and compare them to those of your classmates. Select the best analogies for each of the topics and be ready to say why you think they are good. If you choose, you can then use your analogy as the basis for an extended analogy for this chapter's writing assignment.

ARGUMENTS BY PRECEDENT

Precedent arguments are like analogy arguments in that they make comparisons between an X and a Y. In precedent arguments, however, the Y term is always a past event, usually an event where some sort of decision was reached, often a moral, legal, or political decision. An argument by precedent tries to show that a similar decision should or should not be reached for the present issue X because the situation of X is or is not like the situation of Y.

A good example of a precedent argument is the following excerpt from a speech by President Lyndon Johnson in the early years of the Vietnam War:

> Nor would surrender in Vietnam bring peace because we learned from Hitler at Munich that success only feeds the appetite of aggression. The battle would be renewed in one country and then another country, bringing with it perhaps even larger and crueler conflict, as we have learned from the lessons of history.*

Here the audience knows what happened at Munich: France and Britain tried to appease Hitler by yielding to his demand for a large part of Czechoslovakia, but Hitler's armies continued their aggression anyway, using Czechoslovakia as a staging area to invade Poland. By arguing that surrender in Vietnam would lead to the same consequences, Johnson brings to his argument about Vietnam the whole weight of his audience's unhappy knowledge of World War II. Administration white papers developed Johnson's precedent argument by pointing toward the similarity of Hitler's promises with those of the Viet Cong: You give us this and we will ask for no more. But Hitler didn't keep his promise. Why should the Viet Cong?

---

*From *Public Papers of the Presidents of the United States*, vol. 2: *Lyndon B. Johnson* (Washington, DC: U.S. Government Printing Office, 1965) 794.

FOR CLASS DISCUSSION

1. Consider the following claims of precedent and evaluate just how effective you think each precedent might be in establishing the claim:
   a. Don't vote for Governor Frick for president because governors have not proven to be effective presidents.
   b. Gays should be allowed to serve openly in the U.S. military because they are allowed to serve openly in most other Western countries.
   c. The United States should avoid military involvement in the former Yugoslavia because it will end up in another mess like Vietnam.

2. Recently, voters in the state of Montana considered an initiative to abolish property taxes. Supporters of the initiative responded to predictions that it would have disastrous consequences for public service in the state by saying, "Similar dire predictions were made in Massachusetts and California when they passed initiatives to lower property taxes and none of these predictions came to pass, so you can ignore these nay-sayers."

You have been hired by a lobbying group who opposes the initiative. Your task is to do the background research that your group needs in order to refute the above precedent argument. Working in small groups, make a list of research questions you would want to ask.

CONDITIONS FOR REBUTTAL: TESTING A RESEMBLANCE ARGUMENT

Once you've written a draft of your resemblance argument, you need to test that argument by attempting to refute it. What follows are some typical questions audiences will raise about arguments of resemblance.

Will a skeptic say I am trying to prove too much with my analogy or precedent?   The most common mistake people make with resemblance arguments is to ask them to prove more than they're capable of proving. Too often, an analogy is treated as if it were a syllogism or algebraic ratio wherein necessary truths are deduced (*a* is to *b* as *c* is to *d*) rather than as a useful, but basically playful, figure that suggests uncertain but significant insight. The best way to guard against this charge is to qualify your argument and to find other means of persuasion to supplement an analogy or precedent argument.

For a good example of an analogy that tries to do too much, consider former President Reagan's attempt to prevent the United States from imposing economic sanctions on South Africa. Reagan wanted to argue that harming South Africa's economy would do as much damage to blacks as to whites. In making this argument, he compared South Africa to a zebra and concluded that one couldn't hurt the white portions of the zebra without also hurting the black.

Now, the zebra analogy might work quite well to point up the interrelatedness of whites and blacks in South Africa. But it has no force whatsoever in supporting Reagan's assertion that economic sanctions would hurt blacks as well as whites. To refute this analogy, one need only point out the disanalogies between the zebra stripes and racial groups. (There are, for example, no differences in income, education, and employment between black and white stripes on a zebra.)

Will a skeptic point out disanalogies in my resemblance argument?   Although it is easy to show that a country is not like a zebra, finding disanalogies is sometimes quite tricky. Often displaying the argument in Toulmin terms will help. Here is the Toulmin schema for former President Johnson's "Munich analogy" for supporting the war in Vietnam:

ENTHYMEME:	The United States should not withdraw its troops from Vietnam because doing so will have the same disastrous consequences as did giving in to Hitler prior to World War II.
CLAIM:	The United States should not withdraw its troops from Vietnam.
STATED REASON:	because doing so will have the same disastrous consequences as did giving in to Hitler before World War II
GROUNDS:	evidence that withdrawal of military support backfired in Europe in 1939
WARRANT:	The situation in Europe in 1939 closely parallels the situation in Southeast Asia in 1965.
BACKING:	evidence of similarities (for example, in political philosophy, goals, and military strength of the enemy; the nature of the conflict between the disputants; and the American commitment to its allies) between the two situations
CONDITIONS OF REBUTTAL:	acknowledged differences between the two situations that might make the outcome of the present situation different from the outcome of the first situation

Laid out like this, some of the problems with the analogy are quickly evident. One has to make a considerable leap to go from undeniably true, historically verifiable grounds to a highly problematic claim. This means that the warrant will have to be particularly strong to license the movement. And although there are undeniable similarities between the two events (as there will be between any two sufficiently complex events), the differences are overwhelming. Thus, during the Vietnam era, critic Howard Zinn attacked the warrant of Johnson's analogy by claiming three crucial differences between Europe in 1938 and Vietnam in 1967.

First, Zinn argued, the Czechs were being attacked from without by an external aggressor (Germany), whereas Vietnam was being attacked from within by rebels as part of a civil war; second, Czechoslovakia was a prosperous, effective democracy, whereas the official Vietnam government was corrupt and unpopular; finally, Hitler wanted Czechoslovakia as a base for attacking Poland, whereas the Viet Cong and North Vietnamese aimed at reunification of their country as an end in itself.*

The Munich example shows again how arguments of resemblance depend on emphasizing the similarities between X and Y and playing down the dissimilarities. One could try to refute the counterargument made by Zinn by arguing first that the Saigon government was more stable than Zinn thinks and second that the Viet Cong and North Vietnamese were driven by goals larger than reunification of Vietnam, namely, communist domination of Asia. Such an argument would once again highlight the similarities between Vietnam and prewar Europe.

Will a skeptic propose a counteranalogy?   A final way of testing a resemblance claim is to propose an alternative analogy or precedent that counters the original claim. Suppose you wanted to argue for the teaching of creationism along with evolution in the schools and your opponent said, "Teaching creationism along with evolution is like teaching the stork theory of where babies come from along with the biological theory." After showing the disanalogies between creationism and the stork theory of reproduction, you could counter with your own analogy: "No, teaching creationism along with evolution is like bilingual education, where you respect the cultural heritage of all peoples." To the extent that your audience values pluralism and the preservation of different beliefs, your analogy may well provide them with a new perspective on the topic, a perspective that allows them to entertain an otherwise alien notion.

The readings for this chapter are three brief excerpts that employ resemblance arguments.

READINGS

1. In this first example, the author is arguing that it is not unconstitutional to require drug testing of federal employees. Within the argument the author draws an analogy between testing for drugs and checking for weapons or bombs at an airport. Using the techniques suggested in this chapter, test the soundness of the argument.

> The Constitution does not prohibit all searches and seizures. It makes the people secure in their persons only from "unreasonable" searches and seizures, and there is nothing unreasonable in Reagan's executive order.
>
>   . . . Those who challenge this sensible program [drug testing by urinalysis] ought to get straight on this business of "rights." Like any other employer, the government has

---

*Based on the summary of Zinn's argument in J. Michael Sproule, *Argument: Language and Its Influence* (New York: McGraw-Hill, 1980), 149–50.

a right—within certain well-understood limits—to fix the terms and conditions of employment. The individual's right, if he finds these conditions intolerable, is to seek employment elsewhere. A parallel situation may be observed at every airport in the land. Individuals may have a right to fly, but they have no right to fly without having their persons and baggage inspected for weapons. By the same token, the federal worker who refuses to provide a urine specimen under the president's order can clean out his desk and apply to General Motors or General Electric or Kodak—only to discover that private industry is equally interested in a drug-free work place.*

2. In our second example former NAACP administrator Jack Greenberg defends affirmative action on the basis of analogy to other cases in the free market in which certain groups are given preferences not related to merit.

> The moral legitimacy of affirmative action and quotas favoring racial minorities must be assessed in a social and historical context, in the light of the many conflicting values that our society holds. . . . [There are many examples of instances in which criteria other than merit result in the selection of persons] other than those best qualified.
>
> A tenured professor will hold his position in spite of competition from younger, better, more vigorous scholars. Tenure is thought, however, to serve the important societal interest in academic freedom by enabling teachers to take controversial positions without fear and by shielding them against petty politics.
>
> Seniority rights advance individual security, worker satisfaction and job loyalty by promoting older workers although younger persons may be objectively more qualified, while, paradoxically, compulsory retirement favors younger persons over older, experienced, and perhaps more competent workers. . . .
>
> [Similarly, preference is given to veterans or union members even though non-veterans or non-union members might be more highly qualified. Both examples serve larger national interests.]
>
> Even the most prestigious schools consider more than marks as criteria for admission—to obtain a geographically and otherwise diverse student body and thereby enhance the educational experience of all. . . .†

Analyze Greenberg's argument. Is he right that affirmative action to hire more minorities can be justified by comparison to other instances when criteria other than merit affect hiring decisions: tenure, seniority, union membership, veteran status, geographic diversity?

3. Analyze the strengths and weaknesses of various kinds of resemblance arguments in the following excerpt from Susan Brownmiller's *Against Our Will: Men, Women and Rape.*

---

*From "A Conservative View" by James J. Kilpatrick. © Universal Press Syndicate. Reprinted with permission. All rights reserved.

†"Affirmative Action, Quotas, and Merit," *New York Times* 7 Feb. 1976.

Pornography is the undiluted essence of anti-female propaganda. Yet the very same liberals who were so quick to understand the method and purpose behind the mighty propaganda machine of Hitler's Third Reich, the consciously spewed-out anti-Semitic caricatures and obscenities that gave an ideological base to the Holocaust and the Final Solution, the very same liberals who, enlightened by blacks, searched their own conscience and came to understand that their tolerance of "nigger" jokes and portrayals of shuffling, rolling-eyed servants in movies perpetuated the degrading myths of black inferiority and gave an ideological base to the continuation of black oppression—these very same liberals now fervidly maintain that the hatred and contempt for women that find expression in four-letter words used as expletives and in what are quaintly called "adult" or "erotic" books and movies are a valid extension of freedom of speech that must be preserved as a Constitutional right.

To defend the right of a lone, crazed American Nazi to grind out propaganda calling for the extermination of all Jews, as the ACLU has done in the name of free speech, is, after all, a self-righteous and not particularly courageous stand, for American Jewry is not currently threatened by storm troopers, concentration camps and imminent extermination, but I wonder if the ACLU's position might change if, come tomorrow morning, the bookstores and movie theaters lining Forty-second Street in New York City were devoted not to the humiliation of women by rape and torture, as they currently are, but to a systematized commercially successful propaganda machine depicting the sadistic pleasures of gassing Jews or lynching blacks?

Is this analogy extreme? Not if you are a woman who is conscious of the ever-present threat of rape and the proliferation of a cultural ideology that makes it sound like "liberated" fun. The majority report of the President's Commission on Obscenity and Pornography tried to pooh-pooh the opinion of law enforcement agencies around the country that claimed their own concrete experience with offenders who were caught with the stuff led them to conclude that pornographic material is a causative factor in crimes of sexual violence. The commission maintained that it was not possible at this time to scientifically prove or disprove such a connection.

❧ WRITING ASSIGNMENTS FOR CHAPTER 12

OPTION 1: *An analogy microtheme*   Because few arguments are devoted entirely to a resemblance claim and because many arguments from resemblance are used in service of other claims, this assignment asks you simply to write a piece of an argument. Imagine that you are writing a longer argument for or against an X of your choice. As part of your argument you want to influence your reader's emotional or intellectual understanding of X, in either a positive or a negative direction, by comparing it to a more familiar Y. Write the portion of your argument that develops the extended analogy. A good model for this assignment is the argument on page 182. The writer opposes a proficiency exam in writing by comparing it to a proficiency exam in physical fitness.

OPTION 2:   *A precedence microtheme*   Imagine that you are writing a proposal argument of the kind "We should/should not do X" and that one of your reasons will develop a precedence argument as follows: "We should/should not do X because doing X will lead to the same good/bad consequences that we experienced when we did Y." Write a portion of your argument that develops this precedence claim.

chapter 13

Evaluation Arguments

X Is/Is Not a Good Y

EXAMPLE CASE

When former tennis star Margaret Court argued that Martina Navratilova's admitted homosexuality kept her from being a proper role model for young tennis players, sports writer Steve Kelley disagreed: "Navratilova is, in fact, an excellent role model. . . . She is self-made. She didn't learn the game playing with the privileged classes. She is honest and well-spoken in interviews. She doesn't kiss off questions with stock cliches. . . . Navratilova is a voracious reader, fluent in four languages. She belongs to the Sierra Club, reads several newspapers a day. She is a political junkie who has the courage of her convictions." Additionally, Kelly admires her courage and integrity in openly acknowledging her relationship with her longtime lover Judy Nelson, an admission that "has cost Navratilova millions in endorsements."*

In our roles as citizens and professionals we are continually expected to make difficult evaluations, to defend them, and even to persuade others to accept them. Often we will defend our judgments orally—in committees making hiring and promotion decisions, in management groups deciding which of several marketing plans to adopt, or at parent advisory meetings evaluating the success of school policies. Sometimes, too, we will be expected to put our arguments in writing.

Practice in thinking systematically about the process of evaluation, then, is valuable experience. In this chapter we focus on *evaluation* arguments of the type "X is/is not a good Y" (or "X is a good/bad Y") and the strategy needed for

---

*Steve Kelley, *Seattle Times* 26 Aug. 1990: C3.

conducting such arguments.* In Chapter 15, we will return to evaluation arguments to examine in more detail some special problems raised by ethical issues.

CRITERIA-MATCH STRUCTURE OF EVALUATION ARGUMENTS

An "X is/is not a good Y" argument follows the same criteria-match structure that we examined in definitional arguments (Chapter 10). A typical claim for such an argument has the following form:

X is/is not a good Y because it meets/fails to meet criteria A, B, and C.

The main structural difference between an evaluation argument and a definition argument involves the Y term. In a definition argument, one argues whether a particular Y term is the correct class in which to place X. (Does this swampy area qualify as a *wetland*?) In an evaluation argument, we know the Y term—that is, what class to put X into (Dr. Choplogic is a *teacher*)—but we don't know whether X is a good or bad instance of that class. (Is Dr. Choplogic a *good* teacher?) As in definition arguments, warrants specify the criteria to be used for the evaluation, whereas the stated reasons and grounds assert that X meets these criteria.

Let's look at an example that, for the sake of illustration, asserts just one criterion for "good" or "bad." (Most arguments will, of course, develop several criteria.)

ENTHYMEME:	Computer-aided instruction (CAI) is an effective teaching method because it encourages self-paced learning. (The complete argument would develop other reasons also.)
CLAIM:	Computer-aided instruction is an effective teaching method.
STATED REASON:	Computer-aided instruction encourages self-paced learning.
GROUNDS:	evidence that CAI encourages self-paced learning; examples of different learners working at different paces
WARRANT (CRITERION):	Self-paced learning is an effective teaching method.

---

*In addition to the contrasting words *good/bad*, a number of other evaluative terms involve the same kinds of thinking: *effective/ineffective, successful/unsuccessful, workable/unworkable*, and so forth. Throughout this chapter, terms such as these can be substituted for *good/bad*.

BACKING: explanations of why self-paced learning is effective; research studies or testimonials showing effectiveness of self-pacing

CONDITIONS OF REBUTTAL: *Attacking stated reason and grounds:* Perhaps students don't really pace themselves in CAI.

Attacking the warrant and backing: Perhaps self-paced learning isn't any more effective than other methods; perhaps the disadvantages of other features of CAI outweigh the value of self-pacing.

As this Toulmin diagram shows, the writer needs to show that self-paced learning is an effective teaching method (the warrant or criterion) and that computer-aided instruction meets this criterion (the stated reason and grounds—the match argument).

GENERAL STRATEGY FOR EVALUATION ARGUMENTS

The general strategy for evaluation arguments is to establish criteria and then to argue that X meets or does not meet the criteria. In writing your argument, you have to decide whether your audience is apt to accept your criteria or not. If you want to argue, for example, that pit bulls do not make good pets because they are potentially vicious, you can assume that most readers will share your assumption that viciousness is bad. Likewise, if you want to praise the new tax bill because it cuts out tax cheating, you can probably assume readers agree that tax cheating is bad.

Often, however, selecting and defending your criteria are the most difficult parts of a criteria-match argument. For example, people who own pit bulls because they *want* a vicious dog for protection may not agree that viciousness is bad. In this case, you would need to argue that another kind of dog, such as a German shepherd or a doberman, would make a better choice than a pit bull or that the bad consequences of a vicious dog outweigh the benefits. Several kinds of difficulties in establishing criteria are worth discussing in more detail.

The Problem of Standards: What's Normal or What's Ideal?

To get a sense of this problem, consider again Young Person's archetypal argument with The Parents about her curfew (see Chapter 1). She originally argued that staying out until 2 A.M. is fair "because all the other kids' parents let their kids stay out late," to which The Parents might respond: "Well, *ideally,* all the other parents should not let their kids stay out that late." Young Person based her criterion

for fairness on what is *normal;* her standards arose from common practices of a social group. The Parents, however, argued from what is *ideal,* basing their criteria
on some external standard that transcends social groups.

We experience this dilemma in various forms throughout our lives. It is the
conflict between absolutes and cultural relativism, between written law and customary practice. There is hardly an area of human experience that escapes the
dilemma: Is it fair to get a ticket for going 70 mph on a 65 mph freeway when most
of the drivers go 70 mph or higher? Is it better for high schools to pass out free
contraceptives to students because the students are having sex anyway (what's
normal), or is it better not to pass them out in order to support abstinence (what's
ideal)? When you select criteria for an evaluation argument, you may well have to
choose one side or the other of this dilemma, arguing for what is ideal or for what
is normal. Neither position should be seen as necessarily better than the other; normal practice may be corrupt just as surely as ideal behavior may be impossible.

The Problem of Mitigating Circumstances

When confronting the dilemma raised by the "normal" versus the "ideal," we
sometimes have to take into account circumstances as well as behavior. In particular, we have the notion of *mitigating* circumstances, or circumstances that are extraordinary or unusual enough to cause us to change our standard measure of
judgment. Ordinarily it is wrong to be late for work or to miss an exam. But what
if your car had a flat tire?

When you argue for mitigating circumstances as a reason for modifying judgment in a particular case, you are arguing against the conditions of both normal
behavior and ideal behavior as the proper criterion for judgment. Thus, when you
make such an argument, you will likely assume an especially heavy burden of
proof. People assume the rightness of usual standards of judgment unless there
are compelling arguments for abnormal circumstances.

The Problem of Choosing Between
Two Goods or Two Bads

Not all arguments of value, of course, clearly deal with bad and good, but with
choosing between two bads or two goods. Often we are caught between a rock and
a hard place. Should we cut pay or cut people? Put our parents in a nursing home
or let them stay at home where they have become a danger to themselves? In such
cases one has to weigh conflicting criteria, knowing that the choices are too much
alike—either both bad or both good.

The Problem of Seductive Empirical Measures

The need to make distinctions among relative goods or relative bads has led
many persons to seek quantifiable criteria that can be weighed mathematically.

Thus we use grade point averages to select scholarship winners, MCAT scores to decide who gets into medical school, and student evaluation scores to decide which professor gets the University Teaching Award.

In some cases, such empirical measures can be quite acceptable. But they can be dangerous if they don't adequately measure the value of the people or things they purportedly evaluate. (Some people would argue that they *never* adequately measure anything significant.) To illustrate the problem further, consider the problems of relying on grade point average as a criterion for employment. Many employers rely heavily on grades when hiring college graduates. But according to every major study of the relationship between grades and work achievement, grades are about as reliable as palm reading when it comes to predicting life success. Why do employers continue to rely so heavily on grades? Clearly because it is so easy to classify job applicants according to a single empirical measure that appears to rank order everyone along the same scale.

The problem with empirical measures, then, is that they seduce us into believing that complex judgments can be made mathematically, thus rescuing us from the messiness of alternative points of view and conflicting criteria. Empirical measures seem extremely persuasive next to written arguments that try to qualify and hedge and raise questions. We suggest, however, that a fair evaluation of any X might require such hedging.

The Problem of Cost

A final problem that can crop up in evaluations is cost. In comparing an X to others of its kind, we may find that on all the criteria we can develop, X comes out on top. X is the best of all possible Ys. But if X costs too much, we have to rethink our evaluation.*

If we're looking to hire a new department head at Median State University, and the greatest scholar in the field, a magnificent teacher, a regular dynamo of diplomacy, says she'll come—for a hundred Gs a year—we'll probably have to withdraw our offer. Whether the costs are expressed in dollars or personal discomfort or moral repugnance or some other terms, our final evaluation of X must take cost into account, however elusive that cost might be.

HOW TO DETERMINE CRITERIA FOR YOUR ARGUMENT

Now that we have explored some of the difficulties you may encounter in establishing and defending criteria for your evaluation of X, let's turn to the practical

---

*We can avoid this problem somewhat by placing items into different classes on the basis of cost. For example, a Mercedes may come out far ahead of a Hyundai, but the more relevant evaluative question to ask is, "How does a Mercedes compare to a Cadillac?"

problem of trying to determine criteria themselves. How do you go about finding the criteria you'll need for distinguishing a good teacher from a poor teacher, a good movie from a bad movie, a successful manager from an unsuccessful manager, a healthy diet from an unhealthy diet, and so forth?

Step 1: Determine the Category in Which the Object Being Evaluated Belongs

In determining the quality or value of any given X, you must first figure out what your standard of comparison is. If, for example, you asked one of your professors to write you a letter of recommendation for a summer job, what class of things should the professor put you into? Is he or she supposed to evaluate you as a student? a leader? a worker? a storyteller? a party animal? or what? This is an important question because the criteria for excellence in one class (student) may be very different from criteria for excellence in another class (party animal).

To write a useful letter, your professor should consider you first as a member of the general class "summer job holder" and base her evaluation of you on criteria relevant to that class. To write a truly effective letter, however, your professor needs to consider your qualifications in the context of the smallest applicable class of candidates: not "summer job holder," but "law office intern" or "highway department flagperson" or "golf course groundsperson." Clearly, each of these subclasses has very different criteria for excellence that your professor needs to address.

We thus recommend placing X into the smallest relevant class because of the apples-and-oranges law. That is, to avoid giving a mistaken rating to a perfectly good apple, you need to make sure you are judging an apple under the class "apple" and not under the next larger class "fruit" or a neighboring class "orange." And to be even more precise, you may wish to evaluate your apple in the class "eating apple" as opposed to "pie apple" because the latter class is supposed to be tarter and the former class juicier and sweeter.

Obviously, there are limits to this law. For example, the smallest possible class of apples would contain only one member—the one being evaluated. At that point, your apple is both the best and the worst member of its class. And hence, evaluation of it is meaningless. Also, we sometimes can't avoid apples-and-oranges comparisons because they are thrust upon us by circumstances, tradition, or some other factor. Thus, the Academy Award judges selecting "Best Movie" aren't allowed to distinguish between Great Big Box Office Hits and "serious little films that make socially significant points."

Step 2: Determine the Purpose or Function of This Class

Once you have located X in its appropriate class, you should next determine what the purpose or function of this class is. Let's suppose that the summer job you are applying for is tour guide at the city zoo. The function of a tour guide is to make people feel welcome, to give them interesting information about the zoo, to make their visit pleasant, and so forth. Consequently, you wouldn't want your professor's evaluation to praise your term paper on Napoleon Bonaparte or your successful synthesis of some compound in your chemistry lab. Rather, the professor should highlight your dependability, your neat appearance, your good speaking skills, and your ability to work with groups. On the other hand, if you were applying for graduate school, then your term paper on Bonaparte or your chem lab wizardry would be relevant. In other words, the professor has to evaluate you according to the class "tour guide," not "graduate student," and the criteria for each class derive from the purpose or function of the class.

Let's take another example. Suppose that you are the chair of a committee charged with evaluating the job performance of Lillian Jones, director of the admissions office at Clambake College. Ms. Jones has been a controversial manager because several members of her staff have filed complaints about her management style. In making your evaluation, your first step is to place Ms. Jones into an appropriate class, in this case, the general class "manager," and then the more specific class "manager of an admissions office at a small, private college." You then need to identify the purpose or function of these classes. You might say that the function of the general class "managers" is to "oversee actual operations of an organization so that the organization meets its goals as harmoniously and efficiently as possible," whereas the function of the specific class "manager of an admissions office at a small, private college" is "the successful recruitment of the best students possible."

Step 3: Determine Criteria Based on the Purposes or Function of the Class to Which X Belongs

Once you've worked out the purposes of the class, you are ready to work out the criteria by which you judge all members of the class. Criteria for judgment will be based on those features of Y that help it achieve the purposes of its class. For example, once you determine the purpose and function of the position filled by Lillian Jones, you can develop a list of criteria for managerial success:

1. Criteria related to "efficient operation"
   - articulates priorities and goals for the organization
   - is aggressive in achieving goals
   - motivates fellow employees
   - is well organized, efficient, and punctual
   - is articulate and communicates well

2. Criteria related to "harmonious operation"
   - creates job satisfaction for subordinates
   - is well groomed, sets good example of professionalism
   - is honest, diplomatic in dealing with subordinates
   - is flexible in responding to problems and special concerns of staff members
3. Criteria related to meeting specific goals of a college admissions office
   - creates a comprehensive recruiting program
   - demonstrates that recruiting program works

Step 4: Give Relative Weightings to the Criteria

Even though you have established criteria, you must still decide which of the criteria are most important. In the case of Lillian Jones, is it more important that she bring in lots of students to Clambake College or that she create a harmonious, happy office? These sorts of questions are at the heart of many evaluative controversies. Thus, a justification for your weighting of criteria may well be an important part of your argument.

DETERMINING WHETHER X MEETS THE CRITERIA

Once you've established your criteria, you've got to figure out how well X meets them. You proceed by gathering evidence and examples. The success of the recruiting program at Clambake College can probably be measured empirically, so you gather statistics about applications to the college, SAT scores of applicants, number of acceptances, academic profiles of entering freshmen, and so forth. You might then compare those statistics to those compiled by Ms. Jones's predecessor or to her competitors at other, comparable institutions.

You can also look at what the recruiting program actually does—the number of recruiters, the number of high school visitations, quality of admissions brochures, and other publications. You can also look at Ms. Jones in action, searching for specific incidents or examples that illustrate her management style. For example, you can't measure a trait such as diplomacy empirically, but you can find specific instances where the presence or absence of this trait was demonstrated. You could turn to examples where Ms. Jones may or may not have prevented a potentially divisive situation from occurring or where she offered or failed to offer encouragement at psychologically the right moment to keep someone from getting demoralized. As with criteria-match arguments in definition, one must provide examples of how the X in question meets each of the criteria that have been set up.

Your final evaluation of Ms. Jones, then, might include an overview of her strengths and weaknesses along the various criteria you have established. You might say that Ms. Jones has done an excellent job with recruitment (an assertion you can support with data on student enrollments over the last five years) but was relatively poor at keeping the office staff happy (as evidenced by employee complaints, high turnover, and your own observations of her rather abrasive management style). Nevertheless, your final recommendation might be to retain Ms. Jones for another three-year contract because you believe that an excellent recruiting record is the most important criterion for her position at Clambake. You might justify this heavy weighting of recruiting on the grounds that the institution's survival depends on its ability to attract adequate numbers of good students.

❦ FOR CLASS DISCUSSION

The following small-group exercise can be accomplished in one or two class hours. It gives you a good model of the process you will need to go through in order to write your own evaluation essay. Working in small groups, suppose that you are going to evaluate a controversial member of one of the following classes:

   a. a teacher
   b. a political figure
   c. an athlete
   d. a school newspaper
   e. a school policy
   f. a recent Supreme Court decision
   g. a rock singer or group or MTV video
   h. a dorm or living group
   i. a restaurant or college hangout
   j. an X of your choice

1. Choose a controversial member within one of these classes as the specific person, thing, or event you are going to evaluate (Professor Choplogic, the Wild Dog Bar, Madonna, and so forth).

2. Narrow down the general class by determining the smallest relevant class to which your X belongs (from "athlete" to "basketball guard"; from "college hangout" to "college hangout for people who want to hold late-night bull sessions").

3. Make a list of the purposes or functions of that class and then list the criteria that a good member of that class would have to have in order to accomplish the purposes.

4. If necessary, rank order your criteria.

5. Evaluate your X by matching X to each of the criteria.

❦

ORGANIZING AN EVALUATION ARGUMENT

As you write a draft, you might find useful the following prototypical structures for evaluation arguments. Of course, you can always alter these plans if another structure better fits your material.

Plan 1 (Criteria and Match in Separate Sections)

- Introduce the issue by showing disagreements about how to evaluate a problematic X (Is X a good Y?).
- State your claim.
- Present your criteria for evaluating members of class Y.
  State and develop criterion 1.
  State and develop criterion 2.
  Continue with the rest of your criteria.
- Summarize and respond to possible objections to your criteria.
- Restate your claim asserting that X is/is not a good member of class Y.
  Apply criterion 1 to your case.
  Apply criterion 2 to your case.
  Continue the match argument.
- Summarize and respond to possible objections to your match argument.
- Conclude your argument.

Plan 2 (Criteria and Match Interwoven)

- Introduce the issue by showing disagreements about how to evaluate a problematic X (Is X a good Y?).
- Present your claim.
  State criterion 1 and argue that your X meets (does not meet) this criterion.
  State criterion 2 and argue that your X meets (does not meet) this criterion.
  Continue with criteria-match sections for additional criteria.
- Summarize opposing views.
- Refute or concede to opposing views.
- Conclude your argument.

CONDITIONS FOR REBUTTAL: TESTING AN EVALUATION ARGUMENT

To strengthen your draft of an evaluation argument, you can role-play a skeptic by asking the following questions.

Will a skeptic accept my criteria?   Many evaluative arguments are weak because the writers have simply assumed that readers will accept their criteria. Whenever your audience's acceptance of your criteria is in doubt, you will need to make your warrants clear and provide backing in their support.

Are my criteria based on the "smallest applicable class" for X?   For example, the James Bond movie *Tomorrow Never Dies* will certainly be a failure if you evaluate it in the general class "movies," in which it would have to compete with *Citizen Kane* and other great classics. But if you evaluated it as an "escapist movie" or a "James Bond movie" it would have a greater chance for success and hence of yielding an arguable evaluation. All of this isn't to say that you couldn't evaluate "escapist movies" as a class of, say, "popular films" and find the whole class deficient. Evaluations of this type are, however, more difficult to argue because of the numbers of items you must take into account.

Will a skeptic accept my general weighting of criteria?   Another vulnerable spot in an evaluation argument is the relative weight of the criteria. How much anyone weights a given criterion is usually a function of his or her own interests relative to the X in question. You should always ask whether some particular group affected by the quality of X might not have good reasons for weighting the criteria differently.

Will a skeptic question my standard of reference?   In questioning the criteria for judging X, we can also focus on the standard of reference used—what's normal versus what's ideal. If you have argued that X is bad because it doesn't live up to what's ideal, you can expect some readers to defend X on the basis of what's normal. Similarly, if you argue that X is good because it is better than its competitors, you can expect some readers to point out how short it falls from what is ideal.

Will a skeptic criticize my use of empirical measures?   The tendency to mistake empirical measures for criteria is a common one that any critic of an argument should be aware of. As we have discussed earlier, what's most measurable isn't always significant when it comes to assessing the essential traits needed to fulfill whatever function X is supposed to fulfill. A 95-mph fastball is certainly an impressive empirical measure of a pitcher's ability—but if the pitcher doesn't get batters out, that measure is a misleading gauge of performance.

Will a skeptic accept my criteria but reject my match argument?   The other major way of testing an evaluation argument is to anticipate how readers might object to your stated reasons and grounds. Will readers challenge you by finding sampling errors in your data or otherwise find that you used evidence selectively? For example, if you think your opponents will emphasize Lillian Jones's abrasive management style much more heavily than you did, you may be able to undercut their arguments by finding counterexamples that show Ms. Jones acting diplomatically. Be prepared to counter objections to your grounds.

The following essay by student writer Sam Isaacson responds to the writing assignment on page 204.

Would Legalization of Gay Marriage Be Good
for the Gay Community?

Sam Isaacson (student)

1   For those of us who have been out for a while, nothing seems shocking about a gay pride parade. Yet at this year's parade, I was struck by the contrast between two groups—the float for the Toys in Babeland store (with swooning drag queens and leather clad, whip-wielding, topless dykes) and the Northwest chapters of Integrity and Dignity (Episcopal and Catholic organizations for lesbians and gays), whose marchers looked as conservative as the congregation of any American church.

2   These stark differences in dress are representative of larger philosophical differences in the gay community. At stake is whether or not we gays and lesbians should act "normal." Labeled as deviants by many in straight society, we're faced with various opposing methods of response. One option is to insist that we are normal and work to integrate gays into the cultural mainstream. Another response is to form an alternative gay culture with its own customs and values; this culture would honor deviancy in response to a society which seeks to label some as "normal" and some as "abnormal." For the purposes of this paper I will refer to those who favor the first response as "integrationists" and those who favor the second response as "liberationists". Politically, this ideological clash is most evident in the issue of whether legalization of same-sex marriage would be good for the gay community. Nearly all integrationists would say yes, but many liberationists would say no. My belief is that while we must take the objections of the liberationists seriously, legalization of same-sex marriage would benefit both gays and society in general.

3   Let us first look at what is so threatening about gay marriage to many liberationists. Many liberationists fear that legalizing gay marriage will reinforce current social pressures that say monogamous marriage is the normal and right way to live. In straight society, those who choose not to marry are often viewed as self-indulgent, likely promiscuous, and shallow—and it is no coincidence these are some of the same stereotypes gays struggle against. If gays begin to marry, married life will be all the more the norm and subject those outside of marriage to even greater marginalization. As homosexuals, liberationists argue, we should be particularly sensitive to the tyranny of the majority. Our sympathies should lie with the deviants—the transsexual, the fetishist, the drag queen, and the leather-dyke. By choosing marriage, gays take the easy route into "normal" society; we not only abandon the sexual minorities of our community, we strengthen society's narrow notions of what is "normal" and thereby further confine both straights and gays.

4   Additionally, liberationists worry that by winning the right to marry gays and lesbians will lose the distinctive and positive characteristics of gay culture. Many gay writers have commented on how as a marginalized group gays have been forced to create different forms of relationships that often allow for a greater and often more fulfilling range of life experiences. Writer Edmund White, for instance, has observed that there is a greater fluidity in the relationships of gays than straights. Gays, he says, are more likely than straights to stay friends with old lovers, are more likely to form close friendships outside the romantic re-

lationship, and are generally less likely to become compartmentalized into isolated couples. It has also been noted that gay relationships are often characterized by more equality and better communication than are straight relationships. Liberationists make the reasonable assumption that if gays win the right to marry they will be subject to the same social pressure to marry that straights are subject to. As more gays are pressured into traditional life patterns, liberationists fear the gay sensibility will be swallowed up by the established attitudes of the broader culture. All of society would be the poorer if this were to happen.

I must admit that I concur with many of the arguments of the liberationists that I have 　5 outlined above. I do think if given the right, gays would feel social pressure to marry; I agree that gays should be especially sensitive to the most marginalized elements of society; and I also agree that the unique perspectives on human relationships that the gay community offers should not be sacrificed. However, despite these beliefs, I feel that legalizing gay marriage would bring valuable benefits to gays and society as a whole.

First of all, I think it is important to put the attacks the liberationists make on marriage 　6 into perspective. The liberationist critique of marriage claims that marriage in itself is a harmful institution (for straights as well as gays) because it needlessly limits and normalizes personal freedom. But it seems clear to me that marriage in some form is necessary for the well-being of society. Children need a stable environment in which to be raised. Studies have shown that children whose parents divorce often suffer long-term effects from the trauma. Studies have also shown that people tend to be happier in stable long-term relationships. We need to have someone to look over us when we're old, when we become depressed, when we fall ill. All people, gay or straight, parents or nonparents, benefit from the stabilizing force of marriage.

Second, we in the gay community should not be too quick to overlook the real bene- 　7 fits that legalizing gay marriage will bring. We are currently denied numerous legal rights of marriage that the straight community enjoys: tax benefits, insurance benefits, inheritance rights, and the right to have a voice in medical treatment or funeral arrangements for a dying partner.

Further, just as important as the legal impacts of being denied the right to marriage is 　8 the socially symbolic weight this denial carries. We are sent the message that while gay sex in the privacy of one's home will be tolerated, gay love will not be respected. We are told that it is not important to society whether we form long-term relationships or not. We are told that we are not worthy of forming families of our own. By gaining the same recognitions by the state of our relationships and all the legal and social weight that recognition carries, the new message will be that gay love is just as meaningful as straight love.

Finally, let me address what I think is at the heart of the liberationist argument against 　9 marriage—the fear of losing social diversity and our unique gay voice. The liberationists are wary of society's normalizing forces. They fear that if gays win the right to marry gay relationships will simply become imitations of straight relationships—the richness gained through the gay experience will be lost. I feel, however, this argument unintentionally plays into the hands of conservatives. Conservatives argue that marriage is, by definition, the union between man and woman. As a consequence, to the broad culture gay marriage can only be a mockery of marriage. As gays and lesbians we need to argue that conservatives are imposing arbitrary standards on what is normal and not normal in society. To fight the conservative agenda, we must suggest instead that marriage is, in essence, a contract of love and commitment between two people. The liberationists, I think, unwittingly feed into conservative identification and classification by pigeonholing gays as outsiders. Reacting against social norms is simply another way of being held hostage by them.

10   We need to understand that the gay experience and voice will not be lost by gaining the right to marry. Gays will always be the minority by simple biological fact and this will always color the identity of any gay person. But we can only make our voice heard if we are seen as full-fledged members of society. Otherwise we will remain an isolated and marginalized group. And only when we have the right to marry will we have any say in the nature and significance of marriage as an institution. This is not being apologetic to the straight culture, but is a demand that we not be excluded from the central institutions of Western culture. We can help merge the fluidity of gay relationships with the traditionally more compartmentalized married relationship. Further, liberationists should realize that the decision *not* to marry makes a statement only if one has the ability to choose marriage. What would be most radical, most transforming, is two women or two men joined together in the eyes of society.

 WRITING ASSIGNMENT FOR CHAPTER 13

Evaluate a "controversial" X: Write an argument in which you try to change someone's mind about the evaluation of X.

The X you choose should be controversial or at least problematic. While you are safe in arguing that a Mercedes Benz is a good car or that smoking is bad for your health, your claim is unlikely to surprise anyone. By "controversial" or "problematic," then, we mean that people are apt to disagree with your evaluation of X or that you are somehow opposing the common view of X. By choosing a controversial or problematic X, you will be able to focus on a clear issue. Somewhere in your essay you should summarize alternative views and either refute them or concede to them (see Chapter 8).

Note that this assignment asks you to do something different from a typical movie review, restaurant review, or product review in a consumer magazine. Many reviews are simply informational or analytic, where the writer's purpose is to describe the object or event being reviewed and explain its strengths and weaknesses. In contrast, your purpose here is persuasive. You must change someone's mind about the evaluation of X.

c h a p t e r 14

◆ Proposal Arguments

"We Should/ Should Not Do X"

EXAMPLE CASE

Barry Commoner, director of the Center for the Biology of Natural Systems at Queens College, poses the following dilemma: "To what extent should the choice of production technologies be governed—as it is now—by private, generally short-term, profit-maximizing response to market forces, and to what extent by long-term social concerns like environmental quality?" In examining the problem of atmospheric pollutants, he opts for governmental control based on long-term social concerns. Specifically, he proposes that the government shift from trying to "clean up" pollutants to issuing an outright ban on pollutant-causing technologies.*

THE NATURE OF PROPOSAL ARGUMENTS

Although *proposal* or *should* arguments are the last type we examine, they are among the most common arguments that you will encounter or be called on to write. Their essence is that they call for action. In reading a proposal, the audience is enjoined to make a decision and then to act upon it—to *do* something. Proposal arguments are sometimes called *should* or *ought* arguments because these helping verbs express the obligation to act: "We *should* do X" or "We *ought* to do X."

---

*"Free Markets Can't Control Pollution," *New York Times* 15 April 1990: III, 13:3.

For instructional purposes, we will distinguish between two kinds of proposal arguments, even though they are closely related and involve the same basic arguing strategies. The first kind we will call *practical proposals,* which propose an action to solve some kind of local or immediate problem. A student's proposal to change the billing procedures for scholarship students would be an example of a practical proposal, as would an engineering firm's proposal for the design of a new bridge being planned by a city government. The second kind we will call *policy proposals,* in which the writer offers a broad plan of action to solve major social, economic, or political problems affecting the common good. An argument that the United States should adopt a national health insurance plan or that the terms for senators and representatives should be limited to twelve years would be examples of policy proposals.

THE GENERAL STRUCTURE AND STRATEGY OF PROPOSAL ARGUMENTS

Proposal arguments, whether practical proposals or policy proposals, generally have a three-part structure: (1) description of a problem, (2) proposed solution, and (3) justification for the proposed solution. Luckily, proposal arguments don't require different sorts of argumentative strategies from the ones you have already been using. In the justification section of your proposal argument, you develop because clauses of the kinds you have practiced all along throughout this text.

SPECIAL REQUIREMENTS OF PROPOSAL ARGUMENTS

Although proposal arguments combine elements from other kinds of claims, they differ from other arguments in that they call for action. Calls to action don't entail any strategies that we haven't already considered, but they do entail a unique set of emphases. Let's look briefly at some of the special requirements of proposal arguments.

Adding Presence to Your Argument

It's one thing for a person to assent to a value judgment, but it's another thing to act on that judgment. The personal cost of acting may be high for many people in your audience. That means that you have to engage not only your audience's intellect, but their emotions as well. Thus proposal arguments often require more attention to *pathos* than do other kinds of arguments (see pp. 107–108).

The effect of *pathos* is to give your argument presence as well as intellectual force. An argument is said to have *presence* when the problem being addressed ceases to be an abstraction. Pathetic appeals help the reader sense the urgency and realness of the problem addressed. In an argument with presence, the reader can share the writer's point of view—the writer's emotions, the force of the writer's personal engagement with the issue. Such arguments call the reader beyond assent toward action.

Overcoming the Natural Conservatism of People

Another difficulty faced by a proposal maker is the innate conservatism of all human beings, whatever their political persuasion. One philosopher refers to this conservatism as the law of inertia, the tendency of all things in the universe, including human beings, to remain at rest if possible. The popular adage "If it ain't broke, don't fix it" is one expression of this tendency. Hence, proposers of change face an extraordinary burden of proof. Specifically, they have to prove that something needs fixing, that it can be fixed, and that the cost of fixing it will be outweighed by the benefits of fixing it.

The difficulty of proving that something needs fixing is compounded by the fact that frequently the status quo appears to be working. So sometimes when writing a proposal, you can't argue that what we have is bad, but only that what we could have is better. Often, then, a proposal argument will be based not on present evils but on the evils of lost potential. And getting an audience to accept lost potential may be difficult indeed, given the inherently abstract nature of potentiality.

The Difficulty of Predicting Future Consequences

Further, most proposal makers will be forced to predict consequences of a given act. As we've seen in our earlier discussions of causality, it is difficult enough to argue backward from event Y in order to establish that X caused Y. Think how much harder it is to establish that X will, in the future, cause certain things to occur. We all know enough of history to realize that few major decisions have led neatly to their anticipated results. This knowledge indeed accounts for much of our conservatism. All the things that can go wrong in a causal argument can go wrong in a proposal argument as well; the major difference is that in a proposal argument we typically have less evidence for our conjectures.

The Problem of Evaluating Consequences

A final difficulty faced by all proposal arguments concerns the difficulty of evaluating the consequences of the proposal. In government and industry, managers often turn to a tool known as *cost-benefit analysis* to calculate the potential consequences of a given proposal. As much as possible, a cost-benefit analysis tries to reduce all consequences to a single scale for purposes of comparison. Most often, the scale will be money. Although this scale may work well in some circumstances, it can lead to grotesquely inappropriate conclusions in other situations.

Just how does one balance the money saved by cutting Medicare benefits against the suffering of the people denied benefits? How does one translate the beauty of a wilderness area into a dollar amount? On this score, cost-benefit analyses often run into a problem discussed in the previous chapter: the seductiveness of empirical measures. Because something can't be readily measured doesn't mean it can be safely ignored. And finally, what will be a cost for one group will often be a benefit for others. For example, if social security benefits are cut, those on social security will suffer, but current workers who pay for it with taxes will take home a larger paycheck.

These, then, are some of the general difficulties facing someone who sets out to argue in favor of a proposal. Although not insurmountable, they are at least daunting. Given those difficulties, let's now set forth the writing assignment for this chapter and then turn to the question of how one might put together a proposal argument.

DEVELOPING A PROPOSAL ARGUMENT

Writers of proposal arguments must focus in turn on three main phases or stages of the argument: showing that a problem exists, explaining the proposed solution, and offering a justification.

Convincing Your Readers that a Problem Exists

There is one argumentative strategy generic to all proposal arguments: awakening in the reader a sense of a problem. Typically, the development of a problem occurs in one of two places in a proposal argument—either in the introduction prior to the presentation of the arguer's proposal claim or in the body of the paper as the first main reason justifying the proposal claim. In the second instance the writer's first *because* clause has the following structure: "We should do X *because a problem exists (and X will solve it)."*

At this stage of your argument, it's important to give your problem presence. You must get people to see how the problem affects people, perhaps through examples of suffering or other loss or through persuasive statistics and so forth. Your goal is to awaken your readers to the existence of a problem, a problem they may well not have recognized before.

Besides giving presence to the problem, a writer must also gain the readers' intellectual assent to the depth, range, and potential seriousness of the problem. Suppose, for illustration, that you wanted to propose a special tax to increase funding for higher education in your state. In trying to convince taxpayers in your state that a problem exists, what obstacles might you face? First of all, many taxpayers never went to college and feel that they get along just fine without it. They tend to worry more about the quality of roads, social services, elementary and secondary schools, police and fire protection, and so forth. They are not too convinced that they need to worry about professors' salaries or better-equipped research labs. Thus, it's not enough to talk about the importance of education in general or to cite figures showing how paltry your state's funding of higher education is.

To convince your audience of the need for your proposal, you'll have to describe the consequences of low funding levels in terms they can relate to. You'll have to show them that potential benefits to the state are lost because of inadequate funding. Perhaps you can show the cost in terms of inadequately skilled graduates, disgruntled teachers, high turnover, brain drain to other states, inadequate educational services to farmers and businesspeople, lost productivity, and so forth. Or perhaps you can show your audience examples of benefits realized from better college funding in other states. Such examples give life to the abstract notion of lost potential.

All of this is not to say that you can't or shouldn't argue that higher education is inherently good. But until your reader can see low funding levels as "problematic" rather than "simply the way things are," your proposal stands little chance of being enacted.

Showing the Specifics of Your Proposal

Having decided that there is a problem to be solved, you should lay out your thesis, which is a proposal for solving the problem. Your goal now is to stress the feasibility of your solution, including costs. The art of proposal making is the art of the possible. To be sure, not all proposals require elaborate descriptions of the implementation process. If you are proposing, for example, that a local PTA chapter should buy new tumbling mats for the junior high gym classes, the procedures for buying the mats will probably be irrelevant. But in many arguments the specifics of your proposal—the actual step-by-step methods of implementing it—may be instrumental in winning your audience's support.

You will also need to show how your proposal will solve the problem either partially or wholly. Sometimes you may first need to convince your reader that the problem is solvable, not something intractably rooted in "the way things are," such as earthquakes or jealousy. In other words, expect that some members of your audience will be skeptical about the ability of any proposal to solve the problem you are addressing. You may well need, therefore, to "listen" to this point of view in your refutation section and to argue that your problem is at least partially solvable.

In order to persuade your audience that your proposal can work, you can follow any one of several approaches. A typical approach is to lay out a causal argument showing how one consequence will lead to another until your solution is effected. Another approach is to turn to resemblance arguments, either analogy or precedent. You try to show how similar proposals have been successful elsewhere. Or, if similar things have failed in the past, you try to show how the present situation is different.

The Justification: Convincing Your Reader that Your Proposal Should Be Enacted

This phase of a proposal argument will need extensive development in some arguments and minimal development in others, again depending on your particular problem and the rhetorical context of your proposal. If your audience already acknowledges the seriousness of the problem you are addressing and has simply been waiting for the right solution to come along, then your argument will be successful so long as you can convince your audience that your solution will work and that it won't cost too much. Such arguments depend on the clarity of your proposal and the feasibility of its being implemented.

But what if the costs are high? Or what if your audience doesn't think that the problem you are addressing is particularly serious? In such cases you have to develop your main reasons for believing that X should be done. A good strategy is to use the three-step process described in Chapter 9 when you examined arguments from principle, from consequence, and from resemblance. Here are some examples of how the three-step strategy can be used for proposal arguments.

PROPOSAL CLAIM:	Our university should abolish fraternities and sororities.
PRINCIPLE:	because they are elitist (or "a thing of the past" or "racist" or "sexist" or whatever)
CONSEQUENCE:	because eliminating the Greek system will improve our school's academics (or "fill our dormitories," "allow us to experiment with new living arrangements," "replace rush with a better freshman orientation," and so forth)
RESEMBLANCE:	because other universities that have eliminated the Greek system have reported good results
PROPOSAL CLAIM:	We should eliminate mandatory busing of children to achieve racial equality.
PRINCIPLE:	because it is unjust (or "ineffective," "a misuse of judicial authority," "a violation of individual rights," and so forth)
CONSEQUENCE:	because it puts too many psychological burdens on kids (or "costs too much," "destroys neighborhood schools," "makes it difficult to have parental involvement in the schools," "splits up siblings," "causes kids to spend too much time on buses," and so forth)
RESEMBLANCE:	because busing schoolchildren to solve a social problem such as racism makes about as much sense as sending alcoholics' kids through a detox center to cure their parents

Both of these arguments attempt to appeal to the value system of the audience. Both try to show how the proposed action is within the class of things that the audience already values, will lead to consequences desired by the audience, or is similar to something the audience already values (or will alleviate something the audience disvalues).

Touching the Right Pressure Points

Having defined and weighed the problem, having worked out a feasible solution, and having motivated your audience to act on your proposal, you may well wish to take your argument a step further. You may thus have to determine who has the power to act on your proposal and apply arguments directly to that person's or agency's immediate interests. More than any other form of argument, a proposal argument needs finally to be addressed to those with the power to act on the proposal. You need to know to whom or to what your power source is beholden or responsive and what values your power source holds that can be appealed to. You're looking, in short, for pressure points.

While attempting to get a university to improve wheelchair access to the student union building, one student with multiple sclerosis discovered that the university had recently paid $100,000 to put oak trim in a new faculty office building. She knew officials were a bit embarrassed by that figure, and it became an effective pressure point for her essay. "The university can afford to pay $100,000 for oak trim for faculty, but can't spend one quarter of that amount helping its disabled students get full access to the student union building." This hard-to-justify discrepancy put considerable pressure on the administration to find money for more wheelchair ramps. The moral here is that it makes good sense to tie one's proposal as much as possible to the interests of those in power.

USING THE "STOCK ISSUES" STRATEGY TO DEVELOP A PROPOSAL ARGUMENT

An effective way to generate ideas for a proposal argument is to ask yourself a series of questions based on the "stock issues" strategy. Suppose, for example, you wanted to develop the following argument: "In order to solve the problem of students who won't take risks with their writing, the faculty at Weasel College should adopt a pass/fail method of grading in all writing courses." The stock issues strategy invites the writer to consider "stock" ways (that is, common, usual, frequently repeated ways) that such arguments can be conducted.

Stock issue 1: *Is there really a problem here that needs to be solved?* Is it really true that a large number of student writers won't take risks in their writing? Is this problem more serious than other writing problems such as undeveloped ideas, lack of organization, poor sentence structure, and so forth? This stock issue invites the writer to convince her audience that a true problem exists. Conversely, an opponent to the proposal might argue that a true problem does not exist.

Stock issue 2: *Will the proposed solution really solve this problem?* Is it true that a pass/fail grading system will cause students to take more risks with their writing? Will more interesting, surprising, and creative essays result from pass/fail grading? Or will students simply put less effort into their writing? This stock issue prompts a supporter to demonstrate that the proposal will solve the problem; in contrast, it prompts the opponent to show that the proposal won't work.

Stock issue 3: *Can the problem be solved more simply without disturbing the status quo?* An opponent of the proposal might agree that a problem exists and that the proposed solution might solve it. However, the opponent might say, "Are there not less radical ways to solve this problem? If we want more creative and risk-taking student essays, can't we just change our grading criteria so that we reward risky papers and penalize conventional ones?" This stock issue prompts supporters to show that *only* the proposed solution will solve the problem and that no minor tinkering with the status quo will be adequate. Conversely, opponents will argue that the problem can be solved without acting on the proposal.

Stock issue 4: *Is the proposed solution really practical? Does it stand a chance of actually being enacted?* Here an opponent to the proposal might agree that the proposal would work but that it involves pie-in-the-sky idealism. Nobody will vote to change the existing system so radically; therefore, it is a waste of our time to debate it. Following this prompt, supporters would have to argue that pass/fail grading is workable and that enough faculty are disposed to it that the proposal is worth debating. Opponents might argue that the faculty at Weasel College are so traditional that pass/fail has utterly no chance of being accepted, despite its merits.

Stock issue 5: *What will be the unforeseen positive and negative consequences of the proposal?* Suppose we do adopt a pass/fail system. What positive or negative consequences might occur that are different from what we at first predicted? Using this prompt, an opponent might argue that pass/fail grading will reduce the effort put forth by students and that the long-range effect will be writing of even lower quality than we have now. Supporters would try to find positive consequences—perhaps a new love of writing for its own sake rather than the sake of a grade.

❖ FOR CLASS DISCUSSION

The following collaborative task takes approximately two class days to complete. The exercise takes you through the process of creating a proposal argument.

1. In small groups, identify and list several major problems facing students in your college or university.

2. Decide among yourselves which are the most important of these problems and rank them in order of importance.

3. Take your group's number one problem and explore answers to the following questions. Group recorders should be prepared to present your group's answers to the class as a whole:
   a. Why is the problem a problem?
   b. For whom is the problem a problem?
   c. How will these people suffer if the problem is not solved? (Give specific examples.)
   d. Who has the power to solve the problem?
   e. Why hasn't the problem been solved up to this point?
   f. How can the problem be solved? (That is, create a proposal.)
   g. What are the probable benefits of acting on your proposal?
   h. What costs are associated with your proposal?
   i. Who will bear those costs?
   j. Why should this proposal be enacted?
   k. Why is it better than alternative proposals?

4. As a group, draft an outline for a proposal argument in which you:
   a. Describe the problem and its significance.
   b. Propose your solution to the problem.
   c. Justify your proposal by showing how the benefits of adopting that proposal outweigh the costs.

5. Recorders for each group should write their group's outline on the board and be prepared to explain it to the class.

ORGANIZING A PROPOSAL ARGUMENT

When you write your draft, you may find it helpful to have at hand some plans for typical ways of organizing a proposal argument. What follows are two common methods of organization. Option 1 is the plan most typical for practical proposals. Either Option 1 or Option 2 is an effective plan for a policy proposal.

Option 1

- Presentation of a problem that needs solving:
  - description of problem (give problem presence)
  - background, including previous attempts to solve problem
  - argument that the problem is solvable (optional)

- Presentation of writer's proposal:

  succinct statement of the proposed solution serves as thesis statement

  explain specifics of proposed solution

- Summary and rebuttal of opposing views (in practical proposals, this section is often a summary and rejection of alternative ways of solving the problem)

- Justification persuading reader that proposal should be enacted:

  Reason 1 presented and developed

  Reason 2 presented and developed and so forth

- Conclusion that exhorts audience to act

  Give presence to final sentences.

Option 2

- Presentation of issue, including background
- Presentation of writer's proposal
- Justification

  Reason 1:   Show that proposal addresses a serious problem.

  Reason 2:   Show that proposal will solve problem.

  Reason 3:   Give additional reasons for enacting proposal.

- Summary and refutation of opposing views
- Conclusion that exhorts audience to act

CONDITIONS FOR REBUTTAL: TESTING A PROPOSAL ARGUMENT

As we've suggested throughout the foregoing discussion, proposal arguments are vulnerable on many grounds—the innate conservatism of most people, the difficulty of clearly anticipating all the consequences of the proposal, and so forth. What questions, then, can we put specifically to proposal arguments to help us anticipate these vulnerabilities?

Will a skeptic deny that my problem is really a problem?   The first question to ask of your proposal is "What's so wrong with the status quo that change is necessary?" The second question is "Who loses if the status quo is changed?" Be certain not to overlook this second question. Most proposal makers can demonstrate that some sort of problem exists, but often it is a problem only for certain groups of people. Solving the problem will thus prove a benefit to some people but a cost to others. If your audience examines the problem from the perspective of the potential losers rather than the winners, they can often raise doubts about your proposal.

For example, one state recently held an initiative on a proposed "bottle bill" that would fight litter by permitting the sale of soda and beer only in returnable bottles. Sales outlets would be required to charge a substantial deposit on the bottles in order to encourage people to return them. Proponents of the proposal emphasized citizens as "winners" sharing in the new cleanliness of a landscape no longer littered with cans. To refute this argument, opponents showed consumers as "losers" burdened with the high cost of deposits and the hassle of collecting and returning bottles to grocery stores.

Will a skeptic doubt the effectiveness of my solution?   Assuming that you've satisfied yourself that a significant problem exists for a significant number of people, a number of questions remain to be asked about the quality of the proposed solution to solve the problem. First, "Does the problem exist for the reasons cited, or might there be alternative explanations?" Here we return to the familiar ground of causal arguments. A proposal supposedly strikes at the cause of a problem. But perhaps striking at that "cause" won't solve the problem. Perhaps you've mistaken a symptom for a cause, or confused two commonly associated but essentially unlinked phenomena for a cause-effect relationship. For example, will paying teachers higher salaries improve the quality of teaching or merely attract greedier rather than brighter people? Maybe more good teachers would be attracted and retained if they were given some other benefit (fewer students? smaller classes? more sabbaticals? more autonomy? more prestige?).

Another way to test your solution is to list all the uncertainties involved. This might be referred to as "The Devil you know is better than the Devil you don't know" strategy. Remind yourself of all the unanticipated consequences of past changes. Who, for example, would have thought back in the days when aerosol shaving cans were being developed that they might lead to diminished ozone layers, which might lead to more ultraviolet rays getting through the atmosphere from the sun, which would lead to higher incidences of skin cancer? The history of technology is full of such cautionary tales that can be invoked to remind you of the uncertain course that progress can sometimes take.

Will a skeptic think my proposal costs too much?   The most commonly asked question of any proposal is simply, "Do the benefits of enacting the proposal outweigh the costs?" As we saw above, you can't foresee all the consequences of any proposal. It's easy, before the fact, to exaggerate both the costs and the benefits of a proposal. So, in asking how much your proposal will cost, we urge you to make an honest estimate. Will your audience discover costs you hadn't anticipated—extra financial costs or unexpected psychological or environmental or aesthetic costs? As much as you can, anticipate these objections.

Will a skeptic suggest counterproposals?   Related to all that's been said so far is the counterproposal. Can you imagine an appealing alternative to both the status quo and the proposal that you're making? The more clearly your proposal shows that a significant problem exists, the more important it is that you be able to identify possible counterproposals. Any potential critic of a proposal to remedy an acknowledged problem will either have to make such a counterproposal or have to argue that the problem is simply in the nature of things. So, given the likelihood that you'll be faced with a counterproposal, it only makes sense to anticipate it and to work out a refutation of it before you have it thrown at you. And who knows, you may end up liking the counterproposal better and changing your mind about what to propose!

The following proposal argument by student writer Stephen Bean was written in response to the assignment on page 226, reproduced in typewriter format to illustrate a conventional style for academic research papers. It uses the documentation and stylistic guidelines of the Modern Language Association—referred to in most handbooks as MLA style.

Bean 1

Stephen Bean

Professor Arness

English 110

June 1, 199–

What Should Be Done about the Mentally Ill Homeless?

1   Winter paints Seattle's streets gray with misting rain that drops lightly but steadily into pools. Walking to work through one of Seattle's oldest districts, Pioneer Square, I see an incongruous mixture of people: both successful business types and a large population of homeless. Some walk to offices or lunches grasping cups of fresh ground coffee; others slowly push wobbling carts containing their earthly possessions wrapped carefully in black plastic. These scenes of homelessness have become common throughout America's urban centers—so common, perhaps, that despite our feelings of guilt and pity, we accept the presence of the homeless as permanent. The empty-stomach feeling of confronting a ragged panhandler has become an often accepted fact of living in the city. What can we do besides giving a few cents spare change?

2   Recently, a growing number of commentators have been focusing on the mentally ill homeless. In response to the violent murder of an elderly person by a homeless mentally ill man, New York City recently increased its efforts to locate and hospitalize dangerous homeless mentally ill individuals. New York's plan will include aggressive outreach—actively going out into the streets and shelters to locate mentally ill individuals and then involuntarily hospitalizing those deemed dangerous either to others or themselves (Dugger, "Danger" B1). Although the New York Civil Liberties Union has objected to this action on the grounds that

Bean 2

involuntary hospitalization may violate the rights of the mentally ill, many applaud the city's action as a first step in dealing with a problem which the nation has grossly ignored. One highly influential commentator, Charles Krauthammer, has recently called for widescale involuntary reinstitutionalization of the mentally ill homeless—a seemingly persuasive proposal until one begins to do research on the mentally ill homeless. Adopting Krauthammer's proposal would be a dangerous and wrong-headed policy for America. Rather, research shows that community-based care in which psychiatrists and social workers provide coordinated services in the community itself is a more effective solution to the problems of the mentally ill homeless than widescale institutionalization.

In his article "How to Save the Homeless Mentally Ill," Charles Krauthammer   3
argues that the federal government should assist the states in rebuilding a national system of asylums. He proposes that the criteria for involuntary institutionalization be broadened: The state should be permitted to institutionalize mentally ill persons involuntarily not only if they are deemed dangerous to others or themselves (the current criterion for institutionalization) but also if they are "degraded" or made helpless by their illness. He points to the large number of patients released from state institutions in the 1960s and 1970s who, finding no support in communities, ended up on the streets. Arguing that the mentally ill need the stability and supervision that only an institution can provide, Krauthammer proposes substantial increases in federal taxes to fund rebuilding of asylums. He argues that the mentally ill need unique solutions because of their unique problems; their homelessness, he claims, stems from mental illness not poverty. Finally, Krauthammer rebuts the argument that involuntary hospitalization violates civil liberties. He argues that "liberty" has no meaning to someone suffering from severe psychosis. To let someone suffer the pains of mental illness and the pains of the street when they could be treated and recover is a cruel right indeed. He points to the project HELP program where less than a fifth of those involuntarily hospitalized protested their commitment; most are glad, he claims, for a warm bed, nutritious food, and a safe environment.

Krauthammer's argument, while persuasive on first reading, is based on four   4
seriously flawed assumptions. His first assumption is the widely accepted notion that deinstitutionalization of state mental hospitals in the 1960s and 1970s is a

primary cause of the current homelessness problem in America. Krauthammer talks about the hundreds of thousands released from the hospitals who have become "an army of grate-dwellers" (24). However, recent research has shown that the relationship of deinstitutionalization to homelessness is vastly overstated. Ethnologist Kim Hopper argues that while deinstitutionalization has partly contributed to increased numbers of mentally ill homeless its influence is far smaller than popularly believed. She argues that the data many used to support this claim were methodologically flawed and that researchers who found symptoms of mental illness in homeless people didn't try to ascertain whether these symptoms were the cause or effect of living on the street. Finally, she points out that a lag time of five years existed between the major release of state hospital patients and the rise of mentally ill individuals in shelters. This time lag suggests that other social and economic factors might have come into play to account for the rise of homelessness (156–57). Carl Cohen and Kenneth Thompson also point to this time lag as evidence to reject deinstitutionalization as the major cause of mentally ill homelessness (817). Jonathan Kozol argues that patients released from state hospitals in the late sixties and early seventies didn't go directly to the streets but went to single-room occupancy housing, such as cheap hotels or boarding houses. Many of these ex-patients became homeless, he argues, when almost half of single-room occupancy housing was replaced by more expensive housing between 1970 and 1980 (18). The effects of this housing shortage might account for the lag time that Hopper and Cohen and Thompson cite.

5   Krauthammer's focus on mental illness as a cause of much of the homelessness problem leads to another of the implicit assumptions in his argument: that the mentally ill comprise a large percentage of the homeless population. Krauthammer avoids mentioning specific numbers until the end of his article when he writes:

> The argument over how many of the homeless are mentally ill is endless. The estimates, which range from one-quarter to three-quarters, vary with method, definition, and ideology. But so what if even the lowest estimates are right? Even if treating the mentally ill does not end homelessness, how can that possibly justify not treating the tens, perhaps hundreds of thousands who would benefit from a partial solution? (25)

Bean 4

This paragraph is rhetorically shrewd. It downplays the numbers issue and takes the moral high road. But by citing estimates between one-quarter and three-quarters, Krauthammer effectively suggests that a neutral estimate might place the number around fifty percent—a high estimate reinforced by his leap from "tens" to "perhaps hundreds of thousands" in the last sentence.

Close examination of the research, however, reveals that the percentage of mentally ill people on the streets may be even lower than Krauthammer's lowest figure of 25%. In an extensive study conducted by David Snow and colleagues, a team member lived among the homeless for 12 months to collect data on mental illness. Additionally, the researchers tracked the institutional histories of a random sample of homeless. The study found that only 10% of the street sample and 16% of the tracking sample showed mental illness. The researchers pointed to a number of reasons why some previous estimates and studies may have inflated the numbers of mentally ill homeless. They suggest that the visibility of the mentally ill homeless (their odd behaviors make them stand out) combined with the widespread belief that deinstitutionalization poured vast numbers of mentally ill onto the streets caused researchers to bias their data. Thus researchers would often interpret behavior such as socially inappropriate actions, depression, and sleeping disorders as indications of mental illness, when in fact these actions may simply be the natural response to living in the harsh environment of the street. Additionally, the Snow study points to the medicalization of homelessness. This phenomenon means that when doctors and psychiatrists treat the homeless they focus on their medical and psychological problems while ignoring their social and economic ones. Because studies of the mentally ill homeless have been dominated by doctors and psychologists, these studies tend to inflate the numbers of mentally ill on the streets (419–21).

Another persuasive study showing low percentages of mentally ill homeless—although not as low as Snow's estimates—comes from Deborah Dennis and colleagues who surveyed the past decade of research on mentally ill homeless. The combined findings of all these research studies suggest that the mentally ill comprise between 28% and 37% of the homeless population (Dennis et al. 1130). Thus we see that while the mentally ill make up a significant proportion of the homeless population they do not approach a majority as Krauthammer and others would have us believe.

8   Krauthammer's third assumption is that the causes of homelessness among the mentally ill are largely psychological rather than socioeconomic. By this thinking, the solutions to their problems involve the treatment of their illnesses rather than the alleviation of poverty. Krauthammer writes, "Moreover, whatever solutions are eventually offered the non-mentally ill homeless, they will have little relevance to those who are mentally ill" (25). Closer examination, however, shows that other factors play a greater role in causing homelessness among the mentally ill than mental illness. Jonathan Kozol argues that housing and the economy played the largest role in causing homelessness among the mentally ill. He points to two million jobs lost every year since 1980, an increase in poverty, a massive shortage in low income housing, and a drop from 500,000 subsidized private housing units to 25,000 during the Reagan era (17–18). Cohen and Thompson also place primary emphasis on poverty and housing shortages:

> Data suggest that most homeless mentally ill persons lost their rooms in single-room-occupancy hotels or low-priced apartments not because of psychoticism but because they 1) were evicted because of renewal projects and fires, 2) were victimized by unscrupulous landlords or by other residents, or 3) could no longer afford the rent. (818)

Douglas Mossman and Michael Perlin cite numerous studies which show that mental illness itself is not the primary factor causing homelessness among the mentally ill; additionally, they point out that the severity of mental illness itself is closely linked to poverty. They argue that lack of private health care increases poor health and the frequency of severe mental illness. They conclude, "Homelessness is, if nothing else, a condition of poverty, and poor individuals in general are at increased risk for episodes of psychiatric illness" (952). Krauthammer's article conveniently ignores the role of poverty, suggesting that much of the homeless problem could be solved by moving the mentally ill back into institutions. But the evidence suggests that symptoms of mental illness are often the <u>results</u> of being homeless and that any efforts to treat the psychological problems of the mentally ill must also address the socioeconomic problems.

Krauthammer's belief that the causes of mentally ill homelessness are   9
psychological rather than social and economic leads to a fourth assumption that
the mentally ill homeless are a distinct subgroup who need different treatment
from the other homeless groups. Krauthammer thus divides the homeless into
three primary groups: (1) the mentally ill; (2) those who choose to live on the
street; and (3) "the victims of economic calamity, such as family breakup or job
loss" (25). By believing that the mentally ill homeless are not also victims of
"economic calamity," Krauthammer greatly oversimplifies their problems. As
Cohen and Thompson show, it is difficult to separate the mentally ill homeless
and the non-mentally ill homeless. "On closer examination, 'not mentally ill'
homeless people have many mental health problems; similarly, the 'mentally ill'
homeless have numerous nonpsychiatric problems that arise from the sociopolitical
elements affecting all homeless people" (817). Because the two groups are so
similar, it is counterproductive to insist on entirely different solutions for both
groups.

Krauthammer's proposal thus fails on a number of points. It won't solve nearly   10
as much of the homelessness problem as he leads us to believe. It would commit
valuable taxpayer dollars to building asylums rather than attacking the underlying
causes of homelessness in general. And perhaps most importantly, its emphasis on
involuntary confinement in asylums is not the best long-range method to treat the
mentally ill homeless. Instead of moving the mentally ill homeless away from
society into asylums, we would meet their needs far more effectively through
monitored community-based care. Instead of building expensive institutions we
should focus on finding alternative low cost housing for the mentally ill homeless
and meet their needs through teams of psychiatrists and social workers who could
oversee a number of patients' treatments, monitoring such things as taking
medications and receiving appropriate counseling. Involuntary hospitalization may
still be needed for the most severely deranged, but the majority of mentally ill
homeless people can be better treated in their communities.

From a purely financial perspective, perhaps the most compelling reason to   11
prefer community-based care is that it offers a more efficient use of taxpayer
dollars. In a letter to the <u>New York Times</u> on behalf of the Project for Psychiatric

Outreach to the Homeless, Drs. Katherine Falk and Gail Albert give us the following statistics:

> It costs $105,000 to keep someone in a state hospital for a year. But it costs only $15,000 to $35,000 (depending on the intensity of services) to operate supported residences in the community with the necessary onsite psychiatrists, case workers, case managers, drug counselors, and other rehabilitation services. (A30)

It can be argued, in fact, that the cost of maintaining state hospitals for the mentally ill actually prevents large numbers of mentally ill from receiving treatment. When large numbers of mentally ill persons were released from state hospitals during the deinstitutionalization movement of the 1960s and 1970s, the original plan was to convert resources to community-based care. Even though the number of patients in state institutions has dramatically decreased over the past two decades, institutions have continued to maintain large shares of state funding. According to David Rothman of Columbia University, "Historically, the dollars have remained locked in the institutions and did not go into community mental health" (qtd. in Dugger, "Debate" B2). In fact, cutting New York's state hospital budget would provide enough money for over 20,000 units in supported community residences (Falk and Albert A30). Furthermore, Linda Chafetz points out that having the money to pay for such resources as clothes, bathing facilities, meals, and housing is the most urgent concern among caregivers in treating the mentally ill homeless. According to Chafetz, "The immediate and urgent nature of the resource dilemma can make other issues appear almost frivolous by comparison" (451). With such an obvious shortage of resources, pouring what money we have into the high-cost institutional system would be a grave disservice to the majority of the mentally ill homeless population and to the homeless population as a whole.

12   A second reason to adopt community-based care over widescale institutionalization is that the vast majority of the homeless mentally ill do not need the tight control of the hospital system. Cohen and Thompson cite a number of studies which show "that only 5%–7% of single adult homeless persons are in need of acute inpatient care" (820). Involuntarily hospitalizing a large number of homeless who don't demand institutionalized care is not only a waste of resources but also an unnecessary assault on individual freedom for many.

Finally, the community-based care system is preferable to institutionalization   13
because it most often gives the best treatment to its patients. Although
Krauthammer claims that less than a fifth of involuntarily hospitalized patients have
legally challenged their confinement (25), numerous studies indicate there is
widespread resistance to institutional care by the homeless mentally ill. Mossman
and Perlin cite multiple sources indicating that many mentally ill have legitimate
reasons to fear state hospitals. Moreover, they provide evidence that many would
rather suffer the streets and their mental illness than suffer the conditions of state
hospitals and the side effects of medications. The horrible track record of conditions
of state hospitals supports the logic of this thinking. On the other hand, Mossman
and Perlin point out many mentally ill homeless persons will accept treatment from
the type of alternative settings community-based care offers (953). Powerful
evidence showing the success of community-based care comes from early
evaluation reports of ACCESS (Access to Community Care and Effective Services), a
community-based program of the Center for Mental Health. More than 11,000
mentally ill homeless have received services through this program, which reports
"significant improvements in almost all outcome measures," such as "a 66 percent
decrease in minor criminal activity" and "a 46 percent decrease in reported
psychotic symptoms" ("Articles"). Given that institutionalization can leave mentally
ill persons feeling humiliated and disempowered (Cohen and Thompson 819),
community-based solutions such as ACCESS seem the best approach.

Given the advantages of community-based care, what is the appeal of   14
Krauthammer's proposal? Involuntary institutionalization appeals to our common
impulse to lock our problems out of sight. As crime increases, we want to build
more prisons; when we see ragged men and women mumbling in the street, we
want to shut them up in institutions. But the simple solutions are not often the
most effective ones. Institutionalization is tempting, but alternative methods have
shown themselves to be more effective. Community-based care works better
because it's based on a better understanding of the problem. Community-based
care, by allowing the psychiatrist and social worker to work together, attacks both
the mental and social dimensions of the problem: the client not only receives
psychological counseling and medication, but also help on how to find affordable
housing, how to manage money and shop effectively, and how to live in a

community. Without roots in a community, a patient released from a mental asylum will quickly return to the streets. To pour scarce resources into the expensive project of rebuilding asylums—helping the few while ignoring the many—would be a terrible misuse of taxpayer dollars.

15   Krauthammer's argument appeals in another way also. By viewing the homeless as mentally ill, we see them as inherently different from ourselves. We needn't see any connection to those mumbling bag ladies and those ragged men lying on the grates. When we regard them as mentally ill, we see ourselves as largely unresponsible for the conditions that led them to the streets. Those professional men and women carrying their espresso Starbuck's coffees to their upscale offices in Seattle's Pioneer Square don't have to be reminded that this historic district used to contain a number of single-occupancy boarding houses. The professionals work where the homeless used to live. The rich and the poor are thus interconnected, reminding us that homelessness is primarily a social and economic problem, not a mental health problem. And even the most deranged of the mentally ill homeless are messengers of a nationwide scourge of poverty.

Works Cited*

"Ariticles to Focus on National Effort to Help People Who are Homeless and Have Mental Illness." Press release. 3 March 1997. National Mental Health Services Knowledge Exchange Network (KEN). 23 April 1998. <http://www.mentalhealth.org./resource/praccess.htm>.

Chafetz, Linda. "Withdrawal from the Homeless Mentally Ill." Community Mental Health Journal 26 (1990): 449–61.

Cohen, Carl I., and Kenneth S. Thompson. "Homeless Mentally Ill or Mentally Ill Homeless?" American Journal of Psychiatry 149 (1992): 816–23.

Dennis, Deborah L. et al. "A Decade of Research and Services for Homeless Mentally Ill Persons: Where Do We Stand?" American Psychologist 46 (1991): 1129–38.

Dugger, Celia W. "A Danger to Themselves and Others." New York Times 24 Jan. 1993: B1+.

---. "A Debate Unstilled: New Plan for Homeless Mentally Ill Does Not Address Larger Questions." New York Times 22 Jan. 1993: B2.

*When preparing your own essay using MLA style, begin the works cited list on a separate page.

Bean 10

Falk, Katherine, and Gail Albert. Letter. <u>New York Times</u> 11 Feb. 1993: A30.

Hopper, Kim. "More than Passing Strangers: Homelessness and Mental Illness in
     New York City." <u>American Ethnologist</u> 15 (1988): 155–57.

Kozol, Jonathan. "Are the Homeless Crazy?" <u>Harper's Magazine</u> Sept. 1988: 17–19.

Krauthammer, Charles. "How to Save the Homeless Mentally Ill." <u>New Republic</u> 8
     Feb. 1988: 22–25.

Mossman, Douglas, and Michael L. Perlin. "Psychiatry and the Homeless Mentally
     Ill: A Reply to Dr. Lamb." <u>American Journal of Psychiatry</u> 149 (1992): 951–56.

Snow, David A. et al. "The Myth of Pervasive Mental Illness among the Homeless."
     <u>Social Problems</u> 33 (1986): 407–23.

❧ WRITING ASSIGNMENTS FOR CHAPTER 14

OPTION 1: *A practical proposal addressing a local problem*   Write a practical proposal offering a solution to a local problem. Your proposal should have three main sections: (1) description of the problem, (2) proposed solution, and (3) justification. You may include additional sections or subsections as needed. Longer proposals often include an *abstract* at the beginning of the proposal to provide a summary overview of the whole argument. (Sometimes called the *executive summary*, this abstract may be the only portion of the proposal read by high-level managers.) Sometimes proposals are accompanied by a *letter of transmittal*—a one-page business letter that introduces the proposal to its intended audience and provides some needed background about the writer.

Document design is important in practical proposals, which are aimed at busy people who have to make many decisions under time constraints. Because the writer of a practical proposal usually produces the finished document (practical proposals are seldom submitted to newspapers or magazines for publication), he or she must pay particular attention to the attractive design of the document. An effective design helps establish the writer's *ethos* as a quality-oriented professional and helps make the reading of the proposal as easy as possible. Document design includes effective use of heading and subheadings, attractive typeface and layout, flawless editing, and other features enhancing the visual appearance of the document.

OPTION 2: *A policy proposal as a guest editorial*   Write a two- to three-page policy proposal suitable for publication as a feature editorial in a college or city newspaper or in some publication associated with a particular group or activity such as a church newsletter or employee bulletin. The voice and style of your argument should be aimed at general readers of your chosen publication. Your editorial should have the following features:

1. The identification of a problem (Persuade your audience that this is a genuine problem that needs solving; give it presence.)
2. A proposal for action that will help alleviate the problem
3. A justification of your solution (the reasons that your audience should accept your proposal and act on it)

OPTION 3: *A researched argument proposing public policy*   Write an eight- to twelve-page proposal argument as a formal research paper, using research data for support. Your argument should include all the features of the shorter argument in Option 2 and also a summary and refutation of opposing views (in the form of alternative proposals and/or differing cost-benefit analyses of your proposal.) An example of a researched policy proposal is student writer Stephen Bean's "What Should Be Done about the Mentally Ill Homeless?" on pages 216–225.

c h a p t e r 15

Ethical
Arguments

The line between ethical arguments ("Is X morally good?") and other kinds of values disputes is often pretty thin. Many apparently straightforward practical values issues can turn out to have an ethical dimension. For example, in deciding what kind of car to buy, most people would base their judgments on criteria such as cost, reliability, safety, comfort, stylishness, and so forth. But some people might feel morally obligated to buy the most fuel-efficient car, or not to buy a car from a manufacturer whose investment or labor policies they found morally repugnant. Depending on how large a role ethical considerations played in the evaluation, we might choose to call this an *ethical argument* as opposed to a simpler kind of values argument. In any case, we here devote a separate chapter to ethical arguments because we believe they represent special difficulties to the student of argumentation. Let's take a look now at some of those special difficulties.

SPECIAL DIFFICULTIES OF
ETHICAL ARGUMENTS

One crucial difficulty with ethical arguments concerns the role of "purpose" in defining criteria for judgment. In Chapter 13, we assumed that every class of beings has a purpose, that the purpose should be defined as narrowly as possible, and that the criteria for judgment derive directly from that purpose. For example, the purpose of a computer repairperson is to analyze the problem with my computer, to fix it, and to do so in a timely and cost-efficient manner. Once I formulate this purpose, it is easy for me to define criteria for a good computer repairperson.

In ethics, however, the place of purpose is much fuzzier. Just what is the purpose of human beings? Before I can begin to determine what ethical duties I have to myself and to others, I'm going to have to address this question; and because the chance of reaching agreement on that question remains remote, many ethical arguments are probably unresolvable. In ethical discussions we don't ask what a "manager" or a "judge" or a "point guard" is supposed to do in situations relevant to the respective classes; we're asking what John Doe is supposed to be or what Jane Doe is supposed to do with her life. Who they are or what their social function is makes no difference to our ethical assessment of their actions or traits of character. A morally bad person may be a good judge and a morally good person may be a bad manager.

As the discussion so far has suggested, disagreements about ethical issues often stem from different systems of belief. We might call this problem the problem of warrants. This is, people disagree because they do not share common assumptions on which to ground their arguments.

If, for example, you say that good manners are necessary for keeping us from reverting to a state of raw nature, your implied warrant is that raw nature is bad. But if you say that good manners are a political tool by which a ruling class tries to suppress the natural vitality of the working class, then your warrant is that liberation of the working classes from the corrupt habits of the ruling class is good. It would be difficult, therefore, for people representing these opposing belief systems to carry on a reasonable discussion of etiquette—their whole assumptions about value, about the role of the natural self, and about political progress are different. This is why ethical arguments are often so acrimonious—they frequently lack shared warrants to serve as starting places for argument.

It is precisely because of the problem of warrants, however, that you should try to confront issues of ethics with rational deliberation. The arguments you produce may not persuade others to your view, but they should lay out more clearly the grounds and warrants of your own beliefs. Such arguments serve the purpose of clarification. By drafting essays on ethical issues, you begin to see more clearly what you believe and why you believe it. Although the arguments demanded by ethical issues require rigorous thought, they force us to articulate our most deeply held beliefs and our richest feelings.

AN OVERVIEW OF MAJOR ETHICAL SYSTEMS

When we are faced with an ethical issue, such as the issue of whether terrorism can be justified, we must move from arguments of good or bad to arguments of right or wrong. The terms *right* and *wrong* are clearly different from the terms *good* and *bad* when the latter terms mean simply "effective" (meets purposes of class, as in "This is a good stereo system") or "ineffective" (fails to meet purposes of class, as in "This is a bad cookbook"). But *right* and *wrong* often also differ from what seems to be a moral use of the terms *good* and *bad*. We might say, for example, that warm sunshine is good because it brings pleasure and that cancer is bad because it brings pain and death, but that is not quite the same thing as saying that sunshine is "right" and cancer is "wrong." It is the problem of "right" and "wrong" that ethical arguments confront.

Thus it is not enough to say that terrorism is "bad"; obviously everyone, including most terrorists, would agree that terrorism is "bad" in that it causes suffering and anguish. If we want to condemn terrorism on ethical grounds, we have to say that it's also "wrong" as well as "bad." In saying that something's wrong, we're saying that all people ought to refrain from doing it. We're also saying that acts that are morally "wrong" are in some way blameworthy and deserve censure, a conclusion that doesn't necessarily follow a negative nonethical judgment, which might lead simply to our not buying something or not hiring someone. From a nonethical standpoint, you may even say that someone is a "good" terrorist in that he fully realizes the purposes of the class "terrorist": He causes great damage with a minimum of resources, brings a good deal of attention to his cause, and doesn't get caught. The ethical question here, however, is not whether or not this person is a good member of the class, but whether it is wrong for such a class to exist.

In asking the question "Ought the class 'terrorist' exist?" or, to put it more colloquially, "Are there ever cases where terrorism is justified?" we need to seek some consistent approach or principle. In the phrase used by some philosophers, ethical judgments are typically "universalizable" statements. That is, when we oppose a terrorist act, our ethical argument (assuming it's a coherent one) should be capable of being generalized into an ethical principle that will hold for all similar cases. Ethical disputes usually involve clashes between such principles. For example, a pro-terrorist might say, "My ends justify my means," whereas an antiterrorist might say, "The sanctity of human life is not to be violated for any reason." The differences in principles such as these account for different schools of ethical thought.

There are many different schools of ethical thought—too many to present in this chapter. But to help you think your way through ethical issues, we'll look at some of the most prevalent methods of resolving ethical questions. The first of these methods, "naive egoism," is really less a method than a retreat from method. It doesn't represent a coherent ethical view, but it is a position that many people lapse into on given issues. It represents, in short, the most seductive alternative to rigorous ethical thought.

Naive Egoism

Back in Chapter 1, we touched on the morality of the Sophists and suggested that their underlying maxim was something like "might makes right." That is, in ethical terms, they were essentially egoists who used other people with impunity to realize their own ends. The appeal of this position, however repugnant it may sound when laid out like this, is that it rationalizes self-promotion and pleasure seeking: If we all follow the bidding of our egos, we'll be happy.

On examination, however, this philosophy proves to be incoherent. It should be noted, however, that philosophers don't reject naive egoism simply because they believe "selfishness is bad." Rather, philosophers tend to assess ethical systems according to such factors as their scope (how often will this system provide principles to guide our moral action?) and their precision (how clearly can we analyze a given situation using the tools of the system?) rather than their intuition about whether the system is right or wrong. Although naive egoism has great scope (you can always ask, "What's in it for me?"), it is far from precise, as we'll try to show.

Take the case of young Ollie Unger, who has decided that he wants to quit living irrationally and to join some official school of ethical thought. The most appealing school at the moment—recommended to him by a philosophy major over at the Phi Upsilon Nu house—is the "I'm Number One!" school of scruples. He heads downtown to their opulent headquarters and meets with the school's guru, one Dr. Pheelgood.

"What's involved in becoming a member of your school?" Ollie inquires.

"Ahhh, my apple-cheeked chum, that's the beauty of it. It's so simple. You just give me all your worldly possessions and do whatever I tell you to do."

Ollie's puzzled. He had in mind something a bit more, well, gratifying. He was hoping for something closer to the philosophy of eat, drink, and make merry—all justified through rational thought.

"You seem disappointed," Pheelgood observes. "What's the matter?"

"Well, gee, it just doesn't sound like I'm going to be number one here. I thought that was the idea. To look out for *numero uno*."

"Of course not, silly boy. This is after all the "I'm Number One School of Scruples." And I, *moi*, am the I who's number one.

"But I thought the idea of your school was for everyone to have the maximum amount of enjoyment in life."

Peevishness clouds Pheelgood's face. "Look here, Unger, if I arrange things for you to have a good time, it's going to cost me. Next you'll be asking me to open soup kitchens. If I'm to look out for number one, then you've got to act entirely differently from me. I take, you give. *Capiche?*"

As should be obvious by now, it's very difficult to systematize egoism. You have two sets of demands in constant conflict—the demands of your own personal ego and those of everyone else's. It's impossible, hence, to universalize a statement that all members of the school could hold equally without contradicting all other members of the school.

Some egoists try to get around this problem by conceding that we must limit our self-gratification either by entering into contracts or institutional arrangements with others or by sacrificing short-term interests for long-term ones. We might, for example, give to the poor now in order to avoid a revolution of the masses later. But once they've let the camel's nose of concern for others into the tent, it's tough to hang onto egoistic philosophy. Having considered naive egoism, let's turn to a pair of more workable alternatives.

In shifting to the two most common forms of ethical thought, we shift point of view from "I" to "us." Both groups, those who make ethical judgments according to the consequences of any act and those who make ethical judgments according to the conformity of any act with a principle, are guided by their concern for the whole of humanity rather than simply the self.

Consequences as the Grounds of Ethics

Perhaps the best-known example of evaluating acts according to their ethical consequences is John Stuart Mill's Utilitarianism. The goal of Utilitarianism, according to Mill, is "the greatest good for the greatest number." It is a very down-to-earth philosophy that grew out of nineteenth-century British philosophers' concern to demystify ethics and to make it work in the practical world.

As Mill makes clear, a focus on ethical consequences allows you readily to assess a wide range of acts. You can apply the principle of utility—which says that an action is morally right if it produces a greater net value (benefits minus costs) than any available alternative action—to virtually any situation and it will help you reach a decision. Obviously, however, it's not always easy to make the calculations called for by the principle, since, like any prediction of the future, an estimate of consequences is conjectural. In particular, it's often very hard to assess the long-term consequences of any action. Too often, Utilitarianism seduces us into a short-term analysis of a moral problem simply because long-term consequences are very difficult to predict.

Principles as the Grounds of Ethics

Any ethical system based on principles will ultimately rest on one or two moral tenets that we are duty-bound to uphold, no matter what the consequences. Sometimes the moral tenets come from religious faith—for example, the Ten Commandments. At other times, however, the principles are derived from philosophical reasoning, as in the case of German philosopher Immanuel Kant. Kant held that no one should ever use another person as a means to his own ends and that everyone should always act as if his acts were the basis of universal law. In other words, Kant held that we were duty bound to respect other people's sanctity and to act in the same way that we would want all other people to act. The great advantage of such a system is its clarity and precision. We are never overwhelmed by a multiplicity of contradictory and difficult-to-quantify consequences; we simply make sure we are not violating a principle of our ethical system and proceed accordingly.

The Two Systems Compared

In the eyes of many people, a major advantage of a system such as Utilitarianism is that it impels us to seek out the best solution, whereas systems based on principle merely enjoin us not to violate a principle by our action. In turn, applying an ethical principle will not always help us resolve necessarily relativistic moral dilemmas. For instance, what if none of our available choices violates our moral principles? How do we choose among a host of permissible acts? Or what about situations where none of the alternatives is permitted by our principles? How might we choose the least bad alternative?

To further our comparison of the two systems, let's ask what a Mill or a Kant might say about the previously mentioned issue of terrorism. Here the Kantian position is clear: To kill another person to realize your own ends is palpably evil and forbidden.

But a follower of Mill will face a less clear choice. A Utilitarian could not automatically rule out terrorism or any other means so long as it led ultimately to the greatest good for the greatest number. If a nation is being slowly starved by those around it, if its people are dying, its institutions crumbling and its future disappearing, who's to say that the aggrieved nation is not justified in taking a few hundred lives to improve the lot of hundreds of thousands? The Utilitarian's first concern is to determine if terrorism will most effectively bring about that end. So long as the desired end represents the best possible net value and the means are effective at bringing about the end, the Utilitarian can, in theory anyway, justify almost any action.

Given the shared cultural background and values of most of us, not to mention our own vulnerability to terrorism, the Kantian argument is probably very appealing here. Indeed, Kantian ethical arguments have overwhelming appeal for us when the principle being invoked is already widely held within our culture, and when the violation of that principle will have clear and immediate negative consequences for us. But in a culture that doesn't share that principle and for whom the consequences of violation are positive rather than negative, the argument will undoubtedly appear weaker, a piece of fuzzy-headed idealism.

 FOR CLASS DISCUSSION

Working as individuals or in small groups:

1. Try to formulate a Utilitarian argument to persuade terrorist leaders in a country such as Libya to stop terrorist action.

2. Try to formulate an ethical principle or rule that would permit terrorism.

Some Compromise Positions Between Consequences and Principles

In the end, most of us would not be entirely happy with an ethic that forced us to ignore either principles or consequences. We all have certain principles that we simply can't violate no matter what the consequences. Thus, for example, some of us would not have dropped the bomb on Hiroshima even if it did mean saving many lives ultimately. And certainly, too, most of us will compromise our princi-ples in certain situations if we think the consequences justify it. For instance, how many of us would not deceive, harm, or even torture a kidnapper to save the life of a stolen child? Indeed, over the years, compromise positions have developed on both sides to accommodate precisely these concerns.

Some "consequentialists" have acknowledged the usefulness of general rules for creating more human happiness over the long run. To go back to our terrorism example, a consequentialist might oppose terrorist action on the grounds that "Thou shalt not kill another person in the name of greater material happiness for the group." This acknowledgment of an inviolable principle will still be based on a concern for consequences—for instance, a fear that terrorist acts may lead to World War III—but having such a principle allows the consequentialist to get away from a case-by-case analysis of acts and to keep more clearly before himself the long-range consequences of acts.

Among latter-day ethics of principle, meanwhile, the distinction between ab-solute obligation and what philosophers call *prima facie* obligation has been devel-oped to take account of the force of circumstances. An absolute obligation would be an obligation to follow a principle at all times, no matter what. A *prima facie* obligation, on the other hand, is an obligation to do something "other things being equal," that is, in a normal situation. Hence, to use a classic moral example, you would not, other things being equal, cannibalize an acquaintance. But if there are three of you in a lifeboat, one is dying and the other two will surely die if they don't get food, your *prima facie* obligation not to eat another might be waived. (However, the Royal Commission, which heard the original case, took a more Kantian posi-tion and condemned the action of the seamen who cannibalized their mate.)

These, then, in greatly condensed form, are the major alternative ways of thinking about ethical arguments. Let's now briefly summarize the ways you can use your knowledge of ethical thought to develop your arguments and refute those of others.

DEVELOPING AN ETHICAL ARGUMENT

To help you see how familiarity with these systems of ethical thought can help you develop an ethical argument, let's take an example case. How, for example, might we go about developing an argument in favor of abolishing the death penalty?

Our first task is to examine the issue from the two points of view just dis-cussed. How might a Utilitarian or a Kantian argue that the death penalty should be abolished? The argument on principle, as is usually the case, would appear to be the simpler of the two. Taking another life is difficult to justify under most eth-ical principles. For Kant, the sanctity of human life is a central tenet of ethics. Under Judeo-Christian ethics, meanwhile, one is told that "Vengeance is Mine, saith the Lord" and "Thou shalt not kill."

But, unfortunately for our hopes of simplicity, Kant argued in favor of capital punishment:

> There is no sameness of kind between death and remaining alive even under the most miserable conditions, and consequently there is no equality between the crime and the retribution unless the criminal is judicially condemned and put to death.*

Kant is here invoking an important principle of justice—that punishments should be proportionate to the crime. Kant appears to be saying that this principle must take precedence over his notion of the supreme worth of the individual. Some philosophers think he was being inconsistent in taking this position. Certainly, in establishing your own position, you could support a case against capital punishment based on Kant's principles, even if Kant himself did not reach the same conclusion. But you'd have to establish for your reader why you are at odds with Kant in this case. Kant's apparent inconsistency here illustrates how powerfully our intuitive judgments can affect our ethical judgment.

Likewise, with the Judeo-Christian position, passages can be found in the Bible that would support capital punishment, notably, the Old Testament injunction to take "an eye for an eye and a tooth for a tooth." The latter principle is simply a more poetic version of "Let the punishment fit the crime." Retribution should be of the same kind as the crime. And the commandment "Thou shalt not kill" is often interpreted as "Thou shalt not commit murder," an interpretation that not only permits just wars or killing in self-defense but is also consistent with other places in the Bible that suggest that people have not only the right but the obligation to punish wrongdoers and not leave their fate to God.

So, there appears to be no clearcut argument in support of abolishing capital punishment on the basis of principle. What about an argument based on consequences? How might abolishing capital punishment result in a net good that is at least as great as allowing it?

A number of possibilities suggest themselves. First, in abolishing capital punishment, we rid ourselves of the possibility that someone may be wrongly executed. To buttress this argument, we might want to search for evidence of how many people have been wrongly convicted of or executed for a capital crime. In making arguments based on consequence we must, whenever possible, offer empirical evidence that the consequences we assert exist—and exist to the degree we've suggested.

There are also other possible consequences that a Utilitarian might mention in defending the abolition of capital punishment. These include leaving open the possibility that the person being punished will be reformed, keeping those

---

*From Immanual Kant, *The Metaphysical Elements of Justice.*

charged with executing the murderer free from guilt, putting an end to the costly legal and political process of appealing the conviction, and so forth.

But in addition to calculating benefits, you will need also to calculate the costs of abolishing the death penalty and to show that the net result favors abolition. Failure to mention such costs is a serious weakness in many arguments of consequence. Moreover, in the issue at hand, the consequences that favor capital punishment—deterrence of further capital crimes, cost of imprisoning murderers, and so forth—are well known to most members of your audience.

In our discussion of capital punishment, then, we employed two alternative ways of thinking about ethical issues. In pursuing an argument from principle, we looked for an appropriate rule that permitted or at least did not prohibit our position. In pursuing an argument from consequence, we moved from what's permissible to what brings about the most desirable consequences. Most ethical issues, argued thoroughly, should be approached from both perspectives, so long as irreconcilable differences don't present themselves.

Should you choose to adopt one of these perspectives to the exclusion of the other, you will find yourself facing many of the problems mentioned here. This is not to say that you can't ever go to the wall for a principle or focus solely on consequences to the exclusion of principles; it's simply that you will be hard pressed to convince those of your audience who happen to be of the other persuasion and demand different sorts of proof. For the purpose of developing arguments, we encourage you to consider both the relevant principles and the possible consequences when you evaluate ethical actions.

TESTING ETHICAL ARGUMENTS

Perhaps the first question you should ask in setting out to analyze your draft of an ethical argument is, "To what extent is the argument based on consequences or on ethical principles?" If it's based exclusively on one of these two forms of ethical thought, then it's vulnerable to the sorts of criticism discussed here. A strictly principled argument that takes no account of the consequences of its position is vulnerable to a simple cost analysis. What are the costs in the case of adhering to this principle? There will undoubtedly be some, or else there would be no real argument. If the argument is based strictly on consequentialist grounds, we should ask if the position violates any rules or principles, particularly such commandments as the Golden Rule—"Do unto others as you would have others do unto you"—which most members of our audience adhere to. By failing to mention these alternative ways of thinking about ethical issues, we undercut not only our argument but our credibility as well.

Let's now consider a more developed examination of the two positions, starting with some of the more subtle weaknesses in a position based on principle. In practice people will sometimes take rigidly "principled" positions because they live in fear of "slippery slopes"; that is, they fear setting precedents that might lead to ever more dire consequences. Consider, for example, the slippery slope leading from birth control to euthanasia if you have an absolutist commitment to the sanctity of human life. Once we allow birth control in the form of condoms or pills, the principled absolutist would say, then we will be forced to accept birth control "abortions" in the first hours after conception (IUDs, "morning after" pills), then abortions in the first trimester, then in the second or even the third trimester. And once we have violated the sanctity of human life by allowing abortions, it is only a short step to euthanasia and finally to killing off all undesirables.

One way to refute a slippery-slope argument of this sort is to try to dig a foothold into the side of the hill to show that you don't necessarily have to slide all the way to the bottom. You would thus have to argue that allowing birth control does not mean allowing abortions (by arguing for differences between a fetus after conception and sperm and egg before conception), or that allowing abortions does not mean allowing euthanasia (by arguing for differences between a fetus and a person already living in the world).

Consequentialist arguments have different kinds of difficulties. As discussed before, the crucial difficulty facing anyone making a consequentialist argument is to calculate the consequences in a clear and reliable way. Have you considered all significant consequences? If you project your scenario of consequences further into the future (remember, consequentialist arguments are frequently stronger over the short term than over the long term, where many unforeseen consequences can occur), can you identify possibilities that work against the argument?

As also noted, consequentialist arguments carry a heavy burden of empirical proof. What evidence can you offer that the predicted consequences will in fact come to pass? Do you offer any evidence that alternative consequences won't occur? And just how do you prove that the consequences of any given action are a net good or evil?

In addition to the problems unique to each of the two positions, ethical arguments are vulnerable to the more general sorts of criticism, including consistency, recency, and relevance of evidence. Obviously, however, consequentialist arguments will be more vulnerable to weaknesses in evidence, whereas arguments based on principle are more open to questions about consistency of application.

 FOR CLASS DISCUSSION

1. Read the following essay, "The Case for Torture," by philosopher Michael Levin. Levin creates an argument that torture not only can be justified but is positively mandated under certain circumstances. Analyze Levin's argument in terms of our distinction between arguments from principle and arguments from consequence.

2. In "The Case for Torture," Levin mentions the possibility of some "murkier" cases in which it is difficult to draw a line demarcating the legitimate use of torture. Try to come up with several examples of these "murkier" cases and explain what makes them murky.

The Case for Torture

Michael Levin

It is generally assumed that torture is impermissible, a throwback to a more brutal age. 1
Enlightened societies reject it outright, and regimes suspected of using it risk the wrath of the United States.

I believe this attitude is unwise. There are situations in which torture is not merely 2
permissible but morally mandatory. Moreover, these situations are moving from the realm of imagination to fact.

Death: Suppose a terrorist has hidden an atomic bomb on Manhattan Island which 3
will detonate at noon on July 4 unless . . . (here follow the usual demands for money and release of his friends from jail). Suppose, further, that he is caught at 10 A.M. of the fateful day, but—preferring death to failure—won't disclose where the bomb is. What do we do? If we follow due process—wait for his lawyer, arraign him—millions of people will die. If the only way to save those lives is to subject the terrorist to the most excruciating possible pain, what grounds can there be for not doing so? I suggest there are none. In any case, I ask you to face the question with an open mind.

Torturing the terrorist is unconstitutional? Probably. But millions of lives surely out- 4
weigh constitutionality. Torture is barbaric? Mass murder is far more barbaric. Indeed, letting millions of innocents die in deference to one who flaunts his guilt is moral cowardice, an unwillingness to dirty one's hands. If *you* caught the terrorist, could you sleep nights knowing that millions died because you couldn't bring yourself to apply the electrodes?

Once you concede that torture is justified in extreme cases, you have admitted that the 5
decision to use torture is a matter of balancing innocent lives against the means needed to save them. You must now face more realistic cases involving more modest numbers. Someone plants a bomb on a jumbo jet. He alone can disarm it, and his demands cannot be met (or if they can, we refuse to set a precedent by yielding to his threats). Surely we can, we must, do anything to the extortionist to save the passengers. How can we tell 300, or 100, or 10 people who never asked to be put in danger, "I'm sorry, you'll have to die in agony, we just couldn't bring ourselves to . . . "

Here are the results of an informal poll about a third, hypothetical, case. Suppose a ter- 6
rorist group kidnapped a newborn baby from a hospital. I asked four mothers if they would approve of torturing kidnappers if that were necessary to get their own newborns back. All said yes, the most "liberal" adding that she would like to administer it herself.

7   I am not advocating torture as punishment. Punishment is addressed to deeds irrevocably past. Rather, I am advocating torture as an acceptable measure for preventing future evils. So understood, it is far less objectionable than many extant punishments. Opponents of the death penalty, for example, are forever insisting that executing a murderer will not bring back his victim (as if the purpose of capital punishment were supposed to be resurrection, not deterrence or retribution). But torture, in the cases described, is intended not to bring anyone back but to keep innocents from being dispatched. The most powerful argument against using torture as a punishment or to secure confessions is that such practices disregard the rights of the individual. Well, if the individual is all that important—and he is—it is correspondingly important to protect the rights of individuals threatened by terrorists. If life is so valuable that it must never be taken, the lives of the innocents must be saved even at the price of hurting the one who endangers them.

8   Better precedents for torture are assassination and pre-emptive attack. No Allied leader would have flinched at assassinating Hitler, had that been possible. (The Allies did assassinate Heydrich.) Americans would be angered to learn that Roosevelt could have had Hitler killed in 1943—thereby shortening the war and saving millions of lives—but refused on moral grounds. Similarly, if nation A learns that nation B is about to launch an unprovoked attack, A has a right to save itself by destroying B's military capability first. In the same way, if the police can by torture save those who would otherwise die at the hands of kidnappers or terrorists, they must.

9   **Idealism:**   There is an important difference between terrorists and their victims that should mute talk of the terrorists' "rights." The terrorist's victims are at risk unintentionally, not having asked to be endangered. But the terrorist knowingly initiated his actions. Unlike his victims, he volunteered for the risks of his deed. By threatening to kill for profit or idealism, he renounces civilized standards, and he can have no complaint if civilization tries to thwart him by whatever means necessary.

10   Just as torture is justified only to save lives (not extort confessions or recantations), it is justifiably administered only to those *known* to hold innocent lives in their hands. Ah, but how can the authorities ever be sure they have the right malefactor? Isn't there a danger of error and abuse? Won't We turn into Them?

11   Questions like these are disingenuous in a world in which terrorists proclaim themselves and perform for television. The name of their game is public recognition. After all, you can't very well intimidate a government into releasing your freedom fighters unless you announce that it is your group that has seized its embassy. "Clear guilt" is difficult to define, but when 40 million people see a group of masked gunmen seize an airplane on the evening news, there is not much question about who the perpetrators are. There will be hard cases where the situation is murkier. Nonetheless, a line demarcating the legitimate use of torture can be drawn. Torture only the obviously guilty, and only for the sake of saving innocents, and the line between Us and Them will remain clear.

12   There is little danger that the Western democracies will lose their way if they choose to inflict pain as one way of preserving order. Paralysis in the face of evil is the greater danger. Some day soon a terrorist will threaten tens of thousands of lives, and torture will be the only way to save them. We had better start thinking about this.

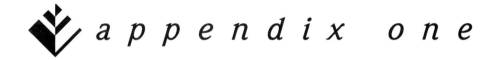 *a p p e n d i x   o n e*

Informal Fallacies

In this appendix we examine *informal fallacies,* which can fool us into thinking that an inconclusive argument is conclusive. Informal fallacies are quirky; they identify classes of less conclusive arguments that recur with some frequency, but they do not contain formal flaws that make their conclusions automatically illegitimate. An informal fallacy makes an argument more or less fallacious, and determining the degree of fallaciousness is a matter of judgment.

In arranging the fallacies we have, for convenience, put them into three categories derived from classical rhetoric: *pathos, ethos,* and *logos.* Fallacies of *pathos* rest on a flawed relationship between what is argued and the audience for the argument. Fallacies of *ethos* rest on a flawed relationship between the argument and the character of those involved in the argument. Fallacies of *logos* rest on flaws in the relationship among statements of an argument.

FALLACIES OF *PATHOS*

Argument to the People (Appealing to Stirring Symbols)

Argument to the people appeals to the fundamental beliefs, biases, and prejudices of the audience in order to sway opinion through a feeling of group solidarity. For example, when a politician says, "My fellow Americans, I stand here, draped in this flag from head to foot, to indicate my fundamental dedication to the values and principles of these sovereign United States," he's linking himself to the prime symbol of the group's nationalistic values, the flag.

Provincialism (Appealing to the Belief that the Known Is Always Better than the Unknown)

Here is an example from the 1960s: "You can't sell small cars in the United States. Americans love their big cars. Those cramped little Japanese tin boxes will never win the hearts of American consumers." Although we may inevitably feel more comfortable with familiar things, ideas, and beliefs, we are not necessarily better off for sticking with them.

Appeal to Emotional Premises
(Appealing to Comforting Reasons
that Have No Basis in Logic)

This mode of short-circuiting reason may take one of three forms:

1. Appeal to common practice. (It's all right to do X because everyone else does it.) "Of course I borrowed money from the company slush fund. Everyone on this floor has done the same in the last eighteen months."

2. Appeal to traditional wisdom. (It's all right because we've always done it this way.) "We've got to require everyone to read *Hamlet* because we've always required everyone to read it."

3. Appeal to popularity—the bandwagon appeal. (It's all right because lots of people like it.) "You should buy a Ford Escort because it's the best-selling car in the world." In all three cases, we say that something is right, good, or necessary based on the comforting but irrational reason that it is common, traditional, or popular.

Red Herring (Shifting the Audience's Attention
from a Crucial Issue to an Irrelevant One)

The *red herring* fallacy deliberately raises an unrelated or irrelevant point to throw an audience off the track. Politicians often employ this fallacy when they field questions from the public press. "You raise a good question about my support of continuing air strikes in country X. Let me tell you about my admiration for the bravery of our pilots."

FALLACIES OF *ETHOS*

Appeals to False Authority and Bandwagon Appeals
(Appealing to the Authority of a Popular Person
or to the "Crowd" Rather than to an Expert)

False authority fallacies offer as support for an argument the fact that a famous person or "many people" support it. Unless the supporters are themselves authorities in the field, their support is irrelevant. "Buy Freeble oil because Joe Quarterback always uses it in his fleet of cars." "How can abortion be wrong if millions of people support a woman's right to choose?"

Keep in mind, however, that occasionally the distinction between a false authority fallacy and an appeal to legitimate authority can blur. Suppose that Arnold Palmer were to praise a particular company's golf club. Because he is an expert on golf, perhaps he speaks from authority about a truly superior golf club. But perhaps he is being paid to endorse a club that is no better than its competitors'. We could better determine the argument's conclusiveness if Palmer presented an *ad rem* ("to the thing") argument showing us scientifically why the golf club in question is superior.

Appeal to the Person or *Ad Hominem* (Attacking the Character of the Arguer Rather than the Argument Itself)

Literally, *ad hominem* means "to the person." When people can't find fault with an argument, they sometimes attack the arguer, substituting irrelevant assertions about that person's character for an analysis of the argument itself. It is better for an argument to be *ad rem* rather than *ad hominem.* Thus an *ad rem* critique of a politician would focus on her voting record, the consistency and cogency of her public statements, her responsiveness to constituents, and so forth. An *ad hominem* argument would shift attention to irrelevant features of her personality or personal life, perhaps a recent divorce or a long-ago reckless driving conviction.

But not all *ad hominem* arguments are *ad hominem* fallacies. It's not always fallacious to address your argument to the arguer. There are indeed times when the credibility of the person making an opposing argument is at issue. Lawyers, for example, in questioning expert witnesses who give damaging testimony, will often make an issue of their motives and credibility—and rightfully so.

Strawperson (Greatly Oversimplifying an Opponent's Argument to Make It Easier to Refute or Ridicule)

In committing a *strawperson* fallacy, you basically make up the argument you *wish* your opponents had made and attribute it to them because it's so much easier to refute than the argument they actually made. Some political debates consist almost entirely of strawperson exchanges, such as "You may think that taxing people out of their homes and onto park benches is the best way to balance the budget, but I don't," or "While my opponent would like to empty our prisons of serial killers and coddle kidnappers, I hold to the sacred principles of swift and sure justice."

FALLACIES OF *LOGOS*

Begging the Question (Supporting a Claim with a Reason that Is Really a Restatement of the Claim in Different Words)

We *beg the question* when we use as a reason the same assertion we make in our claim. "Abortion is murder because it involves the intentional killing of an unborn human being." Since murder is defined as the "intentional killing of a human being," the argument says, in effect, "Abortion is murder because it's murder."

False Dilemma/Either-Or
(Oversimplifying a Complex Issue So
that Only Two Choices Appear Possible)

A good extended analysis of this fallacy is found in sociologist Kai Erickson's analysis of President Harry Truman's decision to drop the A-bomb on Hiroshima. His analysis suggests that the Truman administration prematurely reduced numerous options to just two: either drop the bomb on a major city or suffer unacceptable losses in a land invasion of Japan. Erickson, however, shows there were other alternatives. Typically, we encounter *false dilemma* arguments when people try to justify a questionable action by creating a false sense of necessity, forcing us to choose between two options, one of which is clearly unacceptable.

But of course not all dilemmas are false. People who reject all binary oppositions are themselves guilty of a false dilemma. There are times when we might determine through a rational process of elimination that only two possible choices exist. Deciding whether a dilemma is truly a dilemma or only an evasion of complexity often requires a difficult judgment. Although we should initially suspect any attempt to convert a complex problem into an either/or choice, we may legitimately arrive at such a choice through thoughtful deliberation.

Confusing Correlation for Cause or *Post Hoc, Ergo
Propter Hoc* (After This, Therefore Because of This)
(Assuming that Event X Causes Event Y
Because Event X Preceded Event Y)

Here are two examples in which this fallacy may be at work:

Cramming for a test really helps. Last week I crammed for a psychology test and I got an A on it.

I am allergic to the sound of a lawnmower because every time I mow the lawn I start to sneeze.

We treat this fallacy at length in Chapter 11 in our discussion of correlation versus causation (pp. 163–165). The *post hoc, ergo propter hoc* fallacy occurs when a sequential relationship is mistaken for a causal relationship. The conjunction may be coincidental, or it may be attributable to some as-yet-unrecognized third factor. For example, your A on the psych test may be caused by something other than your cramming. Maybe the exam was easier, or perhaps you were luckier or more mentally alert. And perhaps a lawnmower makes you sneeze because it stirs up pollen rather than because it makes a loud noise.

Slippery Slope (Once We Move Slightly Toward an Unpleasant End, We Will Eventually Have to Go All the Way)

The *slippery-slope* fallacy appeals to the fear that once we take a first step in a direction we don't like, we will have to keep going.

> We don't dare send weapons to Country X. If we do so, next we will send in military advisers, then a special forces battalion, and then large numbers of troops. Finally, we will be in all-out war.

> Look, Blotnik, no one feels worse about your need for open-heart surgery than I do. But I still can't let you turn this paper in late. If I were to let you do it, then I'd have to let everyone turn in papers late.

The slippery-slope fear is that an apparently harmless first step in a dangerous direction dooms us to slide right out of sight.

The problem, of course, is that not every slippery-slope argument exhibits the slippery-slope fallacy. We all know that some slopes *are* slippery and that we sometimes have to draw the line, saying "to here, but no farther." And it is true also that making exceptions to rules is dangerous; the exceptions soon get established as regular procedures. The slippery slope becomes a fallacy, however, when we forget that some slopes don't have to be slippery unless we let them be slippery. Often we do better to imagine a staircase with stopping places all along the way. The assumption that we have no control over our descent once we take the first step makes us unnecessarily rigid.

Hasty Generalization (Making a Broad Generalization on the Basis of Too Little Evidence)

A *hasty generalization* occurs when we leap to a conclusion on insufficient evidence: "The food stamp program supports mostly freeloaders. Let me tell you about my worthless neighbor."

But what constitutes "sufficient" evidence is a knotty problem. No generalization arrived at through empirical evidence would meet a logician's strict standard of certainty. The Food and Drug Administration (FDA), for example, proceeds cautiously before certifying a drug as "safe." However, whenever doubts arise about the safety of an FDA-approved drug, critics accuse the FDA of having made a hasty generalization. At the same time, patients eager to get a new drug, or manufacturers eager to sell it, may lobby the FDA to quit dragging its feet and get the drug to market. Hence, the point at which a hasty generalization about drug safety passes over into the realm of a prudent generalization is nearly always uncertain and contested.

Mistaking the Part for the Whole or *Pars Pro Toto* (Assuming that What Is True for a Part Will Be True for the Whole).

We use the *pars pro toto* fallacy when we attack the whole of something by focusing on a part we don't like. Thus, critics who want to abolish the National Endowment for the Arts might focus on several controversial grants and use them as justification for wiping out all NEA programs.

False Analogy (Claiming that Because X Resembles Y in One Regard, X Will Resemble Y in All Regards)

Arguments by analogy are tricky because there are almost always significant differences between any two things being compared. If the two things differ greatly, the analogy can mislead rather than clarify. "You can't force a kid to become a musician any more than you can force a tulip to become a rose." For further discussion of reasoning by analogy, see Chapter 12.

Non Sequitur (Making a Claim that Doesn't Follow Logically from the Premises, or Supporting a Claim with Irrelevant Premises)

The *non sequitur* (literally, "it does not follow") fallacy is a miscellaneous category that includes any claim that doesn't follow logically from its premises or that is supported with irrelevant premises. Typically, *non sequitur* fallacies take the following forms:

An illogical leap: "Clambake University has one of the best faculties in the United States because a Nobel Prize winner used to teach there." (How does the fact that a Nobel Prize winner used to teach at Clambake University make its present faculty one of the best in the United States?)

Irrelevant premises: "I should not receive a C in this course because I have received Bs or As in all my other courses (here is my transcript for evidence) and because I worked exceptionally hard in this course (here is my log of hours worked)." (Even though the arguer has solid evidence to support each premise, the premises themselves are irrelevant to the claim. Course grades should be based on actual performance, not on previous grades or on effort.)

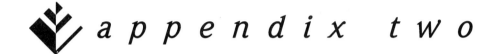

a p p e n d i x   t w o

A Concise Guide
to Documentation

An important convention of academic writing is the meticulous care writers take to cite and document their sources. In this appendix we will briefly explain the following: (1) How to avoid plagiarism, (2) how to cite your sources using the MLA (Modern Language Association) or APA (American Psychological Association) systems, and (3) how to provide complete bibliographic information at the end of your paper. We also include an example of a student argument written in the APA style. (For an example of a student argument in the MLA style, see pages 216–225.) For more complete information, consult a composition handbook or the most recent editions of *The MLA Handbook for Writers of Research Papers* or the *Publication Manual of the American Psychological Association.*

HOW TO AVOID PLAGIARISM

Before discussing how to cite and document your sources, we need to take a brief excursion into the realm of ethics to explain plagiarism. *Plagiarism* occurs whenever you take someone else's work and pass it off as your own. Plagiarism can happen in two ways: by borrowing another person's *ideas* without giving credit through a proper citation and by borrowing another writer's *language* without giving credit through quotation marks or block indentation.

The second kind of plagiarism is far more common than the first, perhaps because inexperienced writers don't appreciate how much they need to change the wording of a source to make the writing their own. It is not enough just to change the order of phrases in a sentence or to replace a few words with synonyms. In the following example, compare an acceptable rewording of a passage with unacceptable plagiarism.

ORIGINAL PASSAGE (FROM A 1984 ARTICLE ON VIOLENCE
IN THE OLD WEST BY ROGER D. MCGRATH)

There is considerable evidence that women in Bodie were rarely the victims of crime. Between 1878 and 1882 only one woman, a prostitute, was robbed, and

245

there were no reported cases of rape. (There is no evidence that rapes occurred but were not reported.)

ACCEPTABLE REWORDING

According to McGrath (1984), women in Bodie rarely suffered at the hands of criminals. Between 1878 and 1882, the only female robbery victim in Bodie was a prostitute. Also rape seemed non-existent, with no reported cases and no evidence that unreported cases occurred (p. 20).

PLAGIARISM

According to McGrath (1984), there is considerable evidence that women in Bodie were seldom the victims of crime. Between 1878 and 1882 only one woman, a prostitute, was robbed, and there were no reported rapes. There is no evidence that unreported cases of rape occurred (p. 20).

Although the writer of the plagiarized passage has correctly used the APA citation system (see next section) to indicate that his data comes from page 20 in the McGrath article, he has nevertheless plagiarized his source because he has copied its language directly without showing the borrowing through quotation marks.

HOW TO CITE SOURCES

When academic writers cite a source, they use the conventions appropriate to their discipline. In the sciences, citation systems often emphasize the date of a research study and refer to researchers only by last names and first initials. In the humanities, citation systems often emphasize the full names of scholars and place less emphasis on dates. Two of the most extensively used systems are those of the Modern Language Association (MLA) in the humanities and the American Psychological Association (APA) in the social sciences. In both systems, complete bibliographic information on all cited sources is placed at the end of the paper in a "Works Cited" list (MLA) or a "References" list (APA). To cite sources, both systems place reference information in parentheses directly in the text rather than using footnotes or endnotes. However, the two systems differ somewhat in the way this reference information is selected and structured.

In-text Citation: MLA System

In the MLA system, you place the author's name and the page number of the cited source in parentheses. (If the author's name is mentioned in a preceding attributive tag such as "according to Michael Levin" or "says Levin," then only the page number needs to be placed in parentheses.)

Torture, claims one philosopher, should only be applied to those "*known* to hold innocent lives in their hands" and only if the person being tortured is clearly guilty and clearly can prevent a terrorist act from occurring (Levin 13).

or

Torture, claims Michael Levin, should only be applied to those "*known* to hold innocent lives in their hands" and only if the person being tortured is clearly guilty and clearly can prevent a terrorist act from occurring (13).

If readers wish to follow up on the source, they will look up the Levin article in the "Works Cited" at the end. If more than one work by Levin has been used as sources in the essay, then you would include in the in-text citation an abbreviated title of the article following Levin's name.

(Levin, "Torture" 13)

Once Levin has been cited the first time and it is clear that you are still quoting from Levin, then you need put in parentheses only the page number and eliminate the author's name.

In-text Citation: APA System

In the APA system, you place the author's name and the date of the cited source in parentheses. If you are quoting a particular passage or citing a particular table, include the page number where the information is found. Use a comma to separate each element of the citation and use the abbreviation *p.* or *pp.* before the page number. (If the author's name is mentioned in a preceding attributive tag, then only the date needs to be placed in parentheses.)

Torture, claims one philosopher, should only be applied to those "*known* to hold innocent lives in their hands" and only if the person being tortured is clearly guilty and clearly can prevent a terrorist act from occurring (Levin, 1982, p. 13).

or

Torture, claims Michael Levin, should only be applied to those "*known* to hold innocent lives in their hands" and only if the person being tortured is clearly guilty and clearly can prevent a terrorist act from occurring (1982, p. 13).

If readers wish to follow up on the source, they will look for the 1982 Levin article in the "References" at the end. If Levin had published more than one article in 1982, the articles would be distinguished by small letters placed alphabetically after the date:

>   (Levin, 1982a)

or

>   (Levin, 1982b)

In the APA style, if an article or book has more than one author, the word *and* is used to join them in the text but the ampersand (&) is used to join them in the parenthetical reference:

>   Smith and Peterson (1983) found that . . .
>   More recent data (Smith & Peterson, 1983) have shown . . .

Citing a Quotation or Other Data from a Secondary Source

Occasionally, you may wish to use a quotation or other kinds of data from a secondary source. For example, suppose you are writing an argument that the United States should reconsider its trade policies with China. You read an article entitled "China's Gilded Age" by Xiao-huang Yin appearing in the April 1994 issue of *The Atlantic.* This article contains the following passage appearing on page 42:

> Dual ownership has in essence turned this state enterprise into a private business. Asked if such a practice is an example of China's "socialist market economy," a professor of economics at Nanjing University, where I taught in the early 1980's, replied, "Nobody knows what the concept means. It is only rhetoric, and it can mean anything but socialism."

In citing material from a secondary source, it is always best, when possible, to locate the original source and cite your data directly. But in the above case, no other source is likely available. Here is how you would cite it in both the MLA and APA systems.

MLA: According to an economics professor at Nanjing University, the term "socialist market economy," has become confused under capitalistic influence. "Nobody knows what the concept means. It is only rhetoric, and it can mean anything but socialism" (qtd. in Yin 42).

APA: According to an economics professor at Nanjing University, the term "socialist market economy," has become confused under capitalistic influence. "Nobody knows what the concept means. It is only rhetoric, and it can mean anything but socialism" (cited in Yin, 1994, p. 42).

In both systems you would place the Yin article in the end-of-text bibliographic list.

HOW TO PROVIDE BIBLIOGRAPHIC INFORMATION AT THE END OF YOUR PAPER

In this section we briefly describe the format for end-of-text bibliographic entries under "Works Cited" (MLA) or "References" (APA).

"Works Cited" Page: MLA

Page 250 shows a sample "Works Cited" page that would go at the end of a paper using the MLA system. On this page, we illustrate the formats for the most commonly used sources: a book with a single author; a book in a revised edition; a book with two or more authors; an article in an anthology; an article in a scholarly journal; an article in a weekly or biweekly popular magazine; an article in a monthly, bimonthly, or quarterly magazine; a newspaper article, and an internet website. (To see how a "Works Cited" list is appended to a complete researched argument written in MLA style, see Stephen Bean's paper on pp. 216–225.)

"References" Page: APA

Page 251 shows a sample "References" page that would go at the end of a paper using the APA system. It contains the same information as the MLA page, only transformed into APA style and format. Note that the APA system places the date immediately after the author's name; that it uses only initials rather than first and middle names; that it capitalizes only the first word of article and book titles; and that it puts a *p.* or *pp.* in front of page numbers.

EXAMPLE OF A RESEARCHED ARGUMENT IN APA STYLE

Pages 252–258 provide an example of a fully documented argument using the APA style.

WORKS CITED: MLA STYLE SHEET FOR THE MOST COMMONLY USED SOURCES

Ross 27

Works Cited

Adler, Freda. <u>Sisters in Crime</u>. New York: McGraw, 1975.

Andersen, Margaret L. <u>Thinking About Women: Sociological Perspectives on Sex and Gender</u>. 3rd ed. New York: Macmillan, 1993.

Bart, Pauline, and Patricia O'Brien. <u>Stopping Rape: Successful Survival Strategies</u>. New York: Pergamon, 1985.

Durkin, Kevin. "Social Cognition and Social Context in the Construction of Sex Differences." <u>Sex Differences in Human Performances</u>. Ed. Mary Anne Baker. New York: Wiley, 1987. 45–60.

Fairburn, Christopher G., et al. "Predictors of 12-month Outcome in Bulimia Nervosa and the Influence of Attitudes to Shape and Weight." <u>Journal of Consulting and Clinical Psychology</u> 61 (1993): 696–98.

Kantrowitz, Barbara. "Sexism in the Schoolhouse." <u>Newsweek</u> 24 Feb. 1992: 62.

Langewiesche, William. "The World in Its Extreme." <u>Atlantic</u> Nov. 1991: 105–40.

"Selected Rights of Homeless Persons." <u>National Law Center on Homelessness and Poverty</u>. 19 April 1998. <http.//www. nlchp.org/rights2.htm>.

Taylor, Chuck. "After Cobain's Death: Here Come the Media Ready to Buy Stories." <u>Seattle Times</u> 10 Apr. 1994: A1+.

Author's last name and page number in upper right corner.

Book entry, one author. Use standard abbreviations for common publishers.

Book entry in a revised edition.

Book with two or three authors. With four or more authors use "et al.", as in Jones, Peter, et al.

Article in anthology; author heads the entry; editor cited after the title. Inclusive page numbers come two spaces after the period following year.

Article in scholarly journal paginated consecutively throughout year. This article has three or more authors.

Weekly or biweekly popular magazine; abbreviate all months except May, June, and July.

Monthly, bimonthly, or quarterly magazine.

Unauthored document online; title in quotations; website underlined; date of access; web address in angle brackets

Newspaper article with identified author; if no author, begin with title.

REFERENCES: APA STYLE SHEET FOR THE MOST COMMONLY USED SOURCES

Women, Health, and Crime

27

References

Adler, F. (1975). Sisters in crime. New York:McGraw-Hill.

Andersen, M. L. (1993). Thinking about women: Sociological perspectives on sex and gender (3rd ed.). New York: Macmillan.

Bart, P., & O'Brien, P. (1985). Stopping rape: Successful survival strategies. New York: Pergamon Press.

Durkin, K. (1987). Social cognition and social context in the construction of sex differences. In M. A. Baker (Ed.), Sex differences in human performances (pp. 45–60). New York: Wiley & Sons.

Fairburn, C. G., Pevaler, R. C., Jones, R., & Hope, R. A. (1993). Predictors of 12-month outcome in bulimia nervosa and the influence of attitudes to shape and weight. Journal of Consulting and Clinical Psychology, 61, 696–98.

Kantrowitz, B. (1992, February 24). Sexism in the schoolhouse. Newsweek, p. 62.

Langewiesche, W. (1991, November). The world in its extreme. Atlantic, pp. 105–40.

Selected rights of homeless persons. [Online] National Law Center on Homelessness and Poverty. Available: http://www.nlchp.org./rights2.htm [1998, April 19]

Taylor, C. (1993, April 10). After Cobain's death: Here come the media ready to buy stories. Seattle Times, pp. A1+.

Running head with page number doublespaced below.

Book entry, one author. Don't abbreviate publisher but omit unnecessary words.

Book entry in a revised edition.

Book with multiple authors; uses ampersand instead of "and" before last name. Authors' names listed last name first.

Article in anthology; no quotes around article. Name of editor comes before book title.

Article in scholarly journal paginated consecutively throughout year. APA lists all authors rather than using "et al." (except when there are six or more authors).

Weekly or biweekly popular magazine; abbreviate all months except May, June, and July.

Monthly, bimonthly, or quarterly magazine.

Unauthored document online; roman title; type of medium in square brackets; website; no period after web address; access date in square brackets

Newspaper article with identified author; if no author, begin with title.

Women Police Officers:

Should Size and Strength Be Criteria for Patrol Duty?

Lynnea Clark

English 301

15 November 19XX

This research paper follows the APA style for format and documentation.

Women Police Officers:
Should Size and Strength Be Criteria for Patrol Duty?

A marked patrol car turns the corner at 71st and Franklin Avenue and 1
cautiously proceeds into the parking lot of an old shopping center. About a dozen
gang members, dressed in their gang colors, stand alert, looking down the alley
that runs behind the store. As the car moves toward the gathering, they suddenly
scatter in all directions. Within seconds, several shots are fired from the alley.
Switching on the overhead emergency lights, the officer bolts from the car when he
sees two figures running past him. "Freeze! Police!" the officer yells. The men dart
off in opposite directions. Chasing one, the policeman catches up to him, and,
observing no gun, tackles him. After a violent struggle, the officer manages to
handcuff the man, just as the backup unit comes screeching up.

This policeman is my friend. The next day I am with him as he sits at a cafe 2
with three of his fellow officers, discussing the incident. One of the officers
comments, "Well, at least you were stronger than he was. Can you imagine if
Connie Jones was on patrol duty last night?" "What a joke," scoffs another officer.
"How tall is she anyway?" "About 4′10″ and 90 pounds," says the third officer.
"She could fit in my backpack." Connie Jones (not her real name) has just
completed police academy training and has been assigned to patrol duty in _____ .
Because she is so small, she has to have a booster seat in her patrol car and has
been given a special gun, since she can barely manage to pull the trigger of a
standard police-issue .38 revolver. Although she passed the physical requirements
at the academy, which involved speed and endurance running, situps, and monkey
bar tests, most of the officers in her department doubt her ability to perform
competently as a patrol officer. But nevertheless she is on patrol because men and
women receive equal assignments in most of today's police forces. But is this a
good policy? Can a person who is significantly small and weak make an effective
patrol officer?

Because the "small and weak" people in question are almost always women, 3
the issue becomes a woman's issue. Considerable research has been done on
women in the police force, and much of it suggests that women, who are on the
average smaller and weaker than men, can perform competently in law

enforcement, regardless of their size or strength. More specifically, most research concludes that female police workers in general perform just as well as their fellow officers in patrolling situations. A major study by Bloch and Anderson (1984), commissioned by the Urban Institute, revealed that in the handling of violent situations, women performed well. In fact, women and men received equally satisfactory evaluation ratings on their overall performances.

4   In another more recent study (Grennan, 1987) examining the relationship between outcomes of police-citizen confrontations and the gender of the involved officers, female officers were determined to be just as productive as male officers in the handling of violent situations. In his article on female criminal justice employment, Potts (1982) reviews numerous studies on evaluation ratings of policewomen and acknowledges that "the predominant weight of evidence is that women are equally capable of performing police work as are men" (p. 11). Additionally, female officers score higher on necessary traits for leadership (p. 10), and it has been often found that women are better at dealing with rape and abuse victims. Again, a study performed by Grennan (1987), concentrating on male and female police officers' confrontations with citizens, revealed that the inborn or socialized nurturing ability possessed by female police workers makes them "just as productive as male officers in the handling of a violent confrontation" (p. 84).

5   This view has been strengthened further by the achievement of Katherine P. Heller, who was honored by receiving the nation's top award in law enforcement for 1990 (Proctor, 1990). Heller, a United States park policewoman, risked her life by stepping in the open to shoot dead an assailant while he levelled his gun to shoot at her fellow police officer. Five feet three inches and 107 pounds, Heller is not only the first woman to be awarded with Police Officer of the Year, but she is also the smallest recipient ever. Maybe Heller's decisiveness will help lay to rest doubts about many women's abilities as police workers.

6   However, despite the evidence provided by the above cited research, I am not convinced. Although these studies show that women make effective police officers, I believe the studies must be viewed with skepticism. My concern is public safety. In light of that concern, the evidence suggests that police departments should set

stringent size and strength requirements for patrol officers, even if these criteria exclude many women.

First of all, the research studies documenting the success of women as patrol   7 officers are marred by two major flaws: the amount of evidence gathered is scanty and the way that the data have been gathered doesn't allow us to study factors of size and strength. Because of minimal female participation in patrol work prior to the past decade, limited amounts of research and reports exist on the issue. And of the research performed, many studies have not been based on representative samples. Garrison, Grant, and McCormick (1988) found that

> [l]iterature on women in patrol or nontraditional police roles tends to be idiosyncratic. . . . Many of the observations written about a relatively small number of women performing successfully in a wider range of police tasks support the assumption that they are exceptions rather than the norm. (p. 32)

Similarly, Bloch and Anderson (1984) note that in the course of their study

> it was not possible to observe enough incidents to be sure that men and women are equally capable in all such situations. It is clear from the incidents which were described that women performed well in the few violent situations which did arise. (p. 61)

Another problem with the available research is that little differentiation has   8 been made within the large group of women being considered; all women officers seem to be grouped and evaluated based on only two criteria: that they are on the police force and that they are female. But like men, women come in all shapes and sizes. To say that women as a class make effective or ineffective police workers is to make too general a claim. The example of women officers such as Katherine Heller proves that some women make excellent patrol cops. But, presumably, some women probably would not make good patrol cops just as some men would not. The available data do not allow us to determine whether size and strength are factors. Because no size differentiation has been made within the groups of women officers under observation in the research studies, it is impossible to conclude whether or not smaller, weaker women performed patrol duties as well as larger, stronger women did. In fact, for Bloch and Anderson's study (which indicates that, from a performance viewpoint, it is appropriate to hire women for patrol assignments on the same basis as men) both men and women had to meet a minimum height requirement of 5'7". Therefore, the performance of smaller, weaker women in handling violent situations remained unevaluated. Thus the data show that many women are great cops; the data do <u>not</u> show that many small women with minimal strength make great cops.

9   The case of Katherine Heller might seem to demonstrate that smaller women can perform patrol duties successfully. Heller acknowledged in an interview in *Parade* magazine that ninety percent of her adversaries will be bigger than herself (Proctor, 1990, p. 5). But she is no fluttering fluffball; rather, she has earned the reputation for being an extremely aggressive cop and has compensated for her size by her bearing. But how many women (or men) of Heller's size or smaller could maintain such "officer presence"? How can we be certain that Heller is in fact representative of small women rather than being an exception?

10   This question leads to my second reason for supporting stringent size and strength requirements: Many police officers, both male and female, have real doubts about the abilities of small and physically weak patrol workers, most of whom are women. For example, police office Elizabeth Demetriou, a six year veteran of the New York Police Department, said in an interview, "Women on the job still depend on men to help them during confrontations, more so than men do. Male police officers want their partners to be 'tough' or big so that automatically excludes women" (Kennedy, 1996, Online). In a study done by Vega and Silverman (1982), almost 75% of male police officers felt that women were not strong enough to handle the demands of patrol duties, and 42% felt women lacked the needed assertiveness to enforce the law vigorously (p. 32). Unfortunately, however, because of frequent media reports of discrimination and sexism among police personnel and because of pressure from the Equal Employment Opportunity Commission (EEOC) on police agencies and other employers (Vega & Silverman, 1982; Lord, 1986), these reservations and attitudes have not been seriously taken into account. The valid concerns and opinions of police workers who feel that some women officers are not strong enough to deal effectively with violent situations

have been asphyxiated by the smoldering accusations of civil rights activists and feminists, who see only layers of chauvinism, conservatism, cynicism, and authoritarianism permeating our law enforcement agencies. These activists view the problem as being only a "women" issue rather than a "size" issue. But the fact remains that both male and female officers think that many patrol workers are incapable of handling violent situations because of small stature and lack of physical strength. Another policewoman belonging to the same department as Connie Jones explained, "She [Jones] doesn't have the authoritarian stance needed to compensate for her size. She's not imposing and is too soft spoken. Once she responded to a call and was literally picked up and thrown out the door" (anonymous personal communication, October 6, 1990).

Finally, patrol duties, unlike other areas of police work, constitute one of the few 11 jobs in our society that may legitimately require above average strength. Because the job involves great personal risk and danger, the concern for public safety overrides the concern for equal rights in this instance. Patrolling is a high visibility position in police departments as opposed to jobs such as radio dispatching, academy training, or clerical duties. Patrol workers directly face the challenges presented by the public, and violence is always a threat for officers on patrol (Vega & Silverman, 1982; Grennan, 1987). Due to the nature of patrol work, officers many times must cope with violent situations by using physical force, such as that needed for subduing individuals who resist arrest. However, pressure from liberal groups has prevented special consideration being given to these factors of patrol duty. As long as student officers pass the standard academy Physical Ability Test (in addition to the other academy requirements), then they are eligible for patrol assignments; in fact, everyone out of the academy must go on patrol. But the minimum physical requirements are not challenging. According to Lord (1986), police agencies "struggle to find a nondiscriminatory, empirically valid entry level physical agility test which does not discriminate against women by overemphasizing upper body strength" (Lord, 1986, p. 91). In short, the liberal agenda leading to women on patrol has forced the lowering of strength requirements.

Without establishing minimum size and strength requirements for patrol 12 workers, police departments are not discharging their duties with maximum competency or effectiveness. Police training programs stress that police officers should be able to maintain an authoritarian presence in the face of challenges and possess the ability to diffuse a situation just by making an appearance. But some individuals who are able to pass basic training programs still lack the size needed to maintain an imposing physical stance. And as many citizens obviously do not respect the uniform, police workers must possess the strength to efficiently handle violent encounters. Even if size and strength requirements have a disproportionate impact on women, these physical standards are lawful, so long as they relate to the demands of the job and "constitute valid predictors of an employee's performance on the job" (Steel & Lovrich, 1987, p. 53). Patrol duties demand highly capable and effective workers, and in order to professionalize law-enforcement practices and to maintain the degree of order necessary for a free society, police agencies must maintain a high level of competency in their street-patrol forces.

References

Bloch, P., & Anderson, D. (1974). <u>Police women on patrol: Final report.</u> Washington, D.C.: Police Foundation.

Garrison, C., Grant, N., & McCormick, K. (1988). Utilization of police women. <u>The Police Chief, 55</u>(9), 32–73.

Golden, K. (1981). Women as patrol officers: A study of attitudes. <u>Police Studies, 4</u>(3), 29–33.

Grennan, S. (1987). Findings on the role of officer gender in violent encounters with citizens. <u>Journal of Police Science and Administration, 15</u>(1), 78–84.

Igbinovia, P. (1987). African women in contemporary law enforcement. <u>Police Studies, 10</u>(1), 31–34.

Kennedy, E.A. (1996). Defense tactics & the female officer. <u>Women Police</u> [Online] Modern Warrior. Available: http://www.mwarrior.com/DT-fem2.htm [1998, May 4].

Lord, L. (1986). A comparison of male and female peace officers' stereotypic perceptions of women and women peace officers. <u>Journal of Police Science and Administration, 14</u>(2), 83–91.

Potts, L. (1981). Equal employment opportunity and female criminal justice employment. <u>Police Studies, 4</u>(3), 9–19.

Proctor, P. (1990, September 30). "I didn't have time to taste the fear." <u>Parade Magazine,</u> pp. 4–5.

Steel, B., & Lovrich, N., Jr. (1987). Equality and efficiency tradeoffs in affirmative action—real or imagined? The case of women in policing. <u>The Social Science Journal, 24</u>(1), 53–67.

Vega, M., & Silverman, I. (1982). Female police officers as viewed by their male counterparts. <u>Police Studies, 5</u>(1), 31–39.

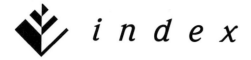

index

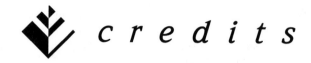 *credits*